Out of Order

Donald J. Wold earned his M.Div. degree from Trinity Evangelical Divinity School and his Ph.D. degree in biblical and Judaic studies from the University of California at Berkeley. He has served as pastor, counselor, and professor of Near Eastern Studies.

Out of Order

*Homosexuality in the Bible
and the Ancient Near East*

Donald J. Wold

Baker Books

A Division of Baker Book House Co
Grand Rapids, Michigan 49516

©1998 by Donald J. Wold

Published by Baker Books
a division of Baker Book House Company
P.O. Box 6287, Grand Rapids, MI 49516-6287

Printed in the United States of America

Unless otherwise indicated, Scripture quotations are adapted from the New American Standard Bible, copyright the Lockman Foundation 1977.

Library of Congress Cataloging-in-Publication Data

Wold, Donald J., 1945–
    Out of order : homosexuality in the Bible and the ancient Near East / Donald J. Wold
      p.   cm.
    Includes bibliographical references and indexes.
    ISBN 0-8010-2114-6 (paper)
    1. Homosexuality in the Bible. 2. Homosexuality—Religious aspects—Biblical teaching. 3. Homosexuality—Religious aspects—History of doctrines. 4. Bible. Criticism, interpretation, etc. 5. Middle East—Religion. I. Title.
BS680.H67W65   1998
261.8′35766—dc21
                                        98-22499

Contents

Preface

Most Christians look to the Bible for guidance on the subject of sexual conduct. The Bible is for them a road map both to eternal life and to the manner in which life is lived here and now. It has much to say about sexual matters from both positive and negative perspectives, but only a few biblical texts address the practice of same-gender sexual relations. These few verses provide the focal point of this book. Their relevance to religious life and to the public debate on homosexuality cannot be overstated. Some denominations have issued statements welcoming homosexuals to membership, lay leadership, and ordination; others have vehemently opposed the acceptance of gay and lesbian lifestyles. The debate within the church reflects diametrically opposed views of Scripture and the role that the Bible plays in determining sexual ethics. Meanwhile, as the Ramsey Colloquium has observed, an intense campaign is being waged through the media and cultural institutions: "The new thing, the novum, is a gay and lesbian movement that aggressively proposed radical changes in social behavior, religion, morality, and law" (1994: 16). Biblical scholars have only recently begun to focus on the homosexuality debate, and much of their work is not readily accessible to the general public. Still lacking in the literature is a thorough investigation of the biblical passages on homosexuality and their relation to ancient Near Eastern sources. It is the purpose of this book to fill this void.

I write from the premise that whatever can be known about homosexuality in the Bible depends first and foremost on the interpretation of certain biblical expressions, which I study in detail from the original Hebrew and Greek texts. Since the Hebrew did not live in a cultural vacuum, I postulate that it is useful to compare the biblical texts to non-Israelite literary sources to see if they might shed some light on the practice of same-gender sexual relations in the larger context of the ancient orient. By no means do I exhaust the comparative data. My purpose in looking to Mesopotamian, Anatolian, and Egyptian records is primarily to construct a framework for the biblical picture of homosexuality. Some points will become clear by comparison, others by contrast. Much work remains to be done on this subject. This book is only a beginning.

Further research will confirm my thesis: the concern for order, both in society and in the cosmos, was of paramount importance to peoples throughout the ancient Near East. Disorder was associated with danger, finding expression in the anomalies of nature and extraordinary events, such as deformity, disease, drought, floods, childlessness, hallucinations, and war. It was customarily thought that behind disorder was a lurking demon, a curse, or an unhappy god. Order might be restored if the demon or god could be appeased in some way. Mesopotamians, Canaanites, and Egyptians sought to establish order in the cosmos through divination and magic. A great number of Babylonian omen texts from the second millennium B.C. attest to these methods of restoring the natural balance of daily life. Cultic, legal, and political institutions were set up to maintain order on the human level.

Among the ancient Hebrews, order was predicated on the creative and sustaining power of Yahweh, the one true God, whose sovereign will and unique presence were manifested in various ways but especially in creation and in Israel's wilderness sanctuary. It is to the creation and the cult that one must look for a rationale against the practice of homosexuality in Hebrew tradition. Creation provided the positive male-female model for sexual union. The levitical laws negated certain illicit sexual relations that defiled the sanctuary and threatened Israel with severe divine sanctions. At the same time, reconciliation for the offender was made possible through the sacrificial system. Even deliberate sin, the category into which homosexual acts fell, could be forgiven on the Day of Atonement, pending the offender's confession and repentance.

New Testament views of homosexuality were crafted on the framework of order in creation and the cult. The apostle Paul's argument in Romans 1 was based on the norm of heterosexual relations in Genesis 1–2. I shall demonstrate that his statements regarding sexual impurity in 1 Corinthians 5–6 are best understood against the background of the levitical laws regarding incest and homosexuality, which specified that illicit sex brought alienation from the people of God and placed the offender in line for divine judgment. The kingdom of God consists of those who conform their conduct to the divine will, and so Paul excluded practicing homosexuals from the company of Christ's followers. True, the church at Corinth welcomed some homosexuals to its communion, but these individuals were transformed and no longer practiced their former lifestyle. Herein lies the New Testament hope for gays and lesbians.

Since no book is without its faults, let me anticipate some possible criticisms that may be leveled against it, providing at the same time some rationale for my approach. First, I may be censured for the narrow focus of my work. The effort to elucidate the biblical teaching on homosexuality against its ancient cultural environment leaves other important topics aside. For example, a thorough history of homosexuality from a Christian perspective still needs to be written. The etiology of homosexuality with respect to recent studies of the hypothalamus (LeVay 1991) and genetic markers (Hamer et al. 1993) weighs heavily in the current debate. The horrible siege of AIDS must be addressed with Christian concern for the sick and dying. The role of the church in relation to homosexuals deserves special treatment. An investigation into the political responsibility of Christians on the subject of sexual ethics and their impact on society would be a worthwhile enterprise. As important as these topics are, they fall beyond the scope of this work.

Second, I treat the biblical text in a "what you see is what you get" fashion. Various types of hermeneutical methods have been espoused for both Old and New Testaments, some of more value than others. Literary critics in particular may object to my method of handling Leviticus 18. This chapter is part of the so-called Holiness Code (Lev. 17–26) and has been viewed as a patchwork by several authors and dated near the time of Ezekiel rather than Moses. I offer a new approach. I see Leviticus 18 as a literary unit based on analogy to the second-millennium Hittite suzerainty treaty pattern. The integrity of this chapter is crucial to understanding the law on homosexuality at Leviticus 18:22.

Third, some readers may think that I go too far in my grammatical analyses to argue against revisionist interpretations. I insist that the biblical text is the main line of defense against moral decay and that careful exegesis is the key to discovering the truth about it. Two issues are raised at this point: the authority of Scripture and the relevance of the biblical text for every generation. If one discounts the authority of Scripture and its relevance, it matters little what the Bible says about homosexuality or any other subject. If, on the one hand, one holds Scripture in high regard and accepts it as the inspired Word of God, it must be allowed to judge the conduct of every individual. Principles of moral conduct should not change with time or place, contrary to the doctrines of situation ethics common in our day. I accept the authority and relevance of Scripture and therefore devote considerable space to Hebrew and Greek lexicography and grammar.

Finally, the sources for the present work encompass a number of foreign languages. The Semitic, Egyptian, and Hittite languages involve signs, scripts, and alphabets quite different from English. Except for Hebrew and Greek, I avoid the original orthographies. The reader must bear with translations and transliterations. These too are not without their problems. For example, English has one orthographic sign for the letter *s*, while Hebrew has four signs: *sāmek* (ס), *ṣādê* (צ), *śîn* (שׂ), and *šîn* (שׁ). Similar problems of transliteration exist in Akkadian, Hittite, Ugaritic, and Egyptian—the languages most often referred to in this book. Transliteration is further complicated since ancient Near Eastern languages contain some sounds not present at all in English, such as Hebrew *ʾālep* (א) and *ʿayin* (ע). Despite the difficulties involved, I include a considerable amount of foreign speech.

The book is divided into three sections. The first provides an introduction to homosexuality in ancient Near Eastern sources. Two fundamental and inseparable concerns dominated the minds—and hence the literatures—of ancient Near Eastern peoples throughout their long history: order and fertility. The perpetuation and stability of society—indeed of human existence—were linked to these concerns. The main problem we have is the lack of sufficient references to homosexual conduct in extrabiblical sources. Apart from certain cultic activities that involved same-gender sexual intercourse and that deserve separate treatment, it is not possible to know the extent to which homosexual acts were practiced at large. Specialists like Jean Bottéro (1992: 191) assert that homosexual relations were not condemned, discouraged, or even considered to be more ignominious than heterosexual relations in Mesopotamia. Only the Middle Assyrian laws at the end of the second millennium B.C. sanction same-gender sex. We can only hope for more texts to come to light. If Bottéro is correct, one must still meet the challenge of fitting the practice of homosexual activities into the larger Mesopotamian value system dominated by order and fertility. The Mesopotamian may have resolved this dilemma by relegating homosexual acts to cultic functionaries. This may explain why laws applying to the general populace do not contain references, either positive or negative, to homosexual acts.

The data for Egyptian sources is also sparse. No laws regarding homosexuality are extant. We find references to same-gender sex in various narrative sources, and these I consider in detail.

Part two takes the reader into the Old Testament texts regarding homosexual conduct. The ideas of order and fertility are foundational for a proper understanding of the biblical view of homosexuality. The Genesis narratives emphasize the importance of fertility as a blessing to humans. The procreative role of male and female is both positive and normative. Heterosexual union is the norm according to Genesis 2:24: "For this cause a man shall leave his father and his mother, and shall

cleave to his wife; and they shall become one flesh." Just as the principles of order and fertility are paramount in the creation accounts, their
importance is self-evident in the Noah and Sodom stories. In the legal
sources, special attention is given to homosexual acts in the context of
impurity. Heavy sanctions for violations are executed by either the community or God. Underlying these sanctions is the concern to maintain
the structure of Israelite society, to provide an order of holiness in keeping with divine requirements. Disorder in the form of homosexual conduct threatens the existence of the community and alienates it from the
divine presence. It is axiomatic to biblical law that individual conduct
has a profound effect on society. Homosexuality falls into the gravest
category of sins punishable by the most severe penalties at the legislator's disposal. At the same time, the sacrificial system provides for reconciliation of the offender, despite the deliberate nature of the violation. Divine punishment may be averted on the Day of Atonement
through the sinner's confession and repentance and the efficacy of the
purification offerings.

In part three, I address the New Testament texts on same-gender sexual relations. I find Pauline teachings to have their roots in the Hebrew
text of the Old Testament rather than in Hellenistic sources. In his letter to the Romans, Paul bases his arguments against homosexual conduct on the Old Testament concepts of creation: order and fertility. He
argues to the Corinthians that same-gender sexual acts, like incest, generate impurity in the body of believers. Such acts lie open to divine punishment and exclude the perpetrator from the kingdom of God. The paradigm for Paul's instruction along these lines is to be found in the Old
Testament narratives and laws dealing with homosexuality.

Finally, the goal of the Bible with respect to homosexual conduct—
as to all sinful conduct—is to transform the sinner, to restore the image
of God, and to empower the individual to overcome any and all forms
of temptation. In this, the New and Old Testaments agree: the divine
requirement is "be holy, for I the LORD your God am holy" (Lev. 19:2).
The steps to achieve this holiness are clearly outlined by the apostle Paul
in 1 Corinthians 6:11. The transformation described in this verse is specific with respect to a list of violations, including homosexual conduct.
Transformation of the homosexual does not come through the sinner's
struggle; it comes when the struggle is over and the victory is owned
through Christ. It is defined by three terms: cleansing, sanctification,
and justification. These are discussed in chapter 13.

There is no better reason to write this book than to lay before my
readers not only the seriousness with which the Bible addresses homosexual conduct but also the joyous prospect of freedom from sexual
bondage. The Bible offers hope for homosexuals. The quest for sexual

purity is a spiritual battle lost unless a transformation occurs within the heart of the individual, restoring the relationship to God that is broken by sin. When the individual is reconciled to God, the moral and ethical requirements of God (in the law and the gospel) can be met. I speak of a kind of metamorphosis that allows one to live on a higher plane, beyond the powers of lust and self-gratification. It is a change that embraces the rule of God in the kingdom of God. This book is presented as a servant to the realization of that end.

Acknowledgments

The writing of this book would not have been possible without the influence of a great many people. First I owe my thanks to an esteemed group of teachers who inspired me and instilled in me the language skills required to research this book. The list begins with Menahem Mansoor at the University of Wisconsin, with whom I began the study of Hebrew some thirty years ago. Next, I thank all my teachers at Trinity Evangelical Divinity School in Deerfield, Illinois, in particular Robert D. Culver for training in systematic theology; Walter Liefeld for courses in New Testament Greek and exegesis; Walter C. Kaiser Jr. for courses in Old Testament history and theology; Thomas E. McComiskey for tutoring in Akkadian and Ugaritic; and Gleason L. Archer Jr. for instruction in Old Testament introduction, Hebrew, Aramaic, and Arabic. Furthermore, I wish to thank my teachers in the department of Near Eastern studies at the University of California, Berkeley, and the Graduate Theological Union: William Fulco of the Jesuit School of Theology for his guidance in Ugaritic, Aramaic, Mandean, and comparative Semitics; Victor L. Gold of the Pacific School of Religion for directing my reading of Biblical Hebrew and the Dead Sea Scrolls; Daniel A. Foxvog for instruction in Akkadian, especially for readings in the Babylonian omen texts and the Mari correspondence; Ariel A. Bloch for leading me through my fellowship in literary Arabic; Anne D. Kilmer for her inspiring seminars in Akkadian, especially in the Nuzi dialect; David Daube, who graciously read my work on *kareth* and served on my dissertation committee; and most of all my mentor and friend Jacob Milgrom, who served as my guide to rabbinics and biblical exegesis throughout my studies at Berkeley. To all of these teachers I owe a debt of gratitude for the tools required to write this book, but to none of them should be attributed any of its shortcomings.

Second, I wish to thank a long line of pastors, counselors, lay leaders, and friends whose words and living examples have guided my spiritual path through the years. How does one estimate the value of their witness week after week, year in and year out? To them, and to all the members of their congregations and families, let this book be a way of returning my thanks for the faithfulness of their testimony to biblical truth. Perhaps they will find it a useful tool in their ministries. If so, I shall be even further gratified.

Third, my thanks are due to those who helped in the collection and compilation of data, especially the library staff of Rolfing Library at Trinity Evangelical Divinity School and to K. C. Hanson for his assistance in providing me with the resources of the library at the Claremont Graduate School of Theology, Claremont, California. To the scholars who have written in the area of homosexuality and the Bible, I pay my debt with references to them in the text. The payment is sincere even when I strongly disagree with their viewpoints.

Above all, I owe my wife, Nadia, and our sons, Ken and Scott, a debt of gratitude for their love and support throughout the process of writing this book. Nadia's inspiration and encouragement have been constant from page one to publication, so it is to her that my greatest appreciation is due. I dedicate this book to her.

Abbreviations

ANET   *Ancient Near Eastern Texts Relating to the Old Testament*

BAGD   Bauer, Arndt, Gingrich, and Danker's *Greek-English Lexicon of the New Testament and Other Early Christian Literature*

CAD   *Chicago Assyrian Dictionary*

EJ   *Encyclopaedia Judaica*

IDB   *Interpreter's Dictionary of the Bible*

TDNT   *Theological Dictionary of the New Testament*

TDOT   *Theological Dictionary of the Old Testament*

1

Introduction

"When I use a word," Humpty Dumpty said, in rather a scornful tone, "it means just what I choose it to mean—neither more nor less."

"The question is," said Alice, "whether you can make words mean so many different things."

"The question is," said Humpty Dumpty, "which is to be master— that's all."

—Lewis Carroll, *Through the Looking Glass*

exual relations are so fundamental to human experience that in every society, at any given point in history, systems of rules governing sexual conduct have been developed. Anthropologists and sociologists study these systems by observation in nonliterate societies. From literate societies, both ancient and modern, documents that reflect the responses of particular peoples to sexual activity are often available for examination. Despite difficulties due to the peculiarities of the languages involved, it is possible to isolate two genres of literature regulating sexual behavior. To one belong all examples of narrative prose, myths, legends, and poetry that have as their theme a sexual motif, whether fictional or historical. To the second category belong legal treatises and hortatory texts designed to regulate individual and corporate conduct. They delineate which sexual acts are acceptable and which are forbidden. My purpose is to examine these two categories of literature as they are found in the Bible and the ancient Near East, focusing on the texts that deal specifically with same-gender sexual intercourse.

I focus on the Bible because it has had a profound influence on Western culture. The Hebrew Scriptures (known to Christians as the Old Testament) are a composite work by many authors from the time of the exodus to the Babylonian exile, a period of about a millennium. Three divisions are recognized: the Law (*Torah*), the Prophets (*Nevi'im*), and the Writings (*Ketuvim*), commonly abbreviated *Tanak*. The *Tanak* is the most important document in Judaism. It records the Hebrew version of the origin of the world, the history of the Israelite nation, and the individual and corporate responsibilities of those who worship Yahweh as the one and only true God. The ethical and moral standards of the Hebrew Bible have been accepted by more than half of the world's population through the vehicles of Judaism, Christianity, and Islam. In short, the widespread use of the Bible to shape views of morality and ethics both now and throughout almost three thousand years of history justifies our study of it on the subject of homosexuality.

Unfortunately, the universal distribution of the Bible makes it vulnerable to misinterpretation. There are two major reasons for this. First is the problem of mistranslating. Few people today have any knowledge of Hebrew and Greek, the original languages of the Bible (the small number of chapters in Aramaic have no bearing on the subject of homosexuality). Fewer still are aware of the literary history of Scripture until its canonization in the first century of our era or of the various textual traditions and mounds of documentation available now for biblical scholars to determine the nature and authenticity of the text. Based on modern research, some excellent translations of the Bible exist in English today. Others, for whatever reason, do not accurately represent the underlying Hebrew or Greek. Even the best translators are restrained by the peculiar idioms of both the original tongue and the language into which it is rendered. This means that every translation must be to some extent an interpretation.

Every effort must be made to avoid errors in translation. In addition to using the primary sources of the Hebrew and Greek Testaments, I shall have occasion to cite the Septuagint. This work, the earliest translation of the Hebrew Bible and an important tool in modern textual criticism and exegesis, was completed at Alexandria, Egypt, probably by the middle of the third century B.C. The Septuagint (commonly referred to by the roman numeral LXX) was widely used not only by Greek-speaking Jews of the Diaspora but also by early Christians. The New Testament writers depended heavily on it. The Septuagint can help to elucidate Hebrew terms and texts that are cryptic. It also often provides an important link between the Old and New Testaments. This is clearly the case on the subject of homosexuality in the Bible.

It is also important to look at what two other groups of material in the biblical tradition—the Apocrypha and Pseudepigrapha—have to say about homosexuality. Written between 200 B.C. and A.D. 100, some of these Jewish compositions relating to the Bible are included in the Septuagint but not canonized in the Hebrew Bible. In addition, the comments of the rabbis from the talmudic academies (A.D. 250–500) will engage our attention from time to time, as will later Jewish and Christian commentaries. These sources make a significant contribution to our effort to avoid errors of interpretation, but they are not sufficient to address the second major cause for misunderstanding the Bible.

Failure to appreciate the Bible's *Sitz im Leben*—its "life situation"— is often a more difficult error to correct than mistranslation. Words cannot be extracted from the Bible, clipped from their contexts, and then assigned meanings based on individual preferences or private agendas in the manner of Humpty Dumpty. The words used by the biblical writers had meanings relevant to and dependent on their specific time and place. Ephraim Speiser exhorts the reader to caution (1967: 188):

> The Bible is first and foremost a unique distillation of history. Now no process of this kind and magnitude can unfold in a vacuum. The people of the Bible, who were to make history in more ways than one, were neither politically nor culturally isolated from other societies. . . . They were an integral part of a larger pattern. Hence the ultimate achievement that is the Bible cannot be properly understood, still less appreciated, except in terms of the setting in which this work originated, and of the initial values which it went on to transfigure and transcend.

The larger pattern to which Speiser alludes is a varied matrix of social, political, legal, and religious customs and ideas, which covers the ancient Orient like a patchwork quilt. On the surface, it is easy to see some similarity in thought and practice among the peoples throughout the region, and one may be quite confident at times to find the original cloth, so to speak, from which the like patches were taken. In other instances, we may be privileged to see only a few pieces that resemble one another, or perhaps we find one of a kind, and we know nothing about where it came from.

On the positive side, archeological discoveries have illuminated the darkness of the ancient Near East to a great extent, making available thousands of documents in several languages. From these documents we know that some forms of homosexuality were practiced in the ancient Near East, but the quilt pieces are very scant indeed. Very possibly, some of what we might hope to learn about ancient sexual conduct remains in documents that are yet unpublished. Nevertheless, it is correct to say that the biblical writers who addressed the issue of same-gender sex did so against the background of customs practiced by Israel's neighbors. What they said must be understood in that original setting if possible. The task is made more difficult because only general references are made in the Bible to Egyptian and Canaanite homosexual practices—blanket statements, if you will, that do not afford us the details of such activities. One must look to a larger pattern of the cultures surrounding ancient Israel in an effort to piece together the biblical view of homosexuality. Only then can one grasp the moral and ethical principles that the biblical writers sought to establish.

To what extent did the cultures of the ancient Near East overlap? There was extensive cross-cultural commerce in both material goods and ideas among the peoples of the ancient Near East as early as the third millennium B.C. and probably before, although we have no literary sources prior to the end of the fourth millennium. Trade with the Aegean flourished, as well as with other regions such as India and Africa, during the second and first millenniums B.C. The amount of Near Eastern influence on Greek culture through the ages has been shown by Walter Burkert in *The Orientalizing Revolution* (1995). There is ample evidence of international diplomacy, illustrated, for example, in the Amarna tablets (from the fourteenth century B.C.), a large collection of documents revealing relations between Egyptian pharaohs and their vassals in the Fertile Crescent (Campbell 1960). The Amarna correspondence is unique because to date it is the only discovery of Akkadian documents in Egypt. The two millenniums before the birth of Christ were characterized by international correspondence in many languages, including Sumerian, Akkadian, Aramaic, Hittite, Ugaritic, Egyptian, Hurrian, Elamite, Hebrew, Eblaite, and Greek.

Ancient Israel was keenly aware of events and customs in other societies, especially those that were proximate in either language or geography. Thus it is legitimate to look at Egyptian, Akkadian, Hittite, and Ugaritic sources for help in explaining the cultural context of Hebrew expressions for homosexuality. This is especially so as we attempt to establish underlying principles for biblical legislation. I do not advocate wholesale borrowing from other cultures on the part of ancient Israel. At the same time, the ancient Near East was a large slate upon which many peoples placed the signatures of their cultures over thousands of years. There can be no doubt that the tiny nation of Israel shared an important place on this slate. Its contribution of monotheism was written large there. But surely Israel was heavily influenced by its neighbors. If this were not so, one could easily discount as fiction the passionate appeals of the Hebrew prophets to reform and the precise biblical laws crafted to prevent apostasy. On the other hand, it is also possible that Israel influenced its neighbors, but this entire discussion goes beyond the scope of this book. My task is to show how the biblical texts on homosexuality can be viewed against the background of other Near Eastern documents. It is not necessary to assume the reciprocal borrowing of practices in order to do this.

If this book were to deal only with the Hebrew Bible, it would be unnecessary to consider ancient Greek customs regarding homosexuality. For the most part, the literary sources reflecting these practices antedate the Hebrew text. However, the New Testament references to homosexuality were written against the background of a dominant Greek culture as well as under the influence of the Hebrew Bible. The Greeks, like the Egyptians and Canaanites before them, were characterized by sexual pursuits that ran counter to biblical tradition. The apostle Paul undoubtedly had such pursuits in mind as he wrote his letters to the Romans and Corinthians. His emphasis is on the dynamic of the gospel to bring about change in the universal setting of sin. His mission is summarized in one verse that introduces his discussion of homosexual conduct: "For I am not ashamed of the gospel, for it is the power of God for salvation to every one who believes, to the Jew first and also to the Greek" (Rom. 1:16).

A discussion of this salvation is an integral part of the biblical view of homosexuality, although it is too often overlooked. I take up the subject of reconciling the homosexual to God both in the levitical system and in the kingdom of God as it is described by the apostle Paul. One cannot understand the New Testament teaching on this important point without first appreciating the requirements of the law. In the same way that the levitical writer established the law against homosexuality and excluded the practice from Israel, so the apostle Paul condemns homosexuality and excludes the homosexual from the kingdom of God. But that is not the end of the story. Provisions are made for even the deliberate sinner to be reconciled to God.

In sum, a proper understanding of the Bible concerning homosexual relations rests on the successful completion of two objectives: (1) the study of the Hebrew and Greek expressions regarding homosexual relations in their respective biblical contexts and (2) the enhancement of this study by referring to ancient Near Eastern sources that touch on same-gender sex.

These goals present challenge enough, but this book would fall short of full value if it does not address modern revisionist attempts to twist the biblical data, in Humpty Dumpty fashion, to their own ends. Therefore, I find it necessary to critique the works of some modern commentators who write from a perspective quite different from my own. In presenting their viewpoints, I make every effort to be accurate and fair. However, I do not deny the apologetic in my method—that the Bible might be read and clearly understood in our day and that the normative principles found in it might find expression in modern life.

Grant for the moment that we have determined what the Bible says about homosexuality, how does one relate the evidence to modern society? One writer observes that there are only two options open to interpreters of the biblical data: one must "either acknowledge that the Bible does not speak directly to the issue of behavior by consenting adults of homosexual orientation, or they must interpret at least some of the passages as disapproving the behavior even if it is based on orientation. At present the second alternative seems stronger than the first" (Hiltner 1980: 229). This stance seems adequate on the surface, but it falls short by allowing modern views of homosexuality to cast a shadow on the biblical perspective. Two methodological errors are made.

First, the Bible speaks directly to the matter of consensual sex between males. It is not optional to think otherwise. Homosexual conduct falls into the category of deliberate action against the divine standard expressed by the law. It matters not whether such action takes place in private or public. In either case, the individual is culpable and, should the community not respond to eradicate the practice, corporate punishment may follow from God himself. A modern situation ethic may shelter any form of conduct under the umbrella of mutual consent or under the rubric of orientation, but this relativistic approach is foreign to the biblical record. It is essential to postulate the idea of intention in the law with respect to homosexuality. The sanctions for same-gender sex would be meaningless otherwise.

In the second place, the use of the term *orientation* as it is generally applied to homosexual identity in modern times is not supported by the biblical text. The Hebrew term *yēṣer* (יֵצֶר) is used of mental purpose or frame of mind and is not far from some modern nuances of *orientation*. But most often the latter is used to denote a biological or environmental cause of homosexuality for which a person bears no moral responsibility when acting it out. The appeal to orientation thus serves to erase the significance and consequences of the action. In the Bible, the cause for all violations against the divine standard is ultimately traceable to the mind-set of the individual: is it subordinated to the will of God? Thus not some but *all* of the passages relating to same-gender sexual intercourse are categorically against it. There are no seams in the biblical view. No concession is made to semantic labels. A bottle of poison labeled with anything but the customary skull and bones is *more* dangerous to society, not less so. Therefore I avoid the use of the term *orientation* in this book.

I do accept the terms *homosexual* and *homosexuality*. Since its coinage by Austrian-born physician K. M. Benkart in 1869, the abstract noun *homosexuality* has been defined broadly as sexual orientation to persons of the same sex or sexual activity with another person of the same sex. Many writers on this subject reject one or the other of these definitions. As long as orientation means only mind-set and not an inherited trait, both definitions are acceptable to me. The term *homosexual* is a hybrid with prefixed *homo-* that, grammatically speaking, should be traced to Greek *homos* meaning "same" or "like" rather than to Latin *homo* meaning "man." Thus, the terms *homosexuality* and *homosexual* in this book refer to anyone engaging in same-gender sexual acts.

A number of causes have been proposed for homosexuality in modern times, but this subject was of no apparent concern to the biblical writer. No reference to causes, apart from the one located in the mind-set of the individual, can be found in the biblical text. I do not discuss the origins of homosexuality.

I have had to leave aside at least two other important topics. First is the relationship of same-gender sex to the larger question of ethics in the Bible. As John Barton observes (1978: 44), this topic remains an intractable aspect of biblical theology. This is especially so when we attempt to use stories (as in Gen. 9; 19; Judg. 19) to establish ethical principles: "Even if we leave on one side the formidable difficulties raised by recent discussions of the dating of the Pentateuch sources, the stories of the judges and the 'Succession Narrative,' and the state of turmoil in study of the historicity of the patriarchs, the fact that the ethical material is embedded in literary narrative is in itself a severe handicap" (p. 55). The point is not that we should disregard the stories; we simply need to define the criteria for extracting ethical standards from such sources. Barton suggests three authorial presuppositions about ethics in narrative (pp. 59–60): (1) obedience to God's revealed will, (2) conformity to a pattern of natural order, where moral norms are detected by reason rather than God's revelation, and (3) imitation of God. Some of what we learn about homosexuality in the Bible is found in narrative sources. These must be carefully evaluated against legal and hortatory texts before the weight of their ethical value can be measured.

Furthermore, in a book this size it is impossible to fit homosexuality into the larger picture of human sexuality. Here the question of homosexuality and moral education comes immediately to mind, and time should be given to critique the work of writers like J. Martin Stafford (1988) on this subject. Sex has always been dangerous. Sex in the Bible is no exception. A full treatment of sexuality must address top-

ics such as the role of women in society, the desacralization of sex, normative heterosexual roles, deviant sexual practices in addition to homosexuality, and cultic prostitution. One might legitimately ask why the
Hebrew Bible does not mention lesbianism directly (Anderson 1993:
10). Moreover, questions about normal eroticism and power in sex lie
beyond the scope of my work. As Tikva Frymer-Kensky notes (1989: 98):
"There is no vocabulary in the Bible in which to discuss such matters,
no divine image or symbolic system by which to mediate it. God does
not model sex, is not the patron of sexual behavior, and is not even
recorded as the guarantor of potency; and there is no other divine fig-
ure who can serve to control or mediate sex."

I do not minimize the importance of looking for causes of homosexuality, but space does not allow for the integration of research on this
subject. A number of controversial areas demand further attention. As
demonstrated by the public response to the writings of Simon LeVay and
Dean Hamer (LeVay 1991; Hamer 1993; LeVay and Hamer 1994), the
supposed biological roots of homosexuality is a hot topic. But as William
Byne shows (1994), the biological evidence is not conclusive—causation
is far from proved. Beyond biology, psychologists continue to debate
what is meant by sexual perversion (Primoratz 1997: 245) and behavior
(Jenkins 1993: 355; Henley 1993: 341; Leahey 1993: 345). Furthermore,
the biblical view of homosexuality must be related to issues relating to
the spread and control of AIDS. Christians cannot avoid the controversy
and must become more involved. I have had to leave untouched in this
book thorny ethical problems surrounding the management of HIV-
positive patients, including the high-profile issue of confidentiality
(Gillett 1987). Last, the role of the church in caring for homosexuals
remains very controversial. I should like to have included a full discussion of the St. Louis Statement on Human Sexuality (1995) and the Ramsey Colloquium (1994) as well as the positions taken by other organiza-
tions such as Homosexuals Anonymous and Exodus on the ex-gay side
and Evangelicals Concerned on the pro-gay side (Grenz 1990: 210), but
this too lies beyond the borders of this book.

As we begin this study, let me emphasize that what is needed in the
current debate regarding the Bible and homosexuality is a spirit of reconciliation rather than condemnation or confrontation on the part of
all who address this issue. Gay-bashing is totally inconsistent with biblical religion. For those in the biblical tradition, dogma should be subordinated to doctrine, and doctrine to exegesis. It is inconceivable that
Christians can be complicit in condemning unbelievers for missing biblical truth that has not been clearly explained to them. Jesus said: "You
hypocrite, first take the log out of your own eye, and then you will see
clearly enough to take the speck out of your brother's eye" (Matt. 7:5).

On the other hand, it is hoped that opponents of the Bible will remain open to an objective reading and evaluation of the data presented here. This presumes a willingness to abandon preconceived notions about what the Bible is and says. My approach to the biblical text is not unlike my analysis of the other documents consulted in preparing this book— let all the texts be treated with equal objectivity and fairness for whatever messages they convey. In the end, however, the Bible stands as a unique document among the ancient Near Eastern and Classical Greek records; and its statements about homosexuality are unique as well.

Finally, a note on the use of the adjectives *moral* and *ethical* and their respective nouns *morality* and *ethics*. Some teachers of ethics will regiment the use of these terms more strictly than I do. Both terms imply a standard for what is right or just in conduct. They presume a knowledge of right and wrong, a sense of conscience. Traced etymologically, what is moral may pertain more specifically to the mind of the individual, to one's own perception of good and bad, right or wrong. One thinks of individual rather than group morality in this sense. On the other hand, ethics may imply more the relation of conduct to society. This distinction, helpful though it may be to us, is not reflected in biblical thought. The Bible affirms individual responsibility for behavior and maintains that whatever the individual does has a direct and profound effect on society. Corporate responsibility is also evident in the biblical record. All activity is measured against the divine standard.

The ultimate biblical model for right conduct is the holiness of God. This standard, absolute and immutable, is revealed both in Scripture and finally in the person and work of Jesus Christ, who said: "I am the way, and the truth, and the life; no one comes to the Father, but through me" (John 14:6). The message of the gospel is essentially one of a new order, a new creation. It effects transformation. It empowers people to change patterns of behavior. As Christians today our task is to bring the truth of God's revelation into the arena of philosophical, religious, social, educational, political, moral, and ethical relativism, as order into chaos. A similar challenge was faced by biblical lawgivers, prophets, priests, and apostles. Relativism and pluralism characterized the cultures of the ancient world as much as our own.

How did the ancients perceive their world? What moral standards governed their conduct? What brought order to their chaos? The quest for order in the ancient Near East receives our attention in the next chapter. The peoples of Mesopotamia and Egypt saw the world in very different ways.

PART 1

Homosexuality in the Ancient Near East

2

Order in the Ancient Near East

In Mesopotamia, where the king is a man, there is perhaps not one rite which does not reflect anxiety and fear, oscillation between pain and joy: because there is no certainty in the interpretation of the will of the gods and in man's conformity with that will. In Egypt, where a god is a king, the rites have a basis of constant serenity: all is well, cannot be otherwise than well.

—Sabatino Moscati, *The Face of the Ancient Orient*

By the time the Hebrews arrived on the scene in antiquity, the two great river civilizations in Mesopotamia and Egypt were already old. High cultures like theirs do not appear, mushroomlike, overnight and mature. From material remains, it is evident that the advance of civilization in both regions took place over several millenniums before Abraham migrated from the Sumerian city of Ur to make his way to Haran and thence to Canaan. Around 3000 B.C. the Sumerians and Egyptians independently developed the first writing systems, one employing cuneiform and the other hieroglyphics (Gelb 1963). It is to this event, at the end of the fourth millennium B.C., that we ascribe the dawn of history. Some slight evidence exists for contact between these two great peoples, probably moving in the direction from Sumer to Egypt, but each civilization grew for the most part independently. While both viewed the world as an ordered system in which gods and humans played important roles, their cosmologies were based on very different underlying presuppositions about the creation of the world and the order required to maintain it. It is our task in this chapter to survey these significant differences.

The Hebrews and other peripheral peoples who settled the arch of the Fertile Crescent are known to us primarily from second-millennium B.C. sources. By the mid-third millennium, the ancient Syrian city of Ebla (modern Tell Mardikh), midway on the arch between Sumer and Egypt, was already a great city (Matthiae 1981), but because this city's written documents have been only recently deciphered, it is too early to ascertain whether these Semitic-speaking people developed their urban culture independently of the Sumerians and Egyptians or under the influence of cultural diffusion from them. Certainly they borrowed the Sumerian cuneiform to record their language.

Much remains to be learned about the manner in which the peoples of western Asia influenced each other in antiquity. Commerce and ideas flowed throughout the region for a long time before the Bible was written. It is against the background of these ideas that one must learn to understand the unique contribution of the Hebrews to Western civilization. Hebrew ideas of creation and order—ideas fundamental to understanding their view of homosexuality—did not emerge instantly and without connection to the ancient world.

Order in Ancient Mesopotamia

The Sumerians were a non-Semitic folk who lived in what is now southern Iraq and developed over the course of several millenniums a very high and sophisticated civilization (on the Sumerians, see Kramer 1963; Woolley 1965; and Jones 1969; on Mesopotamia more generally, see Oates 1986; Lloyd 1978 and 1980; Mallowan 1965; Gordon 1965; Moscati 1962; Knapp 1988; Chiera 1966; Saggs 1968; Oppenheim 1977; Jacobsen 1976; von Soden 1994; Frankfort 1974; and Bottéro 1992). Their modern discovery was an accident, not of archeology but of linguistics, for they were found on clay tablets by scholars looking for information on Babylonia and Assyria. The influence of the Sumerians on the ancient Orient and western civilization is still being measured. In the eloquent testimony of C. Leonard Woolley, the excavator of the great city of Ur, our debt to Sumer is deep indeed: "Their civilization, lighting up a world still plunged in primitive barbarism, was in the nature of a first cause. We have outgrown the phase when all the arts were traced to Greece and Greece was thought to have sprung, like Pallas, full-grown from the brain of the Olympian Zeus; we have learnt how that flower of genius drew its sap from Lydians and Hittites, from Phoenicia and Crete, from Babylon and Egypt. But the roots go farther back: behind all these lies Sumer" (1965: 194).

The prehistoric cemeteries at Ur (dating to about 3500 B.C.) already reflect a long development in human progress. From the First Dynasty of Ur (about 3300 B.C.) to the Semitic destruction of the Third Dynasty of Ur approximately 1500 years later, the Sumerians excelled in innovation. Samuel Noah Kramer lists almost thirty "firsts" in his *History Begins at Sumer* (1981). Among them are the first creation story, the first flood story, the first tower of Babel story, the first belief in a personal god, and the first "Job" story. The Sumerians invented the potter's wheel, brick-making, the dome, and the arch. They gave the world its first law code. Most important, they invented the first system of writing.

So impressive was Sumerian culture that the conquering Semites adapted the Sumerians' cuneiform writing system to their own language, Akkadian (so called after the city Akkad in northern Babylonia). Akkadian is the oldest Semitic language known to us; the earliest texts are dated to about 2500 B.C., but by then the language was already highly sophisticated. Its influence was extensive in both time and place: it became the lingua franca of the Near East for two thousand years and influenced a wide array of related tongues: Amorite, Aramaic, Eblaite, Ethiopic, Hebrew, Hittite, Hurrian (biblical Horite), North Arabic, South Arabic, and Ugaritic. The Sumerians bequeathed to these and other peoples not only their writing system but also their customs, religion, and mythology. The Babylonians added no new gods to the Sumerian pantheon, which they adopted wholesale. The Sumerian creation and flood stories became an integral part of Babylonian lore. Sumerian law was woven into the fabric of Babylonian society as illustrated in the code of Hammurapi. Babylonian art and architecture also show Sumerian influence. In fact, it would be hard to show a single area of Babylonian culture that was not in some way affected by the earlier Sumerians.

The extent of Mesopotamian (both Sumerian and Babylonian) influence on the surrounding cultures was great: "During the nearly three millennia of its documented history, Mesopotamia was in continuous contact with adjacent civilizations and, at times, even with distant civilizations. The region with which Mesopotamia was in contact either directly or through known intermediaries stretches from the Indus Valley across and, at times, even beyond Iran, Armenia, and Anatolia to the Mediterranean coast and into Egypt" (Oppenheim 1977: 63). Mesopotamia had a profound influence on ancient Greek mythology and cultic rituals; for example, the Dionysiac-Orphic myths find close parallels in the *Enûma Elish* and the *Atrahasis Epic*, showing that "the East-West connections went beyond accidental contacts and borrowings and occasionally reached the level of basic anthropological ideas" (Burkert 1995: 127).

Since Mesopotamian influence was so wide, it is reasonable to ask what effect their culture had on the Hebrews. Their influence is greatest in the early chapters of Genesis (1–11), somewhat less obvious in the patriarchal narratives. The Bible reports that the paternal ancestor of the Israelites came from Sumer: "And Terah took Abram his son, and Lot the son of Haran, his grandson, and Sarai his daughter-in-law, his son Abram's wife; and they went out together from Ur of the Chaldeans in order to enter the land of Canaan" (Gen. 11:31). An even greater connection may link the Hebrews to Sumer: Shem, the name of Noah's oldest son, may be equated with Sumer. Kramer (1963: 298) summarizes the implications of this conjecture:

> If . . . Shem is identical with Shumer-Sumer, we must assume that the Hebrew authors of the Bible, or at least some of them, considered the Sumerians to have been the original ancestors of the Hebrew people. . . . There may very well have been considerable Sumerian blood in Abraham's forefathers, who lived for generations in Ur or some other Sumerian cities. As for Sumerian culture and civilization, there is no reason to doubt that these proto-Hebrews had absorbed and assimilated much of the Sumerian way of life. In brief, Sumerian-Hebrew contacts may well have been more intimate than hitherto suspected, and the law which went forth from Zion (Isaiah 2:2) may have had not a few of its roots in the soil of Sumer.

The Sumero-Babylonian accounts of creation antedated the Hebrew version by many centuries; that the writer of Genesis was aware of them cannot be questioned. The Akkadian story, entitled *Enûma Elish* ("When on high . . .") after its opening words, has been the subject of much study. The differences between the biblical and Mesopotamian stories are not in doubt, but their similarities should not be overlooked; both contain the following peculiarities: (1) a primeval body of water existed before creation—a chaos from which order was made; (2) humans were fashioned from clay and enervated by the "breath of life"; (3) creation was effected by divine fiat and by hands-on formation of material; (4) the firmament was created by a separation of waters; and (5) light was created before the luminaries. It is remarkable that the order of the creative process is the same in both versions (Heidel 1951: 129):

Enûma Elish	Genesis
divine spirit and cosmic matter are coexistent and coeternal	divine spirit creates cosmic matter and exists independently of it
primeval chaos; Tiʾâmat enveloped in darkness	the earth a desolate waste, with darkness covering the deep (*tĕhôm*)
light emanating from the gods	light created
	creation of firmament
	creation of dry land
	creation of luminaries
	creation of humans
the gods rest and celebrate	God rests and sanctifies the seventh day

The Hebrew writer probably borrowed his order of creation from an existing model or standardized outline that was generally known throughout the ancient Near East. Both Hebrews and Mesopotamians affirm the importance of order, but the worldviews of the respective peoples are vastly different. The difference is summarized by Leo Oppenheim (1977: 182) in a tone that reflects his own preference for pluralism:

It may be stressed that neither the number of deities worshiped nor the absence or presence of definite (and carefully worded) answers to the eternal and unanswerable questions of man separate decisively a polytheistic from a monotheistic religion. Rather, it seems to be the criterion of a plurality of intellectual and spiritual dimensions that sets off most of the higher polytheistic religions from the narrowness, the one-dimensional pressure of revealed religions. Instead of the symbol of the path and the gate, which may be taken to be the "kenning" of monotheism, a primeval, inevitable, and unchanging design or order (*dharma, ṛta, šimtu*) organizes the multifaceted structures of polytheistic religions. They are characterized by the absence of any centrality and by a deep-seated tolerance to shifting stresses, making possible the adaptability that such religions need to achieve their millennial lifespan.

By contrast, the Hebrew notion of order is predicated on the will of God expressed in creation. The difference is polar, just as it is in modern society where pluralism and secularism are characterized by "deep-seated tolerance to shifting stresses."

The Sumerian term for order is *me*. Every aspect of life in Sumer—music, law, power, truth, peace, strife, terror, the troubled heart, even sexual intercourse and prostitution—was ruled by *me*. The main source of information about *me* is found in the myth "Inanna and Enki: The

Transfer of the Arts of Civilization from Eridu to Erech," which lists some sixty occasions indicated by *me* (Kramer 1963: 116, 160). Wilfred Lambert and Alan Millard (1969: 18) define the term as follows: "A *me* was the concept of any one of the numerous aspects of organized human life, from sexual intercourse to gold-smithery, and all alike were given to man and had to be respected as divine ordinances." According to Sumerian tradition, when the gods created the cosmos they also devised rules and regulations for its smooth operation. It was inconceivable to the Sumerians that the gods would take their hands off once the universe was set in motion.

Not all the deities in the Sumerian pantheon were orderly or, for that matter, ethical and moral. That disorder reigned among them is well illustrated in the *Atrahasis Epic*, the Babylonian flood story. The junior gods, created to do the work of the senior gods, made so much noise that their elders could not sleep. A decision was made to create humankind to do the work. Kingu, one of the rebellious gods, was slain and his blood was mixed with clay to create mankind. Unfortunately the situation was not much improved by this creative effort, for the noise continued. Finally, the idea of a flood was fixed upon to destroy the disorderly creatures, preserving only the righteous Utnapishtim, counterpart of Sumerian Ziusudra and biblical Noah, by means of a reed boat. Just as the world was created from the combined waters of Apsu and Tiᵓâmat, so destruction also came by water.

We learn from these Mesopotamian accounts of creation and the flood that order in the cosmos is disrupted by the rebellious behavior of humankind and that divine punishment ensues to reestablish it (a similar point is made in the biblical account of the tower of Babel). No single moral law exists on the human level since there is no unity on the divine level. Before the gods of nature, the Mesopotamian is left in a state of flux. Sacrifices, magic, and omens are performed to placate the gods and solicit their benevolence. Whatever might be, one's fate (*šimtu*)—the order of one's personal life—is subordinate to the realm of the gods:

> The experience of Nature which produces this mood found direct expression in the Mesopotamian's notion of the cosmos in which he lived. He was in no way blind to the great rhythms of the cosmos; he saw the cosmos as order, not as anarchy. But to him that order was not nearly so safe and reassuring as it was to the Egyptian. Through and under it he sensed a multitude of powerful individual wills, potentially divergent, potentially conflicting, fraught with a possibility of anarchy. . . . To the Mesopotamian, accordingly, cosmic order did not appear as something given; rather it became something achieved—achieved through a continual integration

of the many individual cosmic wills, each so powerful, so frightening. (Frankfort 1974: 139)

Mesopotamian myths also represent disorder on the political level. In the politics of the third millennium B.C., the gods were characterized by disorder. Thorkild Jacobsen suggests (1976: 170) that the myth of creation may reflect political change: from anarchy in the third millennium to primitive democracy in the second and finally to monarchy and order in the first: "In the epic, world order is seen as the outcome of just such a successful drive toward supremacy." The king, however, did not speak on his own, but was a vice-regent of the sky god Anu, who was ultimately the source, the divine will, that brought about world order:

> Human society was to the Mesopotamian merely a part of the larger society of the universe. The Mesopotamian universe—because it did not consist of dead matter, because every stone, every tree, every conceivable thing in it was a being with a will and character of its own—was likewise founded on authority; its members, too, willingly and automatically obeyed orders which made them act as they should act. These orders *we* call laws of nature. So the whole universe showed the influence of the essence peculiar to Anu. (Frankfort 1974: 152)

Disorder in Mesopotamia is the product of people and gods. No god ruled supreme, and chaos constantly strove with order. The myths portray Mesopotamian society (both human and divine) in constant unrest, turmoil, and uncertainty; even the monarchy could not bring intellectual peace or political tranquillity. In Mesopotamian mythology, creation itself comes at the end of a long and boisterous process depicting polarities among the gods. The situation was completely different in Egypt.

Order in Ancient Egypt

The Egyptian term *ma²at* closely expresses the idea of "order" and has a wide range of meanings. It is a dynamic idea fundamental to the Egyptian understanding of the universe. It addresses personal, sociopolitical, and cosmic order (for background on Egyptian history and culture, consult Aldred 1980; Assmann 1990; Bowman 1989; Carter and Mace 1977; Emery 1987; Fagan 1992; Gardiner 1964; Robins 1993; and Seele 1957). Religion in Egypt cannot be understood apart from *ma'at*. Doing the right thing in consonance with *ma'at* has profound implications for felicity in the afterlife. An excellent example of justice/*ma'at* is found in "The Protests of the Eloquent Peasant" (*ANET* 407–10), a story set in the twenty-first century B.C.

A peasant is traveling with his donkeys in search of food for his family when he meets a certain Thut-nakht, a vassal of the pharaoh's chief steward, who covets the poor man's beasts. The peasant is forced off the public road and onto Thut-nakht's private property where one of his donkeys eats a few kernels of the rich man's grain. For this the peasant is subjected to beatings and his donkeys are stolen. Some ten days later the peasant appeals to the chief steward, who directs him to the pharaoh. The peasant makes ten appeals that belabor the idea of *ma'at* against injustice, violence, theft, greed, etc. Ultimately, after more abuse, he is brought a last time to speak, thinking he will be put to death. Instead he is elevated to live with the chief steward at the approval of the pharaoh, and the property of Thut-nakht is transferred to the peasant.

This charming tale emphasizes the social impact of personal *ma'at* and conveys the idea that order is incumbent upon all members of Egyptian society—regardless of their rank. From the lowliest peasant to the pharaoh, all are subject to *ma'at*. Egyptian religion, too, revolved around this notion: *ma'at* "appears to have been a means of expressing the basic unity and solidarity not only of the human community in itself but of that community in a universal setting." The basic idea of religious thought in Egypt was that

> the world and the universe were parts of a strict and unchanging order of stability. This order was an expression of the peculiar Egyptian concept of *Ma'at*. . . . Within this order of *Ma'at*, the universe, the world and the political state all had their appointed place; and it was within this same order that each individual also was able to find meaning and significance for his own existence. . . . Every human action was evaluated not by a prescribed system of laws and rules, but by how far it conformed to the general principle of right and order which was expressed by *Ma'at*. (Tobin 1992: 291)

For the ancient Egyptians, their present order had its locus in the primeval order. Reality was not separated from myth. The Egyptian creation myth "The Primeval Establishment of Order" (*ANET* 9–10) assigns to the god Atum the role of bringing order to the chaotic waters (note the analogy to Mesopotamian and biblical creation stories). The chaotic powers of four pairs of preexistent gods (male-female counterparts) are eclipsed by the ordering force of the self-created Atum. This power of Atum conquers not only chaos in creation but also anxiety (i.e., mental chaos) about the next life. Creation in Egypt was the result of a divine order (Frankfort 1978: 59–70).

Two points should suffice to show the importance of order among the Egyptians: (1) disorder (*izfet*) is intimately related to evil conduct and is associated with the lack of civilization epitomized by the desert, and (2) magic and kingship are the Egyptian solutions to establishing *maʾat* and overcoming disorder. (Two works—both of them pregnant with insight and rich with bibliographical references—address the Egyptian idea of order: Baines, Lesko, and Silverman 1991 and Frankfort 1978; Frankfort's analysis is doubly valuable because it compares Egyptian and Mesopotamian ideas of order.)

Disorder might be created or uncreated, but it never went away. "Disorder lurked at the edges of Egypt—in the desert and in the underworld—and the ordered cosmos was shot through with 'uncreated' elements that threatened to engulf it and had to be countered" (Baines, Lesko, and Silverman 1991: 124). Created disorder is personified in the god Seth, who is represented in one myth as committing a homosexual act (see chap. 3). This antagonist of the goddess Maʾat is characterized by chaos, evil, confusion, and murder—the opposite of balance, harmony, justice, and truth. In fact, evil and disorder are closely linked: "In Egypt, the notion of evil overlapped to a great extent with that of disorder. The fusion of these two ideas would have served the interests of the ruling group by associating publicly sanctioned morality and social subservience with the preservation of the cosmic order. Such a cosmic superstructure for morality is unlikely to be found in a plural society [like Mesopotamia] with divergent and conflicting ideologies" (Baines, Lesko, and Silverman 1991: 163). As in Mesopotamian cosmology, humans generate evil and disorder, and the creator-god disavows responsibility: "I made every man like his fellow. I did not ordain that they do wrong (*izfet*, 'disorder'). It was their desires that damaged what I had said" (p. 163). Egyptian society consisted of four parts— gods, pharaoh, the dead, and humanity—that act together to create and maintain order (p. 129).

Two primary avenues of preserving order were available to ancient Egyptians. Like Mesopotamians, they resorted to magic, which "invoked the most elemental forces in creation and responded to the capricious elements that threatened the essential sense of order" (p. 165). The benefits of magic were many: "If a performance was successful, the proper order of things was reaffirmed. Should it fail, the evocation of drastic consequences in some spells implies the failure would be part of a wider, and in practice almost inconceivable, catastrophe" (p. 169). Beyond the cosmic effects hoped for, doing something by magic at least must have made the Egyptians feel better.

The second avenue was kingship. The pharaoh in Egypt was not perceived as simply representing god; he *was* god incarnate. Kingship was the central feature of Egyptian society. The pharaoh propitiated the gods through cultic offerings, judged humanity, and set order in place of disorder (Baines, Lesko, and Silverman 1991: 128). The pharaoh could not act arbitrarily, for he lived "under the obligation to maintain *maat*" (Frankfort 1978: 51). Stability in Egypt was gained by the mere existence of the pharaoh: "The alignment of society with nature was assumed to be perfect because a divine mediator ruled the land. . . . It was unthinkable that nature and society should follow different courses, for both alike were ruled by *maat*" (p. 277).

Order in Other Ancient Cultures

Mesopotamian and Egyptian ideas of order may be viewed as primary influences on Hebrew thought since these cultures dominated the ancient Near East. Other cultures also influenced the Hebrews, but their extant sources (material and literary) are not as extensive as we might hope. Even though the Bible shows a less direct relationship to other cultures, we should examine the Hittite and Canaanite influence on the Hebrews.

The Hittites ruled a vast kingdom from their capital Hattusas in Anatolia, until the battle of Qadesh in 1286 B.C. (for a general introduction to the Hittites, consult Gurney 1961 and Moscati 1962: 161). For a period of about five centuries Hittite influence was powerful in the ancient Near East. Vestiges of Hittite influence on Hebrew thought can be seen most clearly in the Hebrew cultus and in the system of laws. The idea of order and the administration of the Hittite temple went hand in hand. The Hittite cultus was controlled by purity rules, for impurity was a threat. Since cultus was inseparable from the state, the effect of impurity on the Hittite society was dangerous to the entire society.

The Canaanites also influenced Hebrew thought (for a review of the Canaanites, consult Albright 1965). Ancient Phoenicians who lived in western Syria along the Mediterranean coast spoke a Semitic language. One such dialect is known as Ugaritic, discovered at modern Ras es-Shamra on the Orontes River in 1929. Closely related to Hebrew, Ugaritic is an alphabetic language like Hebrew but is written in cuneiform under the influence of Akkadian.

Ugaritic texts, like other Canaanite literary sources, demonstrate that northwest Semitic cultures were an amalgam of influences by the dominant Egyptian and Mesopotamian peoples that controlled the area for most of the second and third millenniums B.C. Only during brief periods did the local Canaanite population have respite from such influences: "The collapse of Egyptian power in the early 18th century gave the Canaanites freedom to develop the cultural influences which had been streaming from Egypt and Mesopotamia during the preceding two or three centuries" (Albright 1965: 447). The religion of Canaan reflected in the Ugaritic texts reflects practices that did not exist or that had been abandoned in Mesopotamia or Egypt, among them human sacrifice, sacred prostitution of both sexes, eunuch priests, and serpent worship (p. 453).

The crude customs of the Canaanites provide a sharp contrastive background to Hebrew ideas of morality and order in society. On the positive side, however, the Canaanite El traditions may provide a background for creation terminology in the Bible: "El Elyon, procreator of heaven and earth, represents an El tradition that is a forerunner or prototype of Yahweh, maker of heaven and earth. The transition from the former to the latter rendering of the formula is explicable in terms of the development of Israelite religion, especially the modification of Canaanite El traditions in terms of later Yahwism" (Habel 1972: 337).

Finally, the Hebrew cultus can be studied effectively by comparison with practices among peoples far removed from the ancient Orient. I do not suggest that the Hebrews borrowed from these remote cultures, but when analogous customs develop in unrelated cultures, it is worth noting the similarities and differences to clarify the development of society within each native group. For the Hebrews, this development is always represented as a corollary of the will of God. I shall defend later the idea that homosexuality produced disorder in Hebrew society much like adultery and incest do among the Nuer of Africa (Burton 1974: 517). Differences in particulars must be underlined, but the points made by Mary Douglas may also be applied with care to the levitical concept of impurity (see chap. 8 for discussion of Douglas's treatment of the role of purity rules in structuring society).

Conclusion

This brief survey demonstrates that order played a significant role in the lives of ancient Mesopotamians and Egyptians. It was fundamental to cosmology and cosmogony in both cases. Given the influence of these two great river civilizations on the other peoples of the region, it is reasonable to postulate that order was a high priority among them as well. That the Hebrews should have lived in close proximity to Mesopotamians and Egyptians without sharing some of their conceptions of order in creation and the cosmos seems impossible. In fact, the Genesis creation story reflects agreement at several points with the Mesopotamian *Enûma Elish* and with the Egyptian idea that the world came to be by divine fiat. At the same time, striking differences exist between the views of order expressed by the Mesopotamians and Egyptians. In addition, the Hebrews also made their own unique contributions to the idea of order in their cosmology, a view underlined by Henri Frankfort (1978: 241): "The differences between the Egyptian and Mesopotamian manners of viewing the world are very far-reaching. Yet the two peoples agreed in the fundamental assumptions that the individual is part of society, that society is embedded in nature, and that nature is but the manifestation of the divine. This doctrine was, in fact, universally accepted by the peoples of the ancient world with the single exception of the Hebrews."

Let us be clear about what the Hebrews rejected. They agreed with their neighbors that the individual is part of society. They also agreed with both Mesopotamians and Egyptians that society, if not "embedded in nature," should reflect the order characteristic of the creation. Beyond that, the differences are immense. For example, creation in the Bible is the result of divine fiat, not the command of a god like Atum who creates himself, but the word of creation comes forth from the eternal Yahweh who is transcendent and sovereign above the creation—never part of it. The same God who orders nature also orders morality. He creates humanity in his own image (Gen. 1:26–27). As human wrongdoing was the source of disorder among Mesopotamians and Egyptians, so could the gods err. Among the Hebrews, evil is laid squarely on the shoulders of humanity; it is never attributed to the perfect God of the Hebrews. Their neighbors would confront evil with magic; the Hebrews could only confess it and seek the forgiveness of a merciful God. Righteousness, the equivalent of *maʾat*, was conformity to the will of the Creator in keeping with the design of creation. Any conduct contrary to the will of God or out of harmony with the order of creation was deemed by the Hebrews to be out of order. Divine sanctions might ensue.

Ultimately, Hebrew notions of order would be predicated on the holiness of Yahweh their God, an attribute that each Israelite would be expected to emulate. Moral conduct would be expunged of magical and demonic influences, the individual being made accountable solely to the Creator. If disorder in society resulted from violation of pollution rules, the cause would be traced to human error. In this, the Hebrew conception of morality and personal responsibility differed greatly from beliefs held elsewhere throughout ancient western Asia and Egypt. The idea of order, infused with the peculiarities of Hebrew thought and divine inspiration, remained a cornerstone of Israelite society throughout the biblical period. It is especially necessary to grant this when considering the biblical response to same-gender sexual relations.

3

Homosexuality
in the Ancient Near East

If a seignior [free citizen] lay with his [male] neighbor, when they have prosecuted him (and) convicted him, they shall lie with him (and) turn him into a eunuch.

—Middle Assyrian Laws

Each of the respective ancient Near Eastern cultures cast the image of its own shadow on its laws, and it is possible to notice in the shadows definite similarities and differences. These are of particular interest to the student of homosexuality in the Bible, for by the time Leviticus 18:22 and 20:13 were written there was a kind of common law that had existed for centuries and was widely distributed throughout the ancient Near East. The exact relationship between biblical and ancient Near Eastern law, however, has not been definitely established. Unfortunately, no law collections are extant from the many archeological finds in Egypt, but examples of Mesopotamian legal texts abound. Mesopotamian law had a direct influence throughout the ancient world except on the Hittite and the Hebrews, as Ephraim Speiser writes (1967: 552):

The outward signs of foreign dependence on Mesopotamian law are the script, the language and the document. Yet such formal indebtedness fails to reveal the secret of Mesopotamia's appeal. Magnetism on so large a scale would seem to suggest that content as well as form played here a substantial part. Nevertheless, the Hittites certainly did not simply adopt the laws of Hammurabi or the Old Assyrian laws. The Hebrews remain even further apart; for they either never acknowledged the influence of the cuneiform script or they soon emancipated themselves from it in committing their own laws to writing. In content, then, there is nothing like a one-to-one correlation between the laws of Mesopotamia and Hittite or Hebrew law.

This distinction between Hebrew and Mesopotamian law is especially true with regard to homosexuality; there was no law like Hebrew homosexual law among the legal codes of the ancient Near East.

Mesopotamian Law and Homosexuality

I t is often assumed by biblical scholars that homosexual practices were widespread in the ancient Near East (Otto J. Baab, *IDB* 2:639). Mesopotamian law does not categorically prohibit homosexuality, as does biblical law. In fact, I am unaware of any specific reference to homosexuality in Mesopotamian law before the end of the second millennium B.C. The early Mesopotamian laws reflect a variety of legal interests, such as real estate and business transactions, weights and measures, justice for widows, adoption, and family relations; but they do not address homosexuality.

For example, the laws of Eshnunna, an ancient city located not far from modern Baghdad, were composed between the fall of the Third Dynasty of Ur (about 2000 B.C.) and the reign of Hammurapi (1792–1750 B.C.), sixth king of the First Dynasty of Babylon. Comprised of some sixty laws, the Eshnunna code has been of great interest to biblical scholars because it contains legislation that antedates the biblical law of the goring ox (Exod. 21:35–36), but there is no mention of homosexual conduct. The code of Hammurapi consists of a collection of 282 laws and an epilogue that concludes with curses upon all who do not heed his words. It addresses both civil and criminal law, but not homosexuality.

The first explicit reference to homosexuality in Mesopotamia comes in the Middle Assyrian law of the second millennium B.C., quoted in the chapter epigraph (§A20; *ANET* 181). This law occurs in a list of several sexual crimes similar to the stipulations of Leviticus 18 and appears to categorically proscribe male homosexuality. The nature of the homosexual act, however, is debated. According to David Greenberg (1988: 126), it has to do specifically with homosexual rape, the penalty for which is forced anal intercourse ("lie with him") and castration ("turn him into a eunuch") in keeping with the principal of *lex talionis*. He disagrees that this penalty applied to consensual anal homosexual acts:

> Published translations . . . are misleading on this point; they wrongly suggest that the prohibition applied to all acts of anal homosexual intercourse. However, the voice of the verb *na-ku* in this passage implies the use of force. . . . Were the passage to refer to consensual homosexuality, the penalty would make no sense; referring to coercion, it follows the pattern of analogic penalties common to ancient law: "an eye for an eye," "a rape for a rape." Implicitly, the state was willing to sponsor active, aggressive homosexual behavior under special circumstances.

Force is not necessarily implied in the verb, nor is it required to make sense of *lex talionis*. Akkadian *nâku* is used for sexual intercourse of different kinds and may be translated "to have illicit sexual intercourse, to fornicate, to have illicit intercourse repeatedly, to permit intercourse," but not "to rape" (*CAD* N 1:197). According to this Middle Assyrian law, homosexual conduct is illicit; if the offender is brought to trial and convicted, he is given a severe penalty, sufficient enough we may suppose to deter same-gender sexual relations. The penalty consists of two parts: the homosexual is sexually abused by his jurors, perhaps to humiliate him (but not to tacitly legitimize state-sponsored homosexual acts), and then castrated so that he will not perpetrate the crime again. No motive clauses are attached to the penalty as in the levitical laws. Despite the Assyrian legislators' silence on such matters, the rationale for the penalty of castration is evident: it is the principle of *lex talionis*: eye for eye, tooth for tooth, act for act.

Lex talionis remained a fundamental of law throughout the Near East. That the Hebrews took it over is clear from the Pentateuch:

> If a malicious witness rises up against a man to accuse him of wrongdoing, then both the men who have the dispute shall stand before the LORD, before the priests and the judges who will be in office in those days. And the judges shall investigate thoroughly; and if the witness is a false witness and he has accused his brother falsely, then you shall do to him just as he had intended to do to his brother. Thus you shall purge the evil from among you. And the rest will hear and be afraid, and will never again do such an evil thing among you. Thus you shall not show

pity: life for life, eye for eye, tooth for tooth, hand for hand, foot for
foot. (Deut. 19:16–21)

Another Middle Assyrian law touches on homosexuality. In this case
a man is falsely accused of homosexual conduct:

> If a seignior started a rumor against his neighbor in private, saying, "Peo-
> ple have lain repeatedly with him" or he said to him in a brawl in the pres-
> ence of (other) people, "People have lain repeatedly with you; I will pros-
> ecute you," since he is not able to prosecute (him) (and) did not prosecute
> (him), they shall flog that seignior fifty (times) with staves (and) he shall
> do the work of the king for one full month; they shall castrate him and
> he shall also pay one talent of lead. (§A19; *ANET* 181)

Commenting on *nâku*, the *Chicago Assyrian Dictionary* editors make
reference to this law: "referring to homosexuality: 'if a man *ina ṣalte ana
panī* ERÍN.MEŠ *iqbiaššu mā it-ti-ni-ku-ka* says to another man during a
quarrel in front of the men (of the community): Everybody has intercourse with you'" (*CAD* N 1:198). Since the verb *nâku* is iterative in this
case, the action is repeated or customary; this is clearly not a case of
homosexual rape. A reference to consensual relationships could easily
fall under the iterative rubric. Possibly the individual was accused of
being a catamite. Whether he was accused of the active or passive role,
once again a strict and harsh penalty is imposed on the accuser,
although it is not clear that a homosexual act was in fact committed.
Apparently no witnesses could be produced to verify the accusation. If
homosexuality was not a serious offense no major penalty would have
been attached to it, and the false witness would not have been in jeopardy. However, fines are levied, corvée is required, beatings are inflicted,
and castration is imposed as well—implying *lex talionis*. Castration is
the punishment he would have inflicted upon his neighbor. It is apparent from these Middle Assyrian laws that castration was the usual
penalty for homosexual acts in Assyria at the end of the second millennium B.C.

Assuming that the levitical writer was aware of the Assyrian legislation, one might be tempted to see a literal relationship between castration in the Assyrian law and the *kareth* penalty "to cut off." According
to David Greenberg (1988: 125 n. 4), "The provision that the slanderer
be castrated is not entirely unambiguous. Driver and Miles translate the
passage as 'he shall be cut off' and suggest that this may imply social
ostracism. Cardascia . . . understands the passage as specifying some
sort of marking or branding of the offender." It is not likely that marking or branding is implied in the Assyrian penalty, since mutilation and

disfiguring are explicit in other cases (§A16). The periphrastic expression *ana ša rēšen utarruš* ("they shall turn him into a eunuch") found in §A20 makes the law unambiguous. To be "cut off" should be taken literally in the sense of castration in the Assyrian law, not in some figurative sense such as "excommunication." A similar error is made by modern commentators in suggesting that the *kareth* penalty be understood as excommunication. In any event, a one-to-one comparison cannot be made to the *kareth* penalty, for *kareth* is never imposed by humans; it is a divine prerogative (see chap. 9). Herein lies a major difference between biblical law and Middle Assyrian law.

Mesopotamian Practice and Homosexuality

Most of the evidence from Mesopotamian literature and art suggests that homosexuality was limited to the cultus and not commonly practiced outside of it, nor was it morally condemned.

Mesopotamian Literature

Much of the literature of ancient Mesopotamia belongs to the category of magical texts; many of the collections have names like *utukke lemnūti* ("evil demons") or *šumma alû* ("if a ghost"). Every part of Mesopotamian life was thought to be influenced by individual or groups of demons, and fear was an important feature of the Mesopotamian psyche. Disease, death, and misfortune of every kind were ascribed to demons. Past, present, and future concerns were under their control. Inevitably, a variety of means were employed to influence demonic forces. Sheep livers were "read" to determine one's fortune, incantations for potency and disease were recited, and even sexual acts were performed to ward off demons and to predict the future.

Of particular interest for the study of homosexuality are the *šumma alû* texts. Should the *alû*-ghost seize an individual, headache, exhaustion, weakened limbs, or a plethora of other ailments might ensue. In general, the term is defined as "a personal psychic experience often described as a formless and featureless demonic power which engulfs the entire individual" (*CAD* A 1:376). The *šumma alû* prescriptions to ward off this encompassing evil are phrased like the laws of Hammurapi in the familiar protasis-apodosis or "if-then" construction. Five of the instructions touch on same-sex intercourse (D. Greenberg 1988: 126–27):

1. If a man has intercourse with the hindquarters of his equal (male), that man will be foremost among his brothers and colleagues.
2. If a man yearns to express his manhood while in prison and thus, like a male cult prostitute, mating with men becomes his desire, he will experience evil.
3. If a man has intercourse with a (male) cult prostitute, care [in the sense of "trouble"] will leave him.
4. If a man has intercourse with a [male] courtier, for one whole year the worry which plagued him will vanish.
5. If a man has intercourse with a [male] slave, care will seize him.

These passages are summarized by David Greenberg as follows (p. 127):

> None of the acts elicits moral condemnation, but some are auspicious whereas others are not. Homosexuality itself carries no implications; neither here nor anywhere else does the concept of a homosexual person even appear. What matters are the roles and statuses of the parties. To penetrate someone of high social status (an equal, a cult prostitute, a courtier) anally is favorable; to be involved with one's slave, unfavorable. The Babylonians may have felt that a sexual connection would erode a master's authority over his slaves. To prefer the receptive role, perhaps exclusively, appears to have been negatively regarded except in a cultic context. An apodictic curse warns that "one will make him the object of repeated coitus."

Bear in mind that these are omen texts dealing with magic; they are not legal texts and will not, therefore, be concerned with the morality of an act. We should, therefore, analyze this literary genre appropriately.

Anal intercourse with men was viewed in the ancient Near East as a sign of dominance. This view seems to be expressed clearly in that sexual relations with one's equal elevates the aggressor (1), while sexual relations with someone of lower social rank, but not a slave, has a positive effect (4). Conversely, sexual intercourse with a male slave has an inauspicious result (5), perhaps because of the low social status of the servant. Sexual intercourse with a cult prostitute, a guild legitimized in Mesopotamia as in the Canaanite cultures, is deemed effective against the *alû*-ghost (3). However, such activity outside the guild, as with homosexual acts in prison (2), produces unwanted results. It cannot be concluded that the male cult prostitute assumed only the passive role, although this is possible. The *šumma alû* texts do not present a complete view of homosexual practice in Mesopotamia. It is possible that homosexuality was controlled by the cultus for the purpose of generating income and that same-gender sexual relations apart from the cultic activity were neither common nor permitted in Mesopotamia apart from this milieu, at least during the period represented by the Middle Assyrian laws.

Several types of cult personnel are represented in the Mesopotamian sources. According to Marvin Pope (1976: 415), "the *assinnu, kulu'u,* and *kurgarrû,* cult functionaries of the love and war goddess Inanna/ Ishtar, are mentioned in terms suggestive of homosexuality." It is more likely, however, that these terms characterized thespians, musicians, or dancers who performed in conjunction with religious festivals. This is the view of more authoritative scholarship: "The *kurgarrû, assinnu, kulu'u* and others were members of the temple personnel—most often mentioned in connection with Ishtar—performing games, plays, dances and music as part of the ritual (of the great festivals). There is no evidence that they were eunuchs or homosexuals. However, in the Descent of Ishtar the reference to the *kurgarru* as neither male nor female may indicate that they were transvestites performing in female apparel" (*CAD* K 558). It is not possible to deduce from these and associated terms a pattern of homosexual practice in the religious sphere at this time. No single Akkadian term exists for the homosexual.

Tom Horner (1978) finds the earliest reference to homosexual conduct in Mesopotamia in the *Gilgamesh Epic,* the hero and king of Uruk. In his quest for immortality, Gilgamesh encounters Enkidu, and the two become fast friends. Horner (p. 16) interprets the friendship as homosexual because "they kissed each other / and formed a friendship" (*ANET* 79). He regards the following lines (1.3.22) as evidence that Gilgamesh was bisexual:

> Gilgamesh leaves not the son to [his] father;
> [Day] and [night] is unbridled his arro[gance].
> . . . [Gilgamesh] leaves not [the maid to her mother],
> The warrior's daughter, [the noble's spouse]. (*ANET* 73–74)

Horner errs in finding that any reference to friendship between members of the same gender must be characterized as sexual. The two heroes are simply comrades in a tale of adventure as they search for immortality. Nothing in the language of the epic is suggestive of a homosexual relationship. To the contrary, the heterosexual behavior of Gilgamesh and Enkidu is explicit in the poem. Enkidu, a wild man, sleeps with a harlot and is "tamed." Gilgamesh speaks to him as he descends to the netherworld:

Thy wife whom thou lovest thou shalt not kiss,
Thy wife whom thou hatest thou shalt not strike,
Thy son whom thou lovest thou shalt not kiss,
Thy son whom thou hatest thou shalt not strike! (*ANET* 97)

In other words, Gilgamesh is aware that Enkidu will not come back from the dead to experience common human relationships. But does that mean, then, the poet used the word *kiss* equally of Enkidu's wife and son? The kiss between Enkidu and Gilgamesh was in all probability nothing more than the kiss of greeting still customary among Semitic peoples today—there is no sexual component in it. It is strictly a gesture of friendship, as the text of the poem explains.

Mesopotamian Art

Before leaving Mesopotamia, it is of interest to ask whether the art of the area reflects homosexual practice. In fact, unlike Greek art, which vividly portrays homosexual scenes, ancient Near Eastern art noticeably lacks such portrayals, although figurines and statues depicting fertility deities abound. Sometimes, victory steles portray a troop of naked prisoners bound in single file, but in none of them is there a homosexual act of domination or humiliation. In a culture dominated by scenes from nature, by the intimate connection between sex and soil in the annual fertility rites practiced for millenniums, why is there a vacuum in homosexual art? In art, as in literature, Mesopotamia does not appear to be concerned with the practice. Robert Biggs (1969: 103) writes with confidence that "there was apparently no taboo against anal intercourse of either a homosexual or a heterosexual nature, so such activity cannot be considered a perversion."

Reasons for Limited Reference to Homosexuality

The apparent rarity of homosexuality in Mesopotamian society is reflected in the lack of references in Mesopotamian literature and art. Two factors could account for this: (1) the importance of the nuclear family and (2) the concern to generate children to carry on one's name. These intimately related factors combine to assure the Mesopotamian of felicity in the afterlife. Although our knowledge of the family in the ancient Near East is incomplete, homosexuality in the ancient world should be investigated with reference to the larger sphere of family values. Leo Oppenheim (1977: 76–77) provides a good summary regarding the family:

> Through innumerable legal documents from the Sumerian to the Seleucid period we know the individual as father and son (adopted or natural), as brother (as set forth in legacies), and as husband (as mentioned in the marriage and divorce texts). . . . The head of the family had one wife. . . . Emphasis was placed on the virginity of the bride. . . . The first-born son received a preferred share in the paternal estate . . . and provisions were made to insure the daughters' dowries and the younger brothers' marriage expenses.

Extensive legislation on adoption in Mesopotamia emphasizes the integrity of the nuclear family, while pointing to the need for heirs to carry on one's name. Children were an essential asset for economic purposes, and they provided assurance for happiness in the life hereafter. If someone was blessed by Shamas, "he will prolong his life. / He will enlarge his family, gain wealth, / And like the water of a never-failing spring [his] descendants will never fail" (Lambert 1960: 133). Mesopotamians, like Hebrews and Egyptians, believed that life in some form continued after death. At death and upon proper burial, it was expected that one would join the ghosts of ancestors (*ana* GIDIM *kimtišu isniq*). On the other hand, as indicated by this Middle Babylonian *kudurru* or boundary-stone inscription, deprivation of burial was a severe curse for the Mesopotamians: "May his corpse not be buried in the earth, may his ghost not join the ghosts of his relatives (*šalamtašu ina erṣeti aj iqqebir* (GIDIM-*šu*) *ana* GIDIM *kimtišu aj isniq*)" (*CAD* E 398). Parents believed that their children would be responsible to attend to their burial and to maintain their grave. That this belief was shared by the Hebrews and Egyptians is indicated by the respective expressions *go to one's fathers* (Gen. 15:15; 25:8) and *go to one's ka* (*sbj n kꜣ.f*), expressions antithetical to the biblical *kareth* penalty.

If there was widespread homosexuality in Mesopotamia, it would have stood in sharp opposition to the integrity of the nuclear family, to beliefs in afterlife as they related to having children or adopting them, and to the preservation of these fundamental tenets of society as reflected in the genealogical lists from Babylonian and Assyrian sources. It is not surprising that little reference to homosexuality exists in Mesopotamian literature and art. It is difficult to imagine that the practice was common. Very likely it was limited to the cultus.

Hittite Law and Homosexuality

There are significant parallels between the Hebrew and Hittite laws with regard to ritual purity, which separates them both from Mesopotamian law. The moral tone of Hebrew law as well as the legislation concerning homosexual behavior, however, distinguishes it from that of the Hittites. There is also a difference of sanctions between the Hebrews and the Hittites; both use the death penalty, but only the Hebrews use the *kareth* penalty. Hittite moral attitudes toward homosexuality are impossible to deduce from their literature; it is simply not mentioned even though their law code addresses a number of sexual aberrations under the headings of bestiality, rape, and incest, all of which have to do with ritual purity.

Bestiality

Four laws deal with acts of bestiality with cattle, sheep, pigs, dogs, and oxen, all of which are capital crimes. One law specifies an illicit act with cattle: "If a man does evil with a head of cattle, it is a capital crime and he shall be killed" (§187; *ANET* 196; cf. Lev. 18:23; 20:15). Some scholars render the Hittite term *ḥurkel* ("capital crime") as "abomination" (Moyer 1969: 60), giving it a moral quality and a definite connection to Old Testament law. The expression *does evil*, which is the same as that used by Lot regarding the action of the men of Sodom (Lev. 19:7), also indicates a connection with the Old Testament. Copulation with a sheep is forbidden and sanctioned with the death penalty (§188). The offender is brought to the king's court for judgment, but is not allowed an appeal; whatever the king determines to do in the case is his own prerogative. In a similar fashion, relations with a pig, dog, or ox are forbidden: "If anyone does evil with a pig, (or) a dog, he shall die. They will bring them to the gate of the palace and the king may order them killed, the king may spare their lives; but he must not appeal to the king. If an ox leaps at a man, the ox shall die, but the man shall not die. A sheep may be proffered in the man's stead and they shall kill that. If a pig leaps at a man, there shall be no punishment" (§199; *ANET* 196–97). This law is of note inasmuch as it makes the animal culpable for sexual aggression toward man. This is similar to biblical law, which requires death by stoning—the usual method for cases of impurity—for the animal that is penetrated by the male aggressor (Lev. 20:15) and for the animal that mates with a woman (Lev. 20:16). However, the law in Leviticus 18 sanctions these crimes with *kareth*, not the death penalty. The unusual practice of substituting the life of an animal for the life of a man in the Hittite law is also similar to the Old Testament law.

Rape and Adultery

Two laws in the Hittite code deal with rape: "If a man seizes a woman in the mountains, it is the man's crime and he will be killed. But if he seizes her in (her) house, it is the woman's crime and the woman shall be killed. If the husband finds them, he may kill them, there shall be no punishment for him" (§197; *ANET* 196). This law has no parallel in the priestly literature of the Bible, but it has a counterpart at Deuteronomy 22:25–26: "But if in the field the man finds the girl who is engaged, and the man forces her and lies with her, then only the man who lies with her shall die. But you shall do nothing to the girl; there is no sin in the girl worthy of death, for just as a man rises against his neighbor and murders him, so is this case." If a sexual encounter occurred in the woman's house, it is safe to conclude that the relationship was consensual; therefore, the woman who is married is guilty of adultery, and the Hittite law prescribes death. There is no law in the Bible paralleling §198, which permits the offended husband to spare his wife's life by swearing before the king, "My wife shall not be killed" (*ANET* 196). Judgment is then left to the king as to whether the death penalty shall be imposed.

Incest

Of chief interest to us are the Hittite laws addressing incest. These laws have their parallel in Leviticus 18 and 20 and Deuteronomy 27. Immediate consanguineous sexual relations are banned: "If a man violates his own mother, it is a capital crime. If a man violates his daughter, it is a capital crime. If a man violates his son, it is a capital crime" (§189; *ANET* 196). Relations with the stepmother are allowed provided the father is deceased: "If a man violates his stepmother, there shall be no punishment. (But) if his father is living, it is a capital crime" (§190; *ANET* 196). Sexual relations with several women are permitted the Hittite man, as long as they did not occur in the same country: "If a free man cohabits with (several) free women, sisters and their mother, with this one in one country and that one in another country, there shall be no punishment. But if (it happens) in one and the same place knowing (of their relationship), it is a capital crime" (§191; *ANET* 196). This law may be founded on the Hittite concept of impurity, which, like the levitical law, affects the land. If so, illicit sexual relations were perceived to defile Hittite soil.

Hittite law prescribed levirate marriage, a custom also found in the Bible: "If a man has a wife and then the man dies, his brother shall take his wife, then his father shall take her. If in turn also his father dies, one of his brother's sons shall take the wife whom he had. There shall be no punishment" (§193; *ANET* 196). This law provided economically for an otherwise-destitute family member by raising up progeny for the deceased, and perhaps by ensuring well-being in the world to come.

That the marriage contract is inviolable is evident from the law that allows sexual relations with unmarried women and slave-girls or prostitutes: "If a free man cohabits with (several) slave-girls, sisters and their mother, there shall be no punishment. If blood-relations sleep with (the same) free woman, there shall be no punishment. If father and son sleep with (the same) slave-girl or harlot, there shall be no punishment" (§194; *ANET* 196). On the other hand, "if . . . a man sleeps with the wife of his brother while his brother is living, it is a capital crime. If a man has a free woman (in marriage) and then touches also her daughter, it is a capital crime. If a man has the daughter in marriage and then touches also her mother or her sister, it is a capital crime" (§195; *ANET* 196).

None of the Hittite laws proscribes homosexuality, except for the case of incest: "If a man violates his son, it is a capital crime" (§189). It is impossible to project a picture from the silence of the Hittite law on homosexuality during the second millennium B.C. Since considerable attention is given to sexual violations, very possibly the Hittites were unconcerned about homosexuality, or perhaps the practice was commonly accepted; it is impossible to say. That the Hittites were concerned with sexual violations in the nuclear family is clear from incest laws. The manner of execution for capital crimes is not mentioned in Hittite sources. Unfortunately, neither is a rationale provided in the laws, but this is customary for nonbiblical law. Is it possible, however, to deduce a rationale from Hittite practice?

Hittite Practice and Homosexuality

I am unaware of any Hittite text that illustrates the practice of homosexuality. However, a study of sexual intercourse in Anatolian religious texts allows us to establish a rationale for sexual guidelines. Hittite society was dominated by a concept of ritual impurity similar to that in the priestly writings of the Pentateuch.

A Hittite document entitled "Instructions for Palace Personnel to Insure the King's Purity" prescribes the death penalty for contaminating the king (*ANET* 207). Sexual relations are carefully governed for those who come into contact with sacred objects, according to a text entitled "Instructions for Temple Officials" (*ANET* 207). Temple officials are permitted sexual relations with their wives provided they spend the night in the temple and not at home, but a bath is required following intercourse. This is true even for kitchen servants so they will not desecrate the gods' food:

> Whoever sleeps with a woman, if his superior (or) his chief constrains (him), he shall say so. If he himself does not dare tell him, he shall tell his fellow servant and shall bathe anyway. But if he knowingly postpones it and without having bathed approaches the gods' sacrificial loaves (and) libation bowl in an unclean condition, or (if) his fellow servant knows about him—namely that he placed himself first—but nevertheless conceals it, (if) afterward it becomes known, they are liable to the capital penalty; both of them shall be killed. (*ANET* 209)

Here the unclean condition (*šaknuwant*) of the attendant who would resume his official duties is cause for sacrilege. In a document from King Mursilis, a reference is made to sex: "Throughout that night there was sleep (intercourse) with a woman. But when morning came he washed" (Moyer 1969: 56). Semen (*lu-natar*) was probably ritually defiling to the Hittites, as it was for the Hebrews (Lev. 15:8; Deut. 23:10), Egyptians, and Babylonians.

No conclusions about homosexuality among the Hittites can be drawn from either their law codes or their ritual practices as in biblical law. Hittite and Mesopotamian cultures seem to have tolerated the blurring of certain societal categories that the Hebrews could not do, as Tikva Frymer-Kensky (1989: 96–97) explains:

> Deviations from . . . [the] categories are dangerous, and Leviticus proscribes male homosexuality under penalty of death (Lev. 20:13, cf. 18:22). This extreme aversion to homosexuality is not inherited from other Near Eastern laws, and must make sense in the light of biblical thought. It does not really disturb family lines, but it does blur the distinction between male and female, and this cannot be tolerated in the biblical system. Anything that smacks of homosexual blurring is similarly prohibited, such as cross-dressing (Deut. 22:5).

The biblical distinction between male and female is established at creation where God ordains the order and boundaries of all created things, including human society.

Homosexuality in Ancient Egypt

It is impossible to study homosexuality in the laws of Egypt because no legal codes are extant (presumably they were written on papyrus and leather instead of clay tablets). References to homosexuality occur in Egyptian myths and narratives, more so than in the Mesopotamian sources, but without access to legal codes we are unable to ascertain the exact Egyptian attitudes toward homosexuality.

In a secular text dating from the end of the twenty-fourth century B.C., a homosexual relationship is implied between Pharaoh Pepi II and one of his generals (Robins 1993: 74). The incident, however, may not reflect an accurate view of homosexuality in Egypt at large. Since the reign of Pepi II was long and corrupt, it possibly reflects a part of that decay (Posener 1957). A number of scholars still insist that no condemnation of homosexuality is found in this text (D. Greenberg 1988: 129), but it is natural that no condemnation of a pharaoh's activities would have been recorded. Other scholars argue that homosexuality was frowned upon by the Egyptians: "Later folklore depicts Pepy as a voluptuary and (possibly) a homosexual, unflattering labels from an ancient Egyptian viewpoint. In fact, during his lifetime already he may have been held in contempt: in the last half of his reign, in contrast to the beginning, there is a tendency on the part of the nobility to drop titles connected with his pyramid temple" (Redford 1992: 58).

Homosexuality is perhaps depicted in scenes found in a tomb for two manicurists and hairdressers of Pharaoh Niuserre about 2600 B.C.: "Bas-reliefs on the walls of the tomb depict the two men in intimate poses, holding hands, embracing, noses touching. . . . None of the drawings is sexually explicit, but Egyptian art rarely was. If the men were lovers, it would be reasonable to conclude that male homosexuality was fully accepted" (D. Greenberg 1988: 130).

A possible motive for homosexual rape in Egypt may be the struggle for power, as it is with the god Atum, the ancient god of Heliopolis, "the ithyphallic demiurge of the solar cultus who created the universe by an onanistic act" (Aldred 1988: 135). Preserved in a coffin text from the Heracleopolitan Period (Ninth and Tenth dynasties) are the words of the deceased hoping for immortality: "Atum . . . has no power over me, for I copulate between his buttocks." According to David Greenberg (1988: 130), "the formula equates interpersonal power with sexual role performances: he who can force a god to submit to him sexually has nothing to fear from him."

Another incident demonstrating a homosexual act in the struggle for power is the story of Seth, the god of order, and Osiris, the god of disorder, vying for dominance. Disorder was feared and fought; it "lurked at the edges of Egypt—in the desert and in the underworld—and the ordered cosmos was shot through with 'uncreated' elements that threatened to engulf it and had to be countered" (Baines, Lesko, and Silverman 1991: 124). The antagonism between Seth and Osiris continued even after the latter had been abandoned to the netherworld. Horus, represented as a falcon, was established as a symbol of the pharaoh of Lower Egypt, while Seth symbolized the pharaoh of Upper Egypt. In a myth from the Middle Kingdom, Seth and Horus are presented in what appears to be a homosexual activity that may have as its background the political struggle between predynastic Upper and Lower Egypt. The two brothers Seth and Horus are on trial before the gods to determine who shall be the rightful ruler of Egypt after Osiris. During one night of the trial, Seth engages Horus in a sexual act:

> Seth made his penis erect, and put it between Horus' buttocks, and Horus put his hand between his buttocks, and received Seth's semen. Then Horus went to tell his mother Isis: "Help me, Isis my mother! Come, see what Seth has done to me." And he opened his hand and let her see Seth's semen. With a scream she took her weapon and cut off his hand, and threw it in the water, and conjured for him a hand to make up for it. (D. Greenberg 1988: 131)

Before the jury, Seth then claims that he has "played the male role" with Horus, whereupon the Ennead (the nine gods judging the trial) are outraged and spit in Horus's face. This myth suggests, as we know from other sources, that semen was considered to be polluting in Egypt, especially when it is out of order (i.e., out of its natural place in the act of heterosexual coitus). The contempt shown to Horus may indicate the ridicule shown to the passive or female role in the myth, demonstrating at the same time the attempt by Seth to show dominance over his brother. A similar theme is found in Ptolemaic temple inscriptions, where the tables are turned: "They imagine the god Min, identified with Horus, eating lettuce (whose milk-sap is identified with semen) so that he can anally penetrate and impregnate his male enemy (presumably Seth), humiliating him by turning him into a female" (D. Greenberg 1988: 132).

One Egyptian reference to homosexuality suggesting a moral attitude is found in the *Book of the Dead* (chap. 125), in a piece entitled "The Protestation of Guiltlessness" or the so-called Negative Confessions. The deceased appears before the judge in the next world to establish his innocence with regard to the effects of pollution: "I have not had sexual relations with a boy. I have not defiled myself. . . . I have not been perverted; I have not had sexual relations with a boy" (lines A20–21, B27; *ANET* 34–35). This source may more accurately reflect Egyptian attitudes toward homosexual conduct than do the mythological texts. Clearly the act of pederasty jeopardized the individual in the hereafter.

Egyptians, like all peoples of the ancient Near East, were deeply concerned with fertility and the role it played in afterlife. According to Gay Robins (1993: 72), homosexuality would be inconsistent with this belief: "The sterile nature of the relationship could have hindered rebirth into the next world." In all probability, the nonconformance of homosexual roles to the ideals of family life would have precluded exclusive homosexual relationships in ancient Egypt. Gordon Wenham (1991: 361) notes that "it may well be that Egyptians saw nothing immoral in homosexual acts where there was mutual consent. If this is correct, there would appear to be very little difference between their attitude and those of the Assyrians and Hittites." This conclusion, however, is speculative, based as it is on the limited sources from these cultures. A thorough investigation into the complex of beliefs regarding family values, eternal life, fertility versus barrenness, as well as heterosexuality and homosexuality is still needed for the entire ancient Near East.

Three further references to homosexuality in ancient Egypt are found by Hans Goedicke in the "Wisdom of Ptahhotep," the "Suicide" of the *Book of the Dead* (125.19), and a late Heracleopolitan historical inscription. The key term in Ptahhotep's admonitions is the masculine *hmt-hrd*, the object of *nk* ("to have sexual intercourse"). The term is apparently a synecdoche applied to a " 'vulva-boy,' i.e., a boy with whom sexual intercourse is conducted" (Goedicke 1967: 100), thus referring to pederasty (p. 101):

> Maxim 32 is clearly an admonition to abstain from making paederastic advances after meeting objections to the less serious homosexual sports. It strikes one, however, as curious, that there is no strong attitude taken against paederasty *per se*, but that the admonitions stress only a regard for the attitude of the partner and a prohibition against overruling it. Compared with the later indications . . . , the attitude is much more lenient. While later homosexuality seems to be condemned in principle, the earlier view is less dogmatic in its morality, and stresses only the necessity for the consent of the party involved.

In the "Suicide," reference is made to a "lad against whom it is said: 'he belonged to the one whom he hates.' " Apparently a youth had sexual relations under circumstances not to his liking. Goedicke (1967: 102) notes that "the immorality of his deed lies not in the homosexual act, but the lack of an emotional justification. By implication it seems that homosexual relations were not considered morally wrong as long as they were based on mutual consent."

In the Heracleopolitan text, a man claims: "I did not wish to love (*mrt*) a youth. As for a respectable son who does it, his (own) father shall abandon him in court." Goedicke points out this special use of the verb *mr*: "I am not aware of another instance where *mr* 'to love' applies to a homosexual relationship, but this is a special use of the otherwise common term. To find the object of the homosexual interests denoted as *nds* 'youth' is curious, in comparison with the use of *hrd* in Ptahhotep and in the 'Suicide.' " This passage is unique in that it not only denies the action of same-gender sexual contact but also condemns performers of it. Goedicke summarizes (p. 102):

> From this passage it could be concluded that homosexuality was not only morally objectionable, but was at some period legally prosecuted. In its attitude the passage antecedes that reflected in the Book of the Dead. In its stern objection to homosexual practices it conforms with the attitude widely current in the ancient Near East. Why the Instructions of Ptahhotep take a considerably more relaxed stand on the question remains obscure.

Goedicke's observation seems to run counter to Wenham's conclusion, but one must be aware of the time frame with respect to the practice of homosexuality in ancient Egypt. Until the end of the first millennium B.C., no prohibition or legal ramifications of same-gender sexual contact can be found. What effected a change in Egyptian attitudes toward homosexuality, then, cannot be shown. At the very least, it cannot be said that the view of the biblical writer in Leviticus 18:22 and 20:13 was "widely current" in the ancient Near East; some diversity of practice is reflected in the various sources. The categorical position of the Bible against homosexuality was apparently not assumed in Mesopotamia, Anatolia, or Egypt.

Western Semites and Homosexuality

When we consider the subject of homosexuality in the Ugaritic sources, we are faced with the lack of references to same-gender sexual relations. The mythological texts of Ugarit show many of the same themes as Mesopotamian and Egyptian myths, but none presents a homosexual act. Of course, it is possible that texts describing such conduct have not survived or that homosexual acts were practiced in Canaan but are not reflected in the literature. At this point, however, we must say that homosexuality as a common practice in Canaan cannot be identified in the available texts, nor is it represented in the art we have. Fertility, promiscuity, bestiality, incest, yes—but not homosexuality. Canaanite concern for fertility may have overpowered any acceptance of homosexuality as a standard mode of conduct.

Conclusion

A survey of ancient Near Eastern sources regarding homosexuality reveals that the practice existed widely, although it was not mentioned in Mesopotamian legal texts before the Middle Assyrian laws at the end of the second millennium B.C. when homosexual conduct was sanctioned by castration under the principle of *lex talionis*. In Egypt, homosexual conduct is reflected in the myth of Seth and Horus as well as in several other sources, especially in the Negative Confessions, where pederasty is disclaimed. While the *šumma alû* texts portray homosexual acts, we cannot rely on omen texts for a precise evaluation of human conduct at large. There are no references to homosexuality in Canaanite sources. At best, we have only scanty sources to determine the practice of homosexuality in antiquity.

On the other hand, sufficient data is available to give a reasonably clear picture of sexual awareness and the importance of fertility. We may say with confidence that ancient Near Eastern peoples throughout the Fertile Crescent, from Mesopotamia to Egypt, shared a concern for fertility. Fertility beliefs were inexorably connected to the events of nature. Fertility of the soil meant survival in this life, and the abundance of children to carry on one's name meant felicity in the life hereafter. As a result of fertility beliefs, the nuclear family was a central feature of all Near Eastern cultures. The institution of marriage was confined to heterosexuals, and sexual intercourse had procreation as its purpose. Throughout the region, infertility was relieved by adoption. While sex between husband and wife (or concubine) was the norm, other sexual outlets existed in the Near East. For example, anal intercourse was offered in Mesopotamia by the *nadītu*-priestess, whether for strictly ritual purposes or perhaps as a contraceptive method to control over-population (Kilmer 1972: 172). Given the concern for fertility, it is difficult to imagine that the general population had a significant interest in such activity. Incestuous relations were proscribed throughout the Near East, nevertheless they were apparently practiced in some circles, mainly by Egyptian royalty and the gods in Canaanite mythology. Cultic prostitution probably was known throughout the region, but controversy continues among scholars as to the nature of the practice and the specific roles of the participants.

PART 2

Homosexuality
in the Old Testament

4

The Daze of Noah

The offspring of Noah who came forth from the ark were Shem, Ham, and Japheth, Ham being the father of Canaan. These three were the offspring of Noah and from them the entire earth was populated. Noah became a farmer and planted a vineyard. He drank from the wine and became drunk. He was uncovered in his tent and Ham, the father of Canaan, saw the nakedness of his father and told his brothers outside. So Shem and Japheth took a garment, and, placing it upon their shoulders between them, they walked backward and covered the nakedness of their father, and their faces were backward—they did not see their father's nakedness. When Noah awoke from the effects of his wine and became aware of what his youngest son had done to him. He said:

"Cursed be Canaan,
  a servant of servants he shall be to his brothers."
And he said:
  "Blessed be Yahweh the God of Shem
And may Canaan be a servant to him
  May Elohim be sufficient for Japheth,
May he dwell in the tents of Shem.
  And let Canaan be a servant to him."

—Genesis 9:18–27 (author's translation)

Genesis 9 has puzzled students of the Bible for centuries. Two questions have been hard to explain: (1) what was the nature of Ham's act toward his father? and (2) why was Canaan cursed for the behavior of his father? In this chapter, we shall examine these two questions in the light of biblical traditions and ancient Near Eastern sources. We shall determine that the most likely interpretation of the incident portrayed in these verses is gleaned from rabbinic exegesis, namely, that Ham committed an act of rape against his father Noah. As such, Ham's act falls under the category of homosexuality and incest. This narrative and the Sodom story studied in the next chapter may provide background for the biblical legislation against homosexuality and incest in Leviticus 18 and 20, but, since a specific time cannot be established for the narratives (or the law for that matter), it is impossible to determine the relationship. We cannot, however, ignore the nuances in the narrative that may be clues to the customs or practices of the people portrayed. Because of the sketchy nature of this text, any interpretation of this text must be tentative at best. The biblical view of homosexuality cannot be constructed from this chapter; it contributes, however, a small piece to the whole discussion.

The Nature of Ham's Act

Let us consider first the question of Ham's act toward his father, which has met with various interpretations, attesting to its difficulty. One scholar writes that "we are not certain if Ham is guilty solely of voyeurism or if the description of his offense in verse 22 is a euphemism for some act of gross indecency" (Sarna 1989: 64). What did Ham do? Does the passage supply more questions than answers, as another scholar suggests (Speiser 1964: 62)?

The most obvious meaning is the literal one. According to this view, Ham simply looked into the tent, saw his naked father, and told his brothers about what he had seen. This particular interpretation, however, poses several problems concerning custom and intention. Was there a custom that children did not even look into the tent of their parents? How could Ham have known that his father was naked when he opened the tent flap? Perhaps, in his innocence, he meant only to speak with his father. Or, more altruistically, perhaps he knew that his father had taken too much wine and needed assistance of some sort. Perhaps Ham saw his naked father and entertained lewd thoughts (i.e., lusted after him), but did nothing about it. If so, this incident would be one of the earliest examples where an individual is made liable to a curse or penalty for merely intending to do something. Intention plays an important part in the biblical laws on homosexuality, but we are not told what Ham's intentions were. Scholars who accept the literal view maintain that Ham only saw his nude father, but they must defend a custom about which we know nothing. They must also presume an immoral intention based on the severity of the curse imposed by Noah. A further problem with this view is that it does not explain why the curse was pronounced on Ham's son Canaan and not on Ham himself. It was customary throughout the ancient Near East that penalties befell the individual who committed the crime. Of course, to punish Canaan may mean that Ham was punished as well, but this is not explicit in the text.

No narrative or legal source—in either the Bible or the ancient Near East—gives evidence that *seeing* a naked person was offensive or criminal. We will now examine those sources.

Mesopotamian and Egyptian Sources

Marie-Louise Thomsen (1992: 19) discusses Mesopotamian sources relating to the evil eye (Sumerian IGI ḪUL), which is the belief that "someone just by looking, through a kind of witchcraft or power of the eyes, may cause harm to another person, animal, or object." Earlier studies, based on fragmentary bilingual evidence from Nineveh, suggest widespread practice of the evil eye in Mesopotamia. Thomsen maintains (p. 20) to the contrary that "one should expect to find numerous references to the evil eye in the cuneiform texts, but, in fact, IGI ḪUL occurs rarely. Fewer than ten incantations, a few medical recipes, and only one fragmentary ritual directed against the evil eye are known." The eye can be personified as a demon or a monster: "The eye (is) a dragon, the eye of the man (is) a dragon, the eye of the evil man (is) a dragon" (p. 25). Amulets were worn to ward off the evil eye, which was certainly associated with witchcraft, sorcery, and other evils caused by bad people. The effect of the evil eye was apparently less severe than witchcraft or sorcery, being related more to everyday events such as too little rain or a bad batch of cheese as opposed to death or disease. Based on her study of the sources, Thomsen concludes (p. 28):

> The references to the evil eye show that the phenomenon was recorded in ancient Mesopotamia over a very long period of time: from the end of the third millennium until the Late Babylonian period. Most sources are Sumerian, some of them with Akkadian translation, and there is one Akkadian incantation. . . . Considering the enormous number of incantations and ritual texts, however, the rather small number of references concerning the evil eye does not justify speaking of a widespread belief among the ancient cultures of Mesopotamia. The evil eye is connected with witchcraft, but, in fact, witches are rarely accused of looking at their victims, whereas their evil words are frequently mentioned in Maqlû and similar incantations.

One of the Maqlû texts (3.9–14) cited by Thomsen contains a reference to the negative effects of looking at someone. A witch "carried off the young woman's attractiveness; by her angry look she took away her charm. She looked upon the young man and took away his virility. She looked upon the young woman and carried off her attractiveness. The sorceress saw me, she followed me, with her spittle she blocked (my) way" (p. 28). Is it possible that Ham practiced a kind of witchcraft in looking at his naked father to take away his virility? Later rabbinic opinion reflects the belief that Noah lost his virility through this incident (see below), but there is no textual evidence to support the idea that Ham may have given Noah the evil eye and so cursed him in some way. In my opinion, the idea is not far-fetched, but it is purely speculative.

In "The Curse of Agade: The Ekur Avenged," a Sumerian poem composed about 2000 B.C., a sanctuary is desecrated by an unauthorized person looking at it (*ANET* 649), but no extant text describes the punishment of a person for merely looking at someone who is naked. Contact with sanctuaries, worship objects, and priestly garments is forbidden to unauthorized personnel in the biblical and Mesopotamian traditions. Profanation of holy things is a common biblical theme; but even in Ezekiel, where the rules of contact with the sacred are very explicit, it is only the garments that transmit holiness to the people, not the priests themselves: "And when they go out into the outer court, into the outer court to the people, they shall put off their garments in which they have been ministering and lay them in the holy chambers; then they shall put on other garments that they may not transmit holiness to the people with their garments" (Ezek. 44:19).

Akkadian has various expressions for misappropriation of an object forbidden to common touch, for example, the noun *asakku* ("something set apart [for god or king], a taboo") is the object of verbs such as *akālu* ("to eat"), *leqû* ("to take"), and *šarāqu* ("to steal") (*CAD* A 2:327). Other expressions for sacrilege, frequently with the noun *ikkibu* ("sacred, reserved thing, place, or action"; *CAD* I/J 55), do not refer to persons. Violations against the *ikkibu* and the *asakku* typically result in severe punishment, such as a curse or banishment. No reference to punishment for seeing a naked family member has been found.

The standard Akkadian term for "to see" is *amāru*, and its semantic range is wide. An unclean man or woman must not see ritual proceedings (*CAD* A 2:8). Women of good moral character wore veils in the ancient Near East so that their faces might not be seen, but a prostitute who wore the veil was seized by whomever might meet her (*CAD* A 2:10). Examples can be multiplied for the use of *amāru* with numerous objects, but nakedness is not one of them. The Mesopotamian examples of inappropriate looking at or into something or at someone reflect a concern to protect sacred boundaries. No analogs have been found in these sources to illuminate Ham's act of looking at his naked father. If it could be shown that Ham only looked at his naked father, casting upon him the evil eye, we might see in this story the author's intent to devalue the idea of magic and witchcraft through the imposition of the curse that follows.

Unfortunately, there are no Mesopotamian or Egyptian parallels to this incident in Noah's life, unlike the Babylonian and Sumerian narratives of the flood story, where Noah's counterpart is found in Utnapishtim (Heidel 1951; Lambert and Millard 1969). Nevertheless, the literal view has been defended by some respectable commentators, among them Umberto Cassuto (1983: 151–52): "If the covering was an adequate remedy, it follows that the misdemeanour was confined to seeing. And it is the seeing itself, the looking, that is accounted by the refined sensitivity of the Israelite as something disgusting, especially when it is associated, as it is here, with an affront to the dignity of one's father."

Rabbinic Comments

Rabbi Rashi (Solomon ben Isaac, 1040–1105) held that the expression *he saw his father's nakedness* means that Ham castrated Noah, a view supported by Noah's having no more children after the flood. Rabbi Samuel ben Meir (Rashbam; ca. 1080–ca. 1174), however, held that Ham sexually abused his father (Babylonian Talmud, tractate *Sanhedrin* 70a). In fact, a closer examination of the text suggests that Rabbi Samuel was correct: Ham's act was incestuous homosexual rape. Jewish exegesis has given sexual immorality as a rationale for the flood, with particular emphasis on the order of creation. In the expressions *the wickedness of man on earth* (Gen. 6:5) and *all flesh had corrupted their way on the earth* (Gen. 6:12), the rabbis found room for fornication (*Leviticus Rabbah* 23.9), incest (Babylonian Talmud, tractate *Sanhedrin* 56b), and homosexuality (Babylonian Talmud, tractate *Sanhedrin* 108a; *Genesis Rabbah* 27.3). According to Rabbi Akiva, the generation of the flood was to have no portion in the world to come: "The generation of the flood was not blotted out from the world, until they took to composing nuptial songs for marriages between man and man and man and beast as for man and woman" (*Genesis Rabbah* 26.5; cf. *Leviticus Rabbah* 23.9). Samuel Dresner (1991) stresses the point that the flood story bears upon sexual order and disorder:

1. Emphasis is placed on the male-female pairs who entered the ark (Gen. 6:18; 7:7, 13; 8:16, 18).
2. Animals are matched in male-female pairs according to their species.
3. Crossbreeding in all branches of creation is deemed a violation of the laws of natural mating (Gen. 6:1–4).
4. Husbands and wives are listed separately upon entering the ark but together on leaving.
5. The flood story places profound emphasis on the family.

Dresner (1991: 312) summarizes as follows:

> This focus upon the sexual order points to the family. Continuation of human life was threatened by the quality of that life. Promiscuous sexual relations between man and man, man and woman, human and beast, would inevitably cripple the institution of the human couple and that of the human family. Therefore, when humans are chosen to repopulate the world, it is not simply a group of men and women who are designated, but a *family*. Not Noah and "others," but Noah with his "wife," and their sons with their "wives"—which is to say, an entire family unit. So firmly is this teaching embedded in the flood story, *that every animal, every creeping thing, and every bird, everything that stirs on earth came out of the ark "by families."*

The import of Jewish exegesis on Noah and the flood is that sexual immorality is a grave offense against God and leads to destruction. As

Dresner (1991: 314) says: "Divine compassion accounts for human frailty, but the moral law is so set into the very fabric of creation, that, when the measure of toleration is exceeded, it spews forth sinners, whether pagan or Hebrew." This view is found in biblical law with respect to Israel's land; violating the sexual stipulations laid upon Israel as God's vassal will lead to expulsion from the land and other severe sanctions (Lev. 18; 20)—for Canaanite and Israelite alike.

Bearing in mind the perspective of rabbinic teaching on the flood and the importance of the family epitomized in Noah, the new father of the human race, Ham's committing homosexual rape against his father is gross hubris. It suggests that the "new creation" is flawed by the surviving humans (personified by Ham) who are carried into it via the ark. It is against the canvas of the new creation that the biblical writer paints his picture of the Canaanites and the sin of homosexuality.

The Homosexual Rape Theory

Afterr Noah became drunk, "he was uncovered in his tent, and Ham, the father of Canaan, saw the nakedness of his father." Our attention is drawn first to the expression *he was uncovered*. The verb *gālâ* (גָּלָה, "to reveal, uncover"), used in the hithpael conjugation only twice in Scripture (elsewhere Prov. 18:2), may be translated as either reflexive or passive. In the piel conjugation, *gālâ* occurs fifty-seven times. The meaning "to uncover" is supported by the various verbs found in synonymous parallelism with *gālâ*, including *ḥāśap* (חָשַׂף, "to strip off"; Isa. 47:2; Jer. 49:10) and *rā'â* (רָאָה, "to see"): "Your nakedness will be uncovered, / Your shame also will be exposed" (Isa. 47:3). The most frequent object of *gālâ* in the piel is *'erwâ* (עֶרְוָה, "nakedness, shame").

The sexual connotation of the expression *to uncover nakedness* and its parallel *to see one's nakedness* is apparent. Hans-Jürgen Zobel (*TDOT* 2:479) affirms that *gālâ*

> means either "to commit fornication" (Ex. 20:26; Lev. 18:6–19; 20:11, 17–21; Ezk. 16:36, 37; 22:10), which is emphasized in Ezk. 23:18 by the synonymous parallelism between *galah* (in the piel) *taznuth*, "to carry on harlotry openly," and *galah 'ervah*, "to uncover (RSV flaunt) nakedness," or "to rape" (Ezk. 23:10, 29). . . . The expression "to uncover one's nakedness" is found in connection with "uncovering the fountain of her blood" in Lev. 20:18, and "uncovering the skirt of his father" in Dt. 23:1 (22:30);

27:20. We encounter a series of similar expressions as figures for fornication, shame, and utmost insult in the prophetic literature: Isa. 57:8,
"uncover the bed," Hos. 2:12 (10), "uncover lewdness (shame)," Isa. 47:2,
"strip off the robe" and "uncover the legs," and Jer. 13:22 and Nah. 3:5,
"lift up the skirts."

If gālâ were translated reflexively ("he uncovered himself"), the literal interpretation would require that Noah undressed himself in his
drunken state before going to sleep or that he somehow removed his
clothes during sleep. In the morning, upon noticing that he was covered
by a garment not his own, Noah might have inquired of his sons how
the garment came to be in his tent, which was, it is presumed, off limits to everyone except Noah and his wife. He would then have been told
by Shem and Japheth that Ham opened the tent, saw that Noah was
naked, and reported what he had seen to them. Whereupon they took
a garment and covered their father, being careful not to look at him.
For this act of apparent modesty, they received a blessing, and Canaan,
Ham's son, was cursed for his father's indiscretion. The curse apparently befalls Ham's son because Ham dishonors his father.

In light of Rabbi Samuel's view that Noah was sexually abused, is it
possible to establish that Ham was inside his father's tent and that his
intention was to rape him? The text explicitly says that Noah was uncovered inside his tent. It is also recorded that Ham reported something
to his brothers outside the tent. It may be argued that the text would
scarcely mention that the brothers were outside if Ham were also outside at the same time. Furthermore, it is not impossible to argue that
Ham called from inside Noah's tent to his brothers outside or that he
moved from inside the tent to his brothers outside. So based on the
prepositions *inside* and *outside*, let us postulate that Ham actually
entered the tent of his father. We can be certain that Noah was inside
the tent, but it must be shown with probability that Ham was inside the
tent as well.

The Septuagint serves as a clear witness to Ham's being inside Noah's
tent by expanding the Hebrew text of Genesis 9:22 to read, "And Ham,
the father of Canaan, saw the nakedness of his father and went out (*kai
exelthōn*, καὶ ἐξελθών) to tell his two brothers outside." Whether the Septuagint translator had a Hebrew version before him that contained the
past tense of the verb *go out* or whether he relied on his own interpretation of the text, we cannot be sure, but his text is clear witness to
Ham's being inside Noah's tent. If we accept for the moment the text
of the Septuagint, we may confidently place Ham inside his father's tent.
Let us postulate that Ham entered Noah's tent and performed some act.
Let us furthermore postulate (contrary to Cassuto 1983: 152) that the

expression *what his youngest son did to him* at the end of verse 24 implies physical rather than verbal action, for the verb ʿāśâ (עָשָׂה, "to do or make") is best understood in this concrete way. But what exactly did Ham do?

By translating *gālâ* as a passive verb ("he was uncovered"), it could be argued that Noah was uncovered by someone other than himself. If we follow the Septuagint and place Ham inside the tent, given Noah's drunken stupor, it is plausible that Ham did the uncovering. This is the only place in the entire Hebrew Bible where this form (hithpael third-person masculine singular) of the verb *gālâ* appears. Because of the way verses 21–22 are normally punctuated, the reader is made to pause after verse 21 and begin a new thought with verse 22. But the original Hebrew text did not have punctuation marks. If the thought at the end of verse 21 is continued at the beginning of verse 22, with the sequential *waw* (ו, "and") introducing verse 22a in apposition to verse 21b, then Ham may be associated with the verb *gālâ*. It is a passive verb and Noah is the subject. He was acted upon. The implied actor in this view is Ham, and we could understand that Noah was uncovered by Ham.

Whenever we interpret a biblical text, our decisions must be borne out by context. To advance our understanding of Rabbi Samuel's view a step further, notice the beginning of verse 22: "And Ham, the father of Canaan, saw his father's nakedness." Despite Cassuto's objection (1983: 151) that "no evidence can be adduced from the expression '*and* [*Ham*] . . . saw the nakedness of his father*'* (v. 22), which is found elsewhere in the Pentateuch in connection with actual sexual relations," it is precisely this expression that gives the key to this passage. When Cassuto refers to Leviticus 20:17, he quotes only the first half of the verse, "If there is a man who takes his sister, his father's daughter or his mother's daughter, so that he sees her nakedness and she sees his nakedness, it is a disgrace (*ḥesed*, חֶסֶד)." But he should have continued to the end of the verse for full meaning: "And they shall be cut off in the sight of the sons of their people. He has uncovered his sister's nakedness; he bears his guilt." As we shall see later, the penalty *kareth* (from כָּרַת, "to be cut off") is used of deliberate sins against God, especially those that cause impurity, including the sexual sins listed in Leviticus 18 and 20, among them incest and homosexuality.

It is essential to note here that the expressions *to see one's nakedness* and *to uncover one's nakedness* belong to the same semantic field. They are synonymous euphemisms for sexual intercourse. Examples may be found not only in the canonical Old Testament but in later literature as well (De Young 1990). The *kareth* penalty befalls both brother and sister because both give themselves willingly to the incestuous relationship. It is a rare text that imposes a penalty on the female in the Bible. Notice that the verb *gālâ* is used only of the male, since he is the active initiator or aggressor in the sexual act. When the verb *gālâ* is used in connection with sexual intercourse, the male aggressor is its subject.

If this analysis is correct and we transfer the meaning of these expressions from the law, we may postulate that Ham did not "see his father's nakedness" in a literal sense, based on some undocumented psychological theory about sensitivity toward the nakedness of parents. In this view, Ham was not merely a voyeur, for the severity of the curse does not follow from such an innocent act. He deliberately entered his father's tent to perform a sexual act, performed it, and then went outside to tell his brothers what he had done. The point is reinforced by Thomas Schmidt (1995: 88), who cites Anthony Phillips: "This may be a veiled allusion to rape, 'an act so abhorrent that the author is unwilling to spell it out.'"

An objection may be raised at this point: the manner in which the conduct of Shem and Japheth is described suggests that the literal meaning is to be preferred. The point seems to be that they were careful about not looking at their father, keeping their faces turned away. But we must ask if it would have made complete sense for the writer to have ended verse 23 with the expression *and their faces were turned away*? Then we would leave the text knowing that Shem and Japheth literally covered their father's nakedness while keeping their faces turned away as well. The point of the story is that the behavior of Shem and Japheth did not emulate that of Ham. They did something opposite of what he did. Consequently, they were blessed while he was cursed.

If the postulate is granted that Ham had sexual relations with Noah, based on the expressions *uncovered his nakedness* and *saw his nakedness*, is there a contrast between what Ham did and what his brothers did? If we accept the premise that the expression *and they did not see their father's nakedness* means exactly the opposite for Shem and Japheth as it did for Ham, it is stated emphatically that they did not have sexual intercourse with their father as Ham did. Without this statement the contrast would not be complete. So the conclusion is all the more remarkable: Shem and Japheth, morally elevated because they did not have sexual relations with their father, were even more highly elevated because they did not so much as literally look at their father in his naked condition. Their faces were turned away. And bear in mind that their act of covering Noah was not a remedy as Cassuto (1983: 151) suggests, for nothing was fixed by it. When Noah woke from his stupor and realized what had happened to him, probably from the physical pain due to his rape, he proceeded with his curse.

The Curse on Canaan

I f we are able to accept the conclusion that Ham sexually violated his father, how then does the curse come upon Canaan? The interpretation I have suggested so far in adopting Rabbi Samuel's viewpoint also best explains two further points: (1) the severity of the curse on Canaan, Ham's youngest son, and (2) the significance of the blessings upon Shem and Japheth. Let us examine the curse first.

The severity of the curse upon Canaan has puzzled scholars for a long time. They have not been able to see the fairness in punishing Canaan when his father committed the crime. We should remember, however, that the biblical writer is not contemporary with Noah, but he relates this story as one who is familiar with the conduct of the Canaanite people of his own time. It is impossible to know for certain when he wrote. But one scholar attempts to place our writer historically at the time of Israel's conquest of Canaan, suggesting an "alliance between the children of Israel (Shem) and the Sea-Peoples (Japheth) in pursuance of war against the Canaanites" (David Neiman, *EJ* 5:98). Based on literary analysis and legal form, a case also can be made for dating Leviticus 18 to the end of the second millennium b.c., when the Canaanite influences were strong (see the discussion of the suzerainty treaty pattern in chap. 6). Biblical and extrabiblical sources agree that sexual sins were characteristic of the Canaanites. Surely the writer was aware of *lex talionis*, the "eye for an eye, tooth for a tooth," principle in punishing crimes that was common throughout the ancient Near East. If so, it may be that Ham's "seed" in the person of Canaan was punished because his father sinned with his "seed."

This principle is best understood by analogy to the *kareth* penalty as it appears in Leviticus 18:29 and elsewhere in the Torah. According to Leviticus 18, the Israelites are to avoid the sexual crimes of the Canaanites and Egyptians (both descendants of Ham; Gen. 10:6), which include incest and homosexuality. The writer of Genesis 9 identifies at the point of origin (the re-beginning of the human race after the flood) the archetypes of sexual abominations: incest, homosexuality, and rape in the person of Ham. The Canaanites continued the sin of their ancestral father Ham, according to the levitical legislator, which explains why Canaan is cursed and not the other sons of Ham. Since Noah is the prototype of all Gentiles in later Judaism, the story of his drunkenness may be etiologic (a story written long after the event meant to explain an existing condition), perhaps transmitted orally for many generations until it reached the writer. The Canaanites of the writer's day were sexual sinners as was their ancient progenitor Ham; and that they were cursed made the conquest of Canaan a right by divine mandate for the people of Israel.

Finally, the blessings appear in sharp contrast to the curse. Shem, the ancestral father of the Israelites, receives the highest blessing because he hid his face from his father's nakedness, evidencing not even so much as a hint of moral depravity. Japheth, as Shem's assistant in proper conduct, receives a blessing subordinate to Shem, in the same way that the later generations of Japheth were subordinate to Israel, but blessed and not cursed.

Conclusion

The combined picture provided by the language and logic of the Noah story suggests that the sin of Ham was sexual. In particular it was the incestuous, homosexual rape of his father, Noah, while the latter was dazed by too much wine. Genesis 9:18–27 may be an etiologic story meant to explain the origin and continuation of the morally corrupt Canaanites, contemporary with the writer of the biblical text. Known for their sexual aberrations, the Canaanites served as the ultimate contrast to the moral sensitivity of the Israelites, epitomized by their ancestral father Shem in his noble and respectful conduct in covering his father's nakedness. When we understand the meanings of the Hebrew euphemisms *to see one's nakedness* and *to uncover one's nakedness*, it becomes possible to make a case for the sexual nature of Ham's act against his father. This opinion, suggested by Rabbi Samuel, is supported by the Septuagint, which explicitly places Ham inside his father's tent, a textual detail that is superfluous if Ham was guilty of merely looking at his father. "That Ham's descendants through Canaan were cursed indicated that the severity of the sin was more than an unintentional glance at his nude father" (Geisler 1989: 268). If this exegesis is correct and if it is possible to postulate a late-second-millennium b.c. provenance of the Noah story and Leviticus 18, perhaps a closer relationship can be discovered between the early narrative and the law. They are welded together in these texts by the propensity of the Canaanites to involve themselves in incestuous and homosexual behavior offensive to the biblical writer(s). What is hinted at in the narrative is made explicit in the law.

5

Sodom: Inhospitality or Homosexuality?

Now the two angels came to Sodom in the evening as Lot was sitting in the gate of Sodom. When Lot saw them, he rose to meet them and bowed down with his face to the ground. And he said, "Now behold, my lords, please turn aside into your servant's house, and spend the night, and wash your feet; then you may rise early and go on your way." They said however, "No, but we shall spend the night in the square." Yet he urged them strongly, so they turned aside to him and entered his house; and he prepared a feast for them, and baked unleavened bread, and they ate. Before they lay down, the men of the city, the men of Sodom, surrounded the house, both young and old, all the people from every quarter; and they called to Lot and said to him, "Where are the men who came to you tonight? Bring them out to us that we may have relations with them." But Lot went out to them at the doorway, and shut the door behind him, and said, "Please, my brothers, do not act wickedly. Now behold, I have two daughters who have not had relations with man; please let me bring them out to you, and do to them whatever you like; only do nothing to these men, inasmuch as they have come under the shelter of my roof." But they said, "Stand aside." Furthermore, they said, "This one came in as an alien, and already he is acting like a judge; now we will treat you worse than them." So they pressed hard against Lot and came near to break the

*door. But the men reached out their hands and brought Lot into the
house with them, and shut the door. And they struck the men who were
at the doorway of the house with blindness, both small and great, so
that they wearied themselves trying to find the doorway.*

—Genesis 19:1–11

Few biblical narratives are as well known as the Sodom story, and perhaps no other has raised so much controversy, at least in modern times. My purpose in this chapter is to determine if Genesis 19:1–11 reflects an incident of attempted homosexual rape or a case of inhospitality to strangers—the two prominent interpretations of the story.

The City of Sodom

Sodom was a Canaanite city, one of several that made up Canaan's southern border (Gen. 10:19). It was part of a coalition that waged wars with eastern kings, and Lot was involved in one of these skirmishes, captured, and then rescued by his uncle, Abram (Gen. 14:12–16). The Jordan River, Israel's eastern border, flows from north to south and finds its end in the Dead Sea, the lowest spot on earth and famous for its high salt content. From the eastern shore, near the bottom, a tongue of land sticks out to within two miles of the western shore. This peninsula separates the sea into the larger deep body of water to the north and the smaller shallow portion to the south. Depths of up to twelve hundred feet are reached in the north, while the southern depths are only about twenty feet.

It has been argued that Sodom was destroyed by a great fire caused by the ignition of petroleum seepage and natural gas, started by lightning (see Gen. 19:24). The southern end of the Dead Sea may have been filled by an earthquake (J. Penrose Harland, *IDB* 4:396); and it is possible that the ruins of Sodom lie beneath its surface. The ancient city itself is impossible to locate with precision (Michael Avi-Yonah, *EJ* 15:70), despite considerable research (Harland 1942–43: 41). Our only source of information is the biblical text.

Because of the geographical characteristics of the Dead Sea and the surrounding area, some biblical scholars view the Sodom story as an etiology. Georg Fohrer (1968: 90), for example, categorizes this passage as a geographical saga: "The Sodom narrative (Gen. 19) is intended to explain the origin of the southern half of the Dead Sea along with the sterility and desolation of the region, as well as the individual details like a pillar of salt in human shape on the slopes to the southwest." Otto Eissfeldt (1965: 39) holds a similar opinion, adding that this "place or nature saga" explains the situation of the city of Zoar on the southeastern shore of the Dead Sea. Neither scholar, however, mentions homosexuality or inhospitality with regard to this text. Is the Genesis 19 narrative merely etiologic or is there more to it?

The Inhospitality View

The interpretation of the Sodom story rests primarily on the understanding of Genesis 19:5: "And they called to Lot and said to him, 'Where are the men who came to you tonight? Bring them out to us that we may have relations with them.'" The crucial word in this text is the Hebrew verb *yādaʿ* (יָדַע, "to know"), rendered variously by modern translations:

> Bring them out (un)to us, that we may know them. (Authorized Version, Revised Standard Version)

> Bring them out to us that we may get familiar with them. (Speiser 1964: 136)

> Bring them out to us, that we may be intimate with them. (New Jewish Publication Society Version)

These translations reveal the confusion concerning the meaning of *yādaʿ* in this passage. Should it be translated to mean that the men of the city wanted merely to acquaint themselves with the two strangers, or does *yādaʿ* have a sexual connotation in this passage? If so, how can we know? Let us first review a work that rejects the sexual connotation of *yāda*^c in this verse and, therefore, rejects a homosexual interpretation of the whole passage.

John Boswell's 1980 work, *Christianity, Social Tolerance, and Homosexuality*, depends heavily on an earlier work, *Homosexuality and the Western Christian Tradition*, written in 1955 by D. Sherwin Bailey, who suggests that the theme of the story is inhospitality, rejecting the sexual connotations of the story altogether. Boswell (1980: 93–94) summarizes Bailey's thesis as follows:

> Lot was violating the custom of Sodom (where he was himself not a citizen but only a "sojourner") by entertaining unknown guests within the city walls at night without obtaining the permission of the elders of the city. When the men of Sodom gathered around to demand that the strangers be brought out to them, "that they might know them," they meant no more than to "know" who they were, and the city was consequently destroyed not for sexual immorality but for the sin of inhospitality to strangers.

Boswell makes five primary points in support of Bailey's thesis, which will be the focus of my discussion of Genesis 19:1–11:

1. Of the 943 uses of the verb *yāda*^c in the Hebrew Bible, only ten occurrences have a clearly sexual meaning (Gen. 4:1, 17, 25; 19:8; 24:16; 38:26; Judg. 11:39; 19:25; 1 Sam. 1:19; 1 Kings 1:4). Genesis 19:5 is the only place where it is said to refer to homosexual relations.
2. The offering of Lot's daughters as a bribe to the men of Sodom has no sexual overtones. Boswell quotes Bailey (p. 95): "Its connection with the purpose (whatever it was) for which the citizens demanded the production of his guests is purely imaginary. No doubt the surrender of his daughters was simply the most tempting bribe Lot could offer on the spur of the moment to appease the hostile crowd."
3. The story of Judges 19:22–30, which is similar to the Sodom story in using virtually the same language, has been interpreted as a story of inhospitality, not of homosexuality.
4. Boswell maintains (p. 94 n. 4) that the Septuagint "makes no implication of carnal knowledge but uses a Greek expression connoting simply 'making the acquaintance of,' 'becoming familiar with': ʹσυγγενώμεθα αὐτοῖς [*syngenōmetha autois*]'; this is in marked contrast to the verbs employed in reference to Lot's daughters . . . which clearly refer to sexual behavior."

5. Although Sodom is a symbol of evil in many Old Testament texts, none say that the sin of the Sodomites was homosexuality. Boswell cites as an example (p. 94) Ezekiel 16:48–49 where "the sins of Sodom are not only listed categorically but contrasted with the sexual sins of Jerusalem as less serious."

No interpretation of the Sodom story will be satisfactory unless it meets the criterion of consistency. First, it should appeal to the plainest meaning of the text if possible; and, second, it should be supported by extratextual evidence from the native or surrounding cultures when such information is available. With these concerns in mind, I turn my attention to Boswell's argument against a homosexual interpretation of the Sodom story. That hospitality is an important part of Near Eastern culture cannot be denied, but is hospitality the issue in Genesis 19? More specifically how is the verb *yādaᶜ* to be understood in this passage?

The Term Yādaᶜ

Time and distance separate us from the writer of Genesis, which puts us at a disadvantage about the exact meaning of words in the text. Nevertheless, we are not without both linguistic and cultural guidelines. If the interpretation of Bailey and Boswell is persuasive on linguistic and cultural grounds, then clearly we should abandon the homosexual interpretation of the Sodom story. On the other hand, if *yādaᶜ* in this text communicates a message of sexual intercourse, there can be no doubt that the citizens of Sodom are portrayed as seeking homosexual relations with Lot's guests.

General Considerations about Language and Context

Bailey's and Boswell's interpretation of *yādaᶜ* as meaning nothing more than "to be acquainted" in the Genesis 19:5 passage can be supported by neither linguistic nor contextual evidence. For example, the context of Genesis 29:5 makes clear that *yādaᶜ* means "be acquainted with." Jacob is seeking information regarding Laban from the residents of Haran: "And he said to them, 'Do you know (*yādaᶜ*) Laban the son of Nahor?' And they said, 'We know (*yādaᶜ*) him.'" Clearly no sexual meaning is implied in this text, for the context supports the meaning "be acquainted with." However, the context of Genesis 19:5—where the scene is not friendly—is quite different. No doubt Lot's contemporaries were inhospitable, but the issue revolves around the question whether this inhospitality is expressed by the term *yādaᶜ*. Furthermore, the Sodomites were not elders; they were a mixed group, "both young and old, all the people from every quarter" (v. 4). Study of the term *elder* in the various ancient Near Eastern languages, including Hebrew, reveals no support for Bailey's idea that Lot failed to satisfy the custom of obtaining permission from the city elders before a guest might be welcomed.

Before turning to the comparative evidence for the Hebrew term *yādaᶜ*, let us first examine more closely the biblical data. According to G. Johannes Botterweck (*TDOT* 5:464), "in the sense of 'acquaintance' or 'love,' *ydᶜ* then comes to mean sexual intercourse of a man with a woman (Gen. 4:1, 17, 25; 38:26; Jgs. 19:25; 1 S. 1:19; 1 K. 1:4) or a woman with a man (Gen. 19:8; Jgs. 11:39 . . .); for homosexual intercourse, see Gen. 19:5; Jgs. 19:22." Bailey and Boswell are inconsistent about the sexual connotation of *yādaᶜ*, which weakens their argument substantially. Boswell first states (1980: 94 n. 4) that there is no connotation of carnal knowledge in the Septuagint translation of *yādaᶜ* at Genesis 19:5 while there is at 19:8. On his very next page, however, Boswell agrees with Bailey that there is no sexual connotation in the offer of Lot's daughters. Contrary to his view, the Septuagint corroborates the sexual connotation of *yādaᶜ* at Genesis 19:5. Bailey himself (1975: 2) confirms it in 19:8 when he includes this verse in his list of the ten verses where *yādaᶜ* means sexual intercourse.

If we accept for the moment the premise that the context of *yādaᶜ* in Genesis 19 is sexual, would this interpretation be in keeping with what we know about ancient Near Eastern analogs to the verb *yādaᶜ* as a euphemism for sexual intercourse?

Ancient Near Eastern Analogs of Yādaᶜ

Boswell and Bailey maintain that *yādaᶜ* refers to the sex act only ten times out of its 943 biblical occurrences; they do not, however, consider the widespread use of semantic equivalents for the word *yādaᶜ* in the various ancient Near Eastern languages.

Hebrew was not merely a "religious" language of a "religious" people but the common language of the Israelites, closely related to other Semitic languages. The ancient Israelites established their identity as worshipers of Yahweh in reference to the nations surrounding them.

Throughout biblical literature it was the burden of prophets, legislators, and kings to encourage and exhort the people of Israel to abandon the ways of its neighbors. We would expect, therefore, to find expressions that were shared by the ancient Hebrews and their contemporaries, especially one so common to human experience as "to know" a man or woman in the sexual sense.

That is exactly the case, but it is not pointed out by Boswell or Bailey, who would have us believe that the sexual connotation of the word *yādaʿ* is not only unacceptable in our passage but also uncommon in the ancient Near East. But as we shall see, this is not true.

Egyptian. The Egyptian verb *rḫ* ("to know") often carries a sexual connotation, as J. Bergman (*TDOT* 5:455) points out: "Like *yādaʿ*, *rḫ* can also mean 'know' in the sexual sense; in this case it often has a phallus as a determinative. . . . There is a good text to illustrate this sexual usage of *rḫ* in a hymn to Min from Edfu, which substitutes *rḫ* for the *nk*, 'have intercourse with,' of the early version." When two versions of one text are extant, it is possible to establish the meaning of a term by its substitute. When multiple examples of texts using different terms are found, it is possible to build a semantic field of synonymous expressions that clarify the meaning of the related terms. This method is especially useful for euphemistic expressions such as *yādaʿ* in Genesis 19:5. In the later Egyptian version, the term for "know" (*rḫ*) is used where the expression "have intercourse with" (*nk*) appeared in the earlier text. Word substitution may leave the reader with no doubt as to the meaning of a term that might have been misconstrued. The Egyptian text illustrates that *nk* and *rḫ* are interchangeable.

Ugaritic. Hundreds of linguistic parallels to expressions in the Hebrew Bible exist in Ugaritic, another Semitic language and near relative to Hebrew. The close connections between Ugarit and Israel is emphasized by Cyrus Gordon (1987: 112), who writes that the Hebrews did not invent their language or their literary forms but inherited them from the Canaanites:

> It was the content rather than the form of the Old Testament that embodied the original Hebrew contribution. Scripture forbids the Chosen People to commit the abominations of the old native population. Some of the abominations—like copulating with animals—are now attested not only in the Bible, which might be considered biased against the Canaanites, but also in the Ugaritic religious texts, where it [copulating with animals] has a sacred and honored place in the Baal cult.

Like its Hebrew counterpart, Ugaritic *ydʿ* can also be used in the sexual sense. In general, the Ugaritic texts are much more explicit than biblical texts in relating sexual details: Baal "surrounded" (ʿzrt) Anat, "knew" (ydʿ) her, who then "became pregnant" (hry) and "gave birth" (wld) (G. Johannes Botterweck, TDOT 5:460). Nothing is more transparent than this text, which describes a love-making scene with a sequence of verbs: Baal embraces Anat, has sexual intercourse with her, whereupon she conceives and gives birth. The verb ydʿ is an important part of this sequence, and it is defined by its place in the sequence. It means "copulation" since it is followed by conception and birth. It is impossible to give it any other meaning. This Ugaritic evidence demonstrates that the term ydʿ had a wide distribution to the north of ancient Israel.

Akkadian. Closely related to Hebrew, Akkadian was centralized in Mesopotamia, the region between the Tigris and Euphrates rivers comprising the Assyrian Empire in the north and the Babylonian Empire in the south during the second and first millenniums B.C. For twenty-five-hundred years Akkadian was the lingua franca of the ancient Near East. No doubt Abram would have been familiar with this tongue since he migrated from the city of Ur. The great number of extant Akkadian texts includes administrative, literary, religious, historical, and legal documents. In §130 of Hammurapi's code, which dates from the eighteenth century B.C., the verb *idû* (the Akkadian counterpart of Hebrew yādaʿ) is used in a sexual sense, exactly like the Hebrew, Ugaritic, and Egyptian equivalents: "If a man has stopped the cries of a married lady, who has not known (*idû*) a man and is dwelling in her father's house, and has then lain in her bosom and they catch him, that man shall be put to death; that woman then goes free" (Driver and Miles 1952–55: 2.53). This young woman, a virgin ("who has not known a man," *ša zikaram la idû*), has been promised in marriage, but before her marriage is consummated, she is raped violently, her cries for help being stifled by the offender (a similar law is recorded in Deut. 22:25–27). The rapist alone is punished by death. The girl is innocent and suffers no penalty under the law because she did not consent to the sexual act but was forced. There is no question about the sexual meaning of the Akkadian verb *idû* in this text.

This brief look at the ancient Near Eastern languages is sufficient to show that throughout the region and for a long time before Israel came into existence as a nation, all of the Semitic peoples, as well as the non-Semitic Egyptians, apparently shared a common expression for sexual intercourse in their equivalents of the Hebrew verb yādaʿ. From this survey, we may judge accurately that the use of yādaʿ at Genesis 19:5 and 19:8 was a standard Semitic idiom for sexual intercourse.

Yāda͑ in Judges 19:22–30

While the story in Judges 19 is similar to the Sodom story, it differs in that a woman was turned over to the mob. Boswell argues that Judges 19 has not been given a homosexual interpretation; but the sexual connotation of *yāda͑* is clear from the context. Certainly no one would argue that in Judges 19:25 the men of Gibeah "knew" the woman in anything but a sexual sense. They raped her so violently throughout the night that she died. Even Bailey includes Judges 19:25 among the verses where *yāda͑* clearly connotes sexual intercourse. However, he wrongly rejects the sexual context and meaning of *yāda͑* in Judges 19:22. But the context at verse 22 demands a sexual connotation just as it does at verse 25. The Gibeahites say to the old man, "Bring out the man who came into your house that we may have relations (*yāda͑*) with him" (19:22).

The Septuagint renders *yāda͑* in both verses with a form of the verb *ginōskō* (γινώσκω), the same term it uses to translate *yāda͑* in Genesis 19:8, where Boswell (1980: 94) admits that it has a sexual connotation. Once again there is no doubt that the Gibeahites were inhospitable, but this cannot be derived from the meaning of the verb *yāda͑*. The inhospitality is reflected in their attempt at homosexual rape. Inhospitality and homosexuality are not mutually exclusive in these stories, as Bailey and Boswell would have us believe. The narratives portray both inhospitality and homosexual conduct.

Lot's Daughters and the Meaning of Yāda͑

Contextually, it makes no sense to mention that Lot's daughters had "not had relations with man" if *yāda͑* in Genesis 19:8 does not have a sexual meaning as Boswell suggests. If the writer used the verb *yāda͑* in a sexual sense at 19:8 and therefore established the context as sexual, we may deduce that the verb *yāda͑* at 19:5 connotes sexual intercourse as well. Given the sexual meaning of *yāda͑* with reference to Lot's daughters, I contend that they cannot be spoken of in terms of a "bribe" but rather as a substitute for the two men in the house. Hence, Lot offers two daughters and not one.

If my analysis of the homosexual act as a sign of dominance is correct, it would explain why Lot's daughters were not accepted. The issue then would be one of homosexuality not for the sake of sex alone but for the sake of proving social status. It would be meaningless to accept two virgin girls into the equation in a society where women were not valued and were not a threat to the dominance of the men of Sodom.

The Septuagint Contribution

inally, we must consider the linguistic evidence from the Septuagint. It is an important detail because both Bailey and Boswell (1980: 94 n. 4) suggest that the Septuagint translation of yādaᶜ at Genesis 19:5 connotes only "making the acquaintance of" or "becoming familiar with." On this basis, without supporting data, they reject the sexual connotation of yādaᶜ at Genesis 19:5. However, with regard to the Septuagint's interpretation of the term yādaᶜ found in Genesis 19:5, not only can we show that the case made by Boswell and Bailey is weak but it is totally in error.

The Greek word in question in Genesis is syngenōmetha (συγγενώμεθα) a form of the verb synginomai (συγγίνομαι). Proper hermeneutical method dictates that we examine all of the occurrences of this word in the Septuagint to determine its range of meaning. When this is done, it will be apparent that the word means nothing short of sexual intercourse. The term syngenōmetha is rare in the Septuagint: at Genesis 19:5 it is used to translate yādaᶜ; the only other occurrence is at Genesis 39:10, a narrative about Joseph in the Egyptian court. Joseph, well built and handsome, was a servant to Potiphar, a courtier of the pharaoh. In this role, he was in charge of Potiphar's estate, so much so that all Potiphar had to do was to eat. Only Potiphar's wife was off-limits to Joseph. In this story, Joseph defends his honor by resisting seduction by Potiphar's wife:

> And it came about after these events that his master's wife looked with desire at Joseph, and she said, "Lie with me." But he refused and said to his master's wife, "Behold, with me around, my master does not concern himself with anything in the house, and he has put all that he owns in my charge. There is no one greater in this house than I, and he has withheld nothing from me except you, because you are his wife. How then could I do this great evil, and sin against God?" And it came about as she spoke to Joseph day after day, that he did not listen to her to lie beside her, or be with her. (Gen. 39:7–10)

The Hebrew phrase liheyôt ᶜimmāh (לִהְיוֹת עִמָּהּ, "to be with her") is translated by syngenōmetha in the Septuagint. The parallel expression šikěbâ ᶜimmî (שְׁכְבָה עִמִּי, "lie with me") in verse 7 is proof of the sexual context of syngenōmetha. It seems impossible to read this paragraph and believe that this is a case of simple hospitality, of "getting acquainted." Joseph considers it evil (rāᶜâ, רָעָה), a sin against God, to have sexual intercourse with Potiphar's wife, the same term that is used by Lot of the conduct of the Sodomites and of the Gibeahites' request for relations with the Ephraimite in Judges 19. Considering its use in the Septuagint, *syngenōmetha* is a specific term for sexual intercourse, not a general term for getting acquainted.

James De Young (1991) addresses this verb and the subject of cultic prostitution involving male homosexuals in the ancient Near East and supports this interpretation of the Septuagint's use of *syngenōmetha*. He observes that in addition to the two canonical references to *syngenōmetha*, this verb is used of sexual intercourse three times in the apocryphal literature (Judith 12:16; Susanna 11, 39), in Xenophon's *Anabasis* (1.2.12), in Plato's *Republic* (329c) and *Laws* (930d), and in Herodotus's recounting (2.121e) of a plot to snare a thief by having a woman go to bed with him. Philo also interpreted Genesis 19:5 as a reference to homosexuality. De Young concludes (p. 164):

> Certainly Boswell . . . is wrong when he denies that there is any implication of carnal knowledge. More specifically, on the basis of both Septuagintal and secular sources it seems clear that the verb *synginomai* in Gen 19:5 has the meaning "to know carnally." Rather than being ambiguous there is strong evidence that the LXX translators wished to be very explicit in order to communicate a sexual sense, even a homosexual sense. The ambiguity of the Hebrew (if present) is removed by the special term of the LXX, which everywhere else in the LXX refers to carnal knowledge.

Finally, the suggestion that inhospitality is the point of the Sodom story should be rejected not only on linguistic grounds but also by the logical and psychological evidence in the story. Note the following:

1. The intention of the rabble is evil, and Lot perceives it this way. He says in verse 6, "Do not act wickedly." Lot was obviously familiar with the men of the town and knew their history and behavior, despite his not being a native (v. 9). Lot expected that some specific harm would come to his guests, or he would not have used the expression *wicked thing*. Furthermore, the context shows that Sodom was a wicked city: "And the Lord said, 'The outcry of Sodom and Gomorrah is indeed great, and their sin is exceedingly grave. I will go down now, and see if they have done entirely according to its outcry, which has come to me; and if not, I will know' " (Gen. 18:20–21). Following this verse, Abraham makes a long appeal to the Lord on behalf of the righteous in Sodom, but there are apparently fewer than ten righteous people in Sodom who will be spared judgment.

2. Instead of the male guests, Lot offers two virgin daughters, who "have not had relations with man" (the same language as recorded in the Code of Hammurapi §130). Why would Lot have offered two virgins in place of the two men if no sexual content was implied by their request? The implication of the text is that the Sodomites preferred to have sexual relations with the two men (virgins to them) and not with the daughters of Lot. There may, of course, have been other reasons why the daughters were rejected (perhaps sexual intercourse with the daughters implied some responsibility such as marriage or the care and maintenance of the subdued). Whatever the case, such guesses do not detract from the homosexual context of Genesis 19.

3. The violent persistence of the Sodomites does not reflect the demeanor of would-be hospitable folk. If no harm upon his guests was imminent, Lot would have delivered them over to the Sodomites immediately so they could "get acquainted." We have to expect that if the angels had not struck the Sodomites with blindness, they would have found the door and attempted to overpower the new arrivals so as to carry out their evil intentions.

The Sins of Sodom and Ezekiel 16:48–49

To understand Ezekiel 16:48–49, we must begin with verse 43, where Ezekiel says to Jerusalem: " 'Because you have not remembered the days of your youth but have enraged me by all these things, behold, I in turn will bring your conduct down on your own head,' declares the Lord GOD, 'so that you will not commit this lewdness (*zimmâ*) on top of all your other abominations.' " A study of the word *zimmâ* (זִמָּה, "wickedness, lewdness, depravity") shows that it refers to premeditated sexual crimes (Lev. 18:17; 20:14; Judg. 20:6; Ezek. 16:27, 58; 22:9; 23:27, 29, 35, 44, 48; 24:13), is applied to deliberate sin, and sometimes stands parallel to words for lust and harlotry in Ezekiel. It falls under the general category of "abominations" that cause impurity and are repulsive to the God of Israel. Ezekiel uses the language of hyperbole to stress the excesses of Jerusalem's sins against God. In no way does he diminish the sins of Sodom or Samaria in his comparison, nor does he catalogue all the sins of Jerusalem's neighbors. His hortatory emphasis is on converting Jerusalem, not destroying them. He therefore seeks to motivate them to righteous conduct (16:60–63) by shaming them. That is why the prophet seems to make the crimes of Jerusalem more serious than those of Samaria and Sodom (see chap. 7 for a fuller discussion of Ezekiel 16).

Conclusion

We have studied in detail the meaning of the Hebrew verb *yādaᶜ* in Genesis 19 and the related story of the Gibeahites in Judges 19. On the basis of ancient Near Eastern parallels and the Septuagint translation, we can say with confidence that the verb *yādaᶜ* means sexual intercourse in these texts, a view that is supported by logical and psychological data. The inhospitality interpretation of the Sodom story should be rejected. The men of Sodom appeal to Lot to release the strangers for the purpose of homosexual relations—if not rape. It is possible that they do this for sociological reasons as a demonstration of their dominance and power over strangers, but there is no mention of this in the biblical account. According to this view, by raping the men they would effectively turn them into "women" who were powerless in that society. I find no justification for the arguments of Bailey and Boswell that inhospitality was the primary reason for the destruction of Sodom. No doubt this position will disappoint the Bailey school, for he says (1975: 155): "It is much to be hoped that we shall soon hear the last of Sodom and Gomorrah in connection with homosexual practices—though doubtless the term 'sodomy' will always remain as a reminder of the unfortunate consequences which have attended the reinterpretation of an ancient story in the interests of propaganda." This charge must be measured against the need for sound methods of interpretation based on objective findings from the language of the text and from supporting extrabiblical sources. The view that homosexuality should be replaced by inhospitality in the Sodom story cannot be supported from these sources.

6

Order and Leviticus

Virtue, then, is of two kinds, intellectual and moral. Intellectual virtue owes both its inception and its growth chiefly to instruction, and for this very reason needs time and experience. Moral goodness, on the other hand, is the result of habit, from which it actually got its name, being a slight modification of the word ethos. *This fact makes it obvious that none of the moral virtues is engendered in us by nature, since nothing that is what it is by nature can be made to behave differently by habituation. For instance, a stone, which has a natural tendency downward, cannot be habituated to rise, however often you try to train it by throwing it into the air; nor can you train fire to burn downward; nor can anything else that has any other natural tendency be trained to depart from it. The moral virtues, then, are engendered in us neither by nor contrary to nature; we are constituted by nature to receive them, but their full development in us is due to habit.*

—Aristotle, *Ethics*

T he Book of Leviticus has often been considered to be the work of several writers over a rather long period of time, mostly during the era of Israel's Babylonian exile and thereafter. For our pur-

91

poses, I leave this discussion aside to focus on the unity of the book and especially the unity of chapter 18 (for an introduction to Leviticus, see Milgrom 1991). The literary structure of Leviticus is important to a study of homosexuality in the Bible in part because the contents of the book are sometimes viewed as irrelevant to modern issues relating to same-gender sex. A number of issues raised by Simon Parker (1991: 14–16) are typical:

1. If the church invokes the values expressed in Leviticus 18 and 20, should it not raise questions about these practices, not just of some within the group (i.e., those seeking ordination) but of all who apply for membership?
2. If the verses on homosexual acts are cited as bearing on church policies, then the verses on adultery and intercourse during menstruation, for example, must surely also be cited as having the same impact on church policies? And if we cannot understand the common link between these various acts, can we arbitrarily select one of them as a guide for the church?
3. The condemnation of homosexual acts is restricted to one law code in the Old Testament, while adultery, for example, is much more frequently proscribed. If the Bible gives minor importance to homosexuality and puts major stress on adultery, why does the church reverse the emphasis?
4. Since Leviticus refers only to homosexual acts and not to homosexuals, would not the references be to homosexual activity by those whom we know now as heterosexuals? In other words, what does the priestly censure really mean in light of the distinction between sexual activity and sexual identity?
5. Only male acts are in question in Leviticus; why not acts between females? Again, we have to ask whether the categories that the priestly authors were working with are appropriate for understanding these matters.
6. How should we relate the definition of the people of God in these chapters to the gospel's definition of the people of God?

These all are important issues, and Parker is quite right to insist that Leviticus 18:22 and 20:13 "demand extended and thoughtful reflection before they can be expected to yield guidance for us today" (p. 17). I shall consider the details of these laws in the following chapters; in this chapter I address two topics: (1) the literary structure of Leviticus as a whole and (2) the construction of Leviticus 18. In doing so, we shall gain an understanding of the priestly writer's underlying view of order that is essential to comprehending his view of homosexuality.

The Literary Structure of Leviticus

T he Book of Leviticus has a central place in the Pentateuch. The book shares themes with the last part of Exodus and the first part of Numbers: Exodus 25–40 details the construction of the tabernacle at Mount Sinai, Leviticus records the priestly duties and activities relating to Israel's sanctuary, and Numbers 1–10 outlines the requirements of the tabernacle in transit. A unity of theme and purpose thus pervades the entire section from Exodus 25 to Numbers 10.

Leviticus reflects its own literary integrity within this larger section. The careful analysis of the structure of Leviticus by Christopher Smith (1996) may be summarized as follows. The building blocks of Leviticus are individual laws, but these laws are grouped in sections: "They do not in other words, come up like objects in a country auction, jumbled together without regard for purpose or value, first a box of antique postcards, then a butter churn, then a handmade quilt. Instead, they are encountered like objects in a department store, sorted and grouped by common purpose or application" (p. 20). Literary markers, like signs in a store, are used to separate the groups. These standard introductory formulas or concluding summaries are not laws themselves, but each serves to demarcate a specific group of laws.

Beyond groups of laws, Leviticus is divided into a seven-part structure that alternates between law and narrative: law, narrative, law, narrative, law, narrative, law (p. 22). As Smith convincingly analyzes each of these sections to show the logical connections and sequences between them, four major sections emerge in the book, tracing "a movement through increasingly more lofty motives for obedience to the 'statutes and ordinances and laws' of God" (p. 30):

Section one (chaps. 1–7) focuses on the theme of atonement for sin.

Section two (chaps. 11–15) continues the theme of atonement but the emphasis is on uncleanness rather than sin: "The motive for following these cleanness regulations transcends personal exigencies: it is to make a distinction between clean and unclean, just

as God has made a distinction between Israel and the nations"
(p. 30).

Section three (chaps. 17–24) concentrates on holiness: "The believer
is challenged to move from imitating the historical activity of God
to emulating the transhistorical character of God" (p. 31).

Section four (chaps. 25–27) highlights acts of redemption with respect
to real estate, persons in need, and objects devoted to God and with
special emphasis on the people's relationship to the land and the
issue of exile: "The high ethical imperatives of the holiness section
are [here] transcended by an invitation to a life characterized by
acts of pure love for God" (p. 31).

This inquiry into the macrostructure of Leviticus demonstrates the
writer's extreme attention to detail and order. In addition, one can build
a strong rationale for the author's preference for the way in which individual laws are written. Several literary formulas for constructing laws
existed throughout the ancient Near East and are evident in the Bible
as well. Martin Buss emphasizes that Israelite law addresses types of
action, not merely acts (1989: 53):

> One feature of these laws should be noted explicitly, namely that they refer
> to types of actions and not to particular acts. This is not surprising and,
> indeed, is true for anything that is normally called "law." Yet it calls for
> comment. It assumes that one can meaningfully speak of types or kinds
> of realities. Modern ethics has attempted to create alternate approaches
> that attribute rightness or wrongness to particular actions rather than to
> types of them, in line with a strongly particularist orientation in modern
> philosophy. A major branch of utilitarianism is a representative of such
> an approach to ethics. . . . Such particularism, however, is plainly out of
> step with the orientation of the Hebrew Bible.

The deontic logic (dealing with norms) investigated by Buss bears
also the notion of sanctions, especially as it relates to divine retribution.
Once again, let him speak for himself (p. 55):

> How should divine sanctions be understood? One may regard them sim-
> ply as the consequence of wishful thinking or as a cultural device to
> encourage socially beneficial (and discourage contrary) behavior. God
> would then be a more or less useful fiction. But what if consequences
> are rooted in the very nature of community life, which is an integral part
> of the cosmos? For a believer in such an order, the "is" and the "ought"
> (the actual and the ideal) need not be completely separate, although they
> are not identical or strictly derivable one from the other. In any case, in

biblical thought morality is not valued simply for its own sake apart from the consequences for oneself and others.

Now to my point. When we read the individual laws about homosexuality in Leviticus, we must consider together the macrostructure and microstructure of the priestly writer's thought. His perspective on order was different from ours. It may be described as a hierarchy: cosmos-community-conscience. Actions performed on the individual level would automatically have an effect on the community and the world. His world, both vertically and horizontally, was controlled or ordered by God; ours is horizontal and lacks in general a revelatory influence. This is a great problem in modern discussions of homosexuality that attempt to limit the proscriptions against homosexuality to specific acts. It is true that the act of homosexuality is forbidden, of course, but all types of acts in the category of same-gender sex will be encompassed by the law, not merely a singular act or a singular act in a specific position. We must avoid particularistic methods of interpretation and think of types of action as regards the priestly laws.

Occasionally, specific regulations are placed beside general rules. This point is illustrated by Anthony Phillips in a discussion (1980: 39) of the expression *uncovering the father's skirt* (Deut. 22:30), which he interprets as a homosexual act, consistent with my interpretation of the rape of Noah by Ham. Thus, commenting on Leviticus 18:7, he notes:

> Homosexual practices are prohibited neither in the Book of the Covenant nor in Deuteronomy, but are first made criminal in the Holiness Code (Lev. 18:22; 20:13). These provisions are intended to govern *all sexual relations* between males rather than the specific case of a son seducing his father. But in Lev. 18:7 we find specific reference to such relations: "The nakedness of your father and the nakedness of your mother, you shall not uncover: she is your mother, you shall not uncover her nakedness." (italics mine)

Rejecting the view that this verse applies to the mother, he concludes: "But it is much more natural to understand Lev. 18:7a in its present form as prohibiting sexual relations with either of one's parents." The "nakedness of the father" is understood literally.

Just as the larger unit of Leviticus and the still larger unit of the priestly legislation reflect a literary schematic, so also does Leviticus 18 (the specific chapter in which the first legislation on homosexuality occurs) reflect a literary schematic. Let us examine next the literary construction of Leviticus 18.

Leviticus 18 and Suzerainty Treaties

C hapter 18 of Leviticus comprises a complete unit within the book
and establishes a pattern of holiness, or perfect moral virtue, as
the ground of sexual conduct. The form of Leviticus 18 is remarkably similar to covenant and suzerainty treaty patterns found elsewhere
in ancient Near Eastern literature. George Mendenhall (1954: 50)
describes the standardized form with respect to Hittite sources as a uni-
lateral agreement between a great king who stipulated the obligations
incumbent upon a vassal (e.g., "Treaty between Mursilis and Duppi-
Tessub of Amurru"; *ANET* 203). This treaty pattern has parallels in Aramaic and Assyrian documents of the first millennium b.c. (Fitzmyer
1967: 2) and was common to many peoples, including the ancient
Israelites (McCarthy 1978; Baltzer 1971). It has significant implications
for Leviticus 18 because it correlates to an early date in the history of
Israel. In order to demonstrate the similarities, I will first list the characteristics of the Hittite treaties and then of Leviticus 18.

Hittite Treaties

Six features characterize Hittite suzerainty treaties:

1. Preamble: a short section identifying the author of the treaty or
   covenant.
2. Historical prologue: a reminder to the vassal of the benefits given
   by the great king, showing why the subject was obligated to obey
   the stipulations placed upon him.
3. Stipulations: governing the conduct of the vassal before the sovereign.
4. Provision for deposit: usually in a shrine or temple for periodic
   public readings.
5. Witnesses: a list of gods summoned as authorities to enforce the
   stipulations.
6. Curse formula: motivation for compliance with the stipulations
   (sometimes blessings were included).

It is not necessary that all the features correspond exactly between the
Hittite treaties and Leviticus 18, for in the ancient Near Eastern litera-

ture similar treaties differed in several points (Fitzmyer 1967: 122). The order of the features may also vary.

Leviticus 18 as Treaty

While Mendenhall recognized the connections between the suzerainty treaty patterns and Exodus 20 and Joshua 24, the similarity between the Hittite treaties and Leviticus 18 has not been delineated. The pattern may be demonstrated as follows:

1. Preamble/identification of the sovereign (vv. 1–2): "I am the LORD your God."
2. Historical prologue (vv. 3–5): a reminder of God's past actions on Israel's behalf. Because he saved them out of Egypt and brought them to Canaan (vv. 3–4), he invokes upon vassal Israel an obligation to observe his statutes and judgments (v. 5).
3. List of stipulations (vv. 6–23): the essence of the contract with Israel. All the features have to do with sexual crimes: (a) incest (vv. 6–17), (b) bigamy (v. 18), (c) intercourse with menstruants (v. 19), (d) adultery (v. 20), (e) Molech worship (v. 21), (f) homosexuality (v. 22), and (g) bestiality (v. 23).
4. Rationale for compliance (vv. 24–28): the stipulations are motivated by a concern for impurity that defiles the land. The crimes listed are described as abominations that cause impurity, which in turn threatens removal of the population from the land. The native Israelite, as well as the resident alien, is under obligation to observe the stipulations of the treaty. A contrast is drawn between Israelites and previous inhabitants of the land of Canaan.
5. Witness of the treaty (v. 30): Yahweh reminds the people that it is he alone who originates this contract. The treaty ends as it begins: "I am the LORD your God."
6. Curse for noncompliance (v. 29): Anyone who commits the abominations outlined by the treaty will be "cut off from among their people."

The expression *cut off from among their people* is a conditional divine curse of extinction that befalls the person who deliberately violates certain of God's ordinances. Jewish scholars refer to this expression as the *kareth* penalty (from כָּרַת, "to cut off"), and because the penalty is so severe it is clear that the stipulations were important to the God of

Israel. (In chap. 9, I will examine this penalty as well as the death penalty imposed for homosexual violations at Lev. 20:13.)

Leviticus 18 is different from Hittite treaties in that it lacks the provision for deposition in a shrine or temple. The biblical writer describes a time when ancient Israel did not have a permanent temple or shrine but only the portable ark of the covenant, which contained the Decalogue (Deut. 10:1–5; 1 Kings 8:21; 2 Chron. 6:11), the "constitution" of the Israelites. Since the writer of Leviticus contemplates a nomadic people confined to the wilderness for forty years in the preconquest era, he did not stipulate that his treaty be placed in the temple. It is assumed that sacred documents would be stored in the temple when Israel became settled and the temple became the focal point of their worship.

The Uniqueness of Leviticus 18

Two observations may be drawn from the treaty form of Leviticus 18. First, the chapter must be considered as an independent unit, which is supported by (a) the sexual nature of all the crimes listed, (b) the position of the curse at the end of the chapter so as to encompass the entire series, (c) the position of the statement *I am the Lord your God* at the beginning and end of the chapter, and (d) the rationale of impurity for all the crimes. These considerations are of great value for the study of homosexuality in the Bible because they provide an exegetical context for it. Second, the treaty form of Leviticus 18 attests to a date earlier than the Aramaic inscriptions, since the pattern is characteristic of the second millennium only (Mendenhall 1954: 36). It derives from an era when Israel did not exist as a nation but as an extended family in a seminomadic state (Porter 1976: 144; see also Bigger 1979: 203).

In structure, Leviticus 18 stands alone; it is possible that it was originally a separate document inserted into its present location. The content of Leviticus 18 is markedly different from that of the preceding and following chapters, with the exception of chapter 20. The theme of chapter 17, the disposition of the fellowship or peace offerings (*zebaḥ šĕlāmîm*, זֶבַח שְׁלָמִים), is repeated in Leviticus 19:1–8. Hence, chapters 17 and 19 logically belong together, while chapter 18 interrupts the continuity. The impurity caused by deliberate desecration of sacred offerings or aberrant sexual activities provides a rationale for the *kareth* penalty in

Leviticus 17:1–16 and 19:1–8. Perhaps for this reason, Leviticus 18 was placed in its current location.

The relationship between Leviticus 18 and 20 deserves further study. Both chapters deal with similar laws, but Leviticus 20 adds the death penalty whereas chapter 18 has only *kareth*. If one supposes that these penalties are mutually exclusive, some distance may be placed between the two chapters, assigning the latter perhaps to a period when the social nucleus in ancient Israel shifted from the family to the community and then to the state. One could imagine under these circumstances that chapter 20 was written as a separate document. However, I think that the penalties are not mutually exclusive and assign the composition of Leviticus 20 to a period congruent with or shortly after that of Leviticus 18.

Conclusion

L eviticus 18 establishes holiness, the levitical term for the highest moral virtue, as the ground of sexual conduct. The ancient Israelites were not endowed by nature with it, but were, as Aristotle wrote, "constituted by nature" as humans to receive it through the habitual practice of the statutes and ordinances of Yahweh their sovereign. Biblical law presumes that human beings, unlike a stone or fire, may change the course of their moral development and conform in varying measures to higher standards of virtue than their own. In the arena of sexual morality, it is furthermore presumed that some deviation will occur in the practice of achieving the highest virtue, and on this basis, the biblical legislator provides for means of reconciliation and sanctions to enforce the law.

The lifetime process of holiness leads to happiness for those who observe God's law. Aristotle is quite right when he says that happiness as the chief good for human beings "is an activity of soul in accordance with virtue, or if there are more kinds of virtue than one, in accordance with the best and most perfect kind. There is a further qualification: in a complete lifetime. One swallow does not make a summer; neither does one day. Similarly neither can one day, or a brief space of time, make a man blessed and happy" (*Ethics* 76). All action leads to some end, and all action comes with consequences, leading either closer to the goal of holiness (i.e., perfect virtue) or farther from it, and moral responsibility is inherent in the quest. In the biblical writer's perspective, the qual-

ity of one's conduct is not measured by the relative or subjective standards of the moment; the rule is rather the eternal, immutable will of
Yahweh as expressed in the law.

I began this chapter with an epigraph in which Aristotle emphasizes
that nature has no role in the achievement of moral excellence. As we
give our attention to the legislation on homosexuality, which presumes
the importance of choice as the ground for moral action, it is fitting that
I close with Aristotle's own conclusion regarding the pursuit of virtue.
Here is ancient, sage advice for anyone seeking to understand the biblical law on homosexuality (*Ethics* 92):

> Again, the causes or means that bring about any form of excellence are
> the same as those that destroy it, and similarly with art; for it is as a result
> of playing the harp that people become good and bad harpists. The same
> principle applies to builders and all other craftsmen. Men will become
> good builders as a result of building well, and bad ones as a result of build-
> ing badly. Otherwise there would be no need of anyone to teach them:
> they would all be born either good or bad. Now this holds good also of
> the virtues. It is the way that we behave in our dealings with other peo-
> ple that makes us just or unjust, and the way that we behave in the face
> of danger, accustoming ourselves to be timid or confident, that makes us
> brave or cowardly. Similarly with situations involving desires and angry
> feelings: some people become temperate and patient from one kind of
> conduct in such situations, others licentious and choleric from another.
> In a word, then, like activities produce like dispositions. Hence we must
> give our activities a certain quality, because it is their characteristics that
> determine the resulting dispositions. So it is a matter of no little impor-
> tance what sort of habits we form from the earliest age—it makes a vast
> difference, or rather all the difference in the world.

7

Biblical Law and Homosexuality

You shall not lie with a male as one lies with a female; it is an abomination.

—Leviticus 18:22

If there is a man who lies with a male as those who lie with a woman, both of them have committed a detestable act; they shall surely be put to death. Their bloodguiltiness is upon them.

—Leviticus 20:13

Leviticus 18:22 and 20:13 set forth the biblical legislator's view of homosexuality. Written in the language of law, both verses are concise and precise, for their purpose is to regulate behavior and to stipulate the provisions for punishment or correction should violations occur. To understand the biblical law on homosexuality, I have set out to accomplish three goals: first, to analyze the Hebrew terms and the syntax of these crucial verses (the task of this chapter); second, to explain the rationale for prohibiting same-gender sexual relations (chap. 8); and, finally, to address the exact nature and the implications for the execution of the two severe penalties attached to the homosexual act (chap. 9). (For the related task of exploring the analogous terms for sexual relations and the statements regarding homosexuality found in the languages and literatures of the ancient Near East, see chap. 3.)

Contrary to the opinions presented by many contemporary scholars, the language of the two biblical laws on homosexuality is clear. The law in Leviticus 20:13 is phrased in the casuistic manner customary to other codes in the ancient Near East (e.g., Hammurapi's). Casuistic law is comprised of a protasis (the subordinate clause of a conditional sentence: "if a man") and the apodosis (the main clause of the conditional sentence: "both of them have committed an abomination"). On the other hand, the law in Leviticus 18:22 is stated in the apodictic style characteristic of the Ten Commandments, introduced by "you shall not." Given the form of Leviticus 18, the penalty is not included in verse 22 but is delayed until verse 29, in the curse formula at the end of a long list of prohibitions. In contrast, Leviticus 20:13 appends two additional statements to invoke the death penalty. (For a thorough discussion of the forms of casuistic and apodictic law, see Alt 1968: 112–71.)

We must first address three legal Hebrew terms found in both Leviticus 18:22 and 20:13: (1) zākār (זָכָר, "male"), (2) miškĕbê ʾiššâ (מִשְׁכְּבֵי אִשָּׁה, "after the manner of lying with a woman"), and (3) tôʿēbâ (תּוֹעֵבָה, "abomination"). Confusion about these three terms results in a compromised view of the legislator's attitude toward homosexuality.

Zākār

In examining zākār, it is important to note the syntax of Leviticus 18:22: the normal verb-subject-object order is altered to place the direct object zākār first. This "fronting" of the direct object emphasizes the noun, as seen in a literal rendering: "The *male* you must not lie with as with a female."

Some of the confusion regarding the meaning of Leviticus 18:22 and 20:13 is generated by various translations of the term zākār. While the differences in translation may seem small, in some instances they mask the Hebrew original and suggest a misleading interpretation. Consider the following translations of Leviticus 18:22:

Do not lie with a male as one lies with a woman; it is an abhorrence. (New Jewish Publication Society Version)

You shall not lie with a male as with a woman; it is an abomination. (Revised Standard Version)

Do not lie with a man as one lies with a woman; that is detestable. (New International Version)

Thou shalt not lie with mankind, as with womankind: it is abomination. (Authorized Version)

These translations leave room for diverse interpretations. *Male* includes all members of the gender: infants, children, adolescents, and adults of every age. *Man*, on the other hand, may be used exclusively of the adult of the male gender. Since a man is always a male, but a male is not necessarily a man, pederasty could be legitimated according to some translations. Furthermore, *mankind* may include both male and female genders, encompassing the entire human species. Clearly, these English renderings of *zākār* do not mean exactly the same thing; the word, therefore, needs clarification.

Neither *man* nor *mankind* is accurate; hence, the New International Version and Authorized Version should be rejected in favor of the New Jewish Publication Society Version and Revised Standard Version renderings. Hebrew *zākār* is cognate to Akkadian *zakru/zikaru* (*CAD* Z 23, 110). Both terms mean the "male" as opposed to the "female" of the species. Hebrew has another word for man as an individual (ʾîš, אִישׁ) and still another that can refer to either an individual man or to humankind (ʾādām, אָדָם). The former is used in the casuistic law at Leviticus 20:13. The ambiguity of ʾîš and ʾādām may cause some confusion, but context normally makes clear which idea is meant. There is no ambiguity in the term *zākār*; it always refers to the male gender. The Arabic cognate *dhakar* (male) preserves the proto-Semitic meaning of this term precisely; by synecdoche, *dhakar* is also translated "penis" (Wehr 1976: 310). Thus, the term *zākār* refers to anyone with a penis, and its antonym is *něqēbâ* (נְקֵבָה, "female"). A clear picture of this contrast is found in the creation story (Gen. 1:26–27):

Then God said, "Let us make man (ʾādām, אָדָם) in our image, according to our likeness; and let them rule over the fish of the sea and over the birds of the sky and over the cattle and over all the earth, and over every creeping thing that creeps on the earth." And God created man (hāʾādām, הָאָדָם) in his own image, in the image of God he created him; male (zākār, זָכָר) and female (něqēbâ, נְקֵבָה) he created them.

All creatures were created according to a species "after their kind," and it was enjoined upon them to reproduce. Two unique features describe the creation of the archetypal human pair: (1) they enjoyed a special relationship with their Creator inasmuch as they were made "in the image of God," and (2) they were given the responsibility to serve as overseers of creation. Their identity as male and female is part of the established order of creation. When the levitical legislator chose the term *zākār* in Leviticus 18:22, he proscribed all sexual relationships between males of the human species. In his view, the normal or natural sexual orientation of the male was for the female in accordance with the paradigm of creation. The legislator could have expanded upon this term to prohibit sexual intercourse between specific categories of males (e.g., between boys, between adult males and boys, between adult males, between boys and old men, between adult males and old men), since Hebrew words exist for these various categories of individuals within the male species. But it would have been unnecessary because the term *zākār* in Leviticus 18:22 excludes all male sexual relations.

On the other hand, if the writer had chosen *ʾādām* or *ʾîš* instead of *zākār*, it could be argued on the basis of grammar alone that, while sexual intercourse between adult males is forbidden, the text does not explicitly prohibit sexual relations between two males of any age, including the crime of pederasty. At the same time, it might be suggested that singular *ʾîš* really means that group sex between men is permitted since the standard plural (*ʾănāšîm*, אֲנָשִׁים) was not used. Or, had *ʾādām* been used, it could be argued that sexual asceticism is prescribed, or worse, that sexual relations with animals is the preferred course. But the reasons that could be used in defense of same-gender sexual intercourse or bestiality are precluded by the term *zākār*. The law on homosexuality forbids sex between all males of the species. The use of *ʾîš* at Leviticus 20:13 must be understood against the use of *zākār* at Leviticus 18:22; the latter is demonstrably an earlier piece of legislation.

Miškĕbê ʾiššâ

Some writers suggest that the phrase *the lying (down) of a woman* (*miškĕbê ʾiššâ*) is ambiguous. John Boswell (1980: 101 n. 4), for example, says, "It might also be observed that there is considerable room for doubt about precisely what is being prohibited. The Hebrew

reads literally, 'You shall not sleep the sleep of a woman with a man.'
Jewish moralists have debated for a millennium about exactly what constitutes 'the sleep of a woman' and who is technically a 'man.' " Boswell
is clearly under the influence of Bailey at this point, and both authors
fail to appreciate the full significance of the term *zākār*. At least Bailey
recognizes the translation "male," but he misses the target completely
on the meaning of *miškěbê ᵓiššâ* (1975: 58–59, 156):

> This qualification may mean that the intention was to penalize only such
> homosexual acts as approximated to normal heterosexual coitus in so
> far as they involved penile intromission, and that either no cognizance
> was taken of other acts, or they were dealt with as pollution and were pun-
> ished less severely. On the other hand, *mīshkᵉbhēy ᵓīshshāh* may signify
> any lying with a male by another male for sexual purposes, such inter-
> course being only permissible heterosexually. Probably the latter is the
> more likely interpretation, but it is not certain; and the alternative sug-
> gested should not be overlooked when considering the application of the
> Mosaic laws to modern problems. . . .
> Although the laws in the Holiness Code of Leviticus refer to "lying with
> mankind as with womankind," the meaning of this phrase is ambiguous.
> All that can be said with any assurance is that it must at any rate include
> sodomy, which one law forbids as an abomination to the Lord, and
> another punishes as a capital offense; but whether or not it also relates
> to other acts must remain a matter for conjecture.

To propose that the legislator is suggesting that certain sexual positions
that a man might assume with a woman are forbidden with men while
others are acceptable or that pederasty or any other sexual union
between males is permitted by this text is to revert once again to Humpty
Dumpty's methodology of twisting words. The issue here is not how sexual intercourse should be practiced between males, but that it cannot
be practiced between males under any circumstances. This is clear from
the use of the imperative. Moreover, it is wrong to assume that acts that
caused pollution were dealt with less severely in ancient Israel. Exactly
the opposite is the case. As I shall show in the discussion of sanctions
(chap. 9), the most severe penalty available to the biblical legislator was
imposed for violations against pollution rules.

The expression *miškěbê ᵓiššâ* is preceded by a negative command:
"You shall not lie (with). . . ." The Hebrew expression is formed with
two words, the negative particle *lōᵓ* (לֹא) and the imperfect of the verb
šākab (שָׁכַב, "to lie down, to have intercourse"), and the object of the
verb is *zākār*: "Do not have sexual intercourse (with . . .)." There are two
ways to express a negative command in Biblical Hebrew, and the one
that appears in this verse is the stronger of the two. Wilhelm Gesenius

(1910: 317) says that the negative command is used "to express the definite expectation that something will not happen." The expression *to lie with* is a designation for sexual intercourse, synonymous with the use of the term *yādaᶜ* in the Sodom story (Gen. 19:5, 8). The use of the term *šākab* for sexual intercourse in the legal sense is also parallel to the expression *to be with* in Genesis 39:10, where Joseph, tempted by Potiphar's wife, "did not . . . lie beside her, or be with her." The legislator expects his audience to understand that same-gender sexual relations are strictly forbidden.

A further inference may be suggested by the negative command. In much of the modern literature on homosexuality, there is disagreement between those who say that homosexuality is a biological condition and those who say it is an individual choice. The law presumes that all the sexual activities considered in Leviticus 18 are deliberate choices. It would not be just for God to demand that an activity dictated by a physical condition be avoided. The verbs used throughout the chapter also imply choice. Leviticus 18:3 also uses a strong negative command: "You shall not do (*lōʾ taᶜăśû*, לֹא תַעֲשׂוּ)" as the Egyptians and the Canaanites have done. On the positive side, the Israelites are told: "You are to perform (*taᶜăśû*, תַעֲשׂוּ) my judgments and keep (*tišmĕrû*, תִּשְׁמְרוּ) my statutes" (v. 4). These verbs clearly indicate that the Israelites had a choice in the matter. Furthermore, the penalty of *kareth*, imposed for violations of the sexual-purity rules in this chapter, is exacted only for deliberate or "high-handed" violations against God's law (Num. 15:30–31). The law is based on the ability of the individual to choose whether he or she will obey or face the consequences. The choice to obey the law results in God's blessing; the choice to disobey results in the curse of *kareth* (see chap. 9 for details).

The masculine singular noun *miškāb* (מִשְׁכָּב) is derived from the verb *šākab* (שָׁכַב). Substantively, the noun is the "place of lying," that is, a couch or bed, but the verbal idea is not lost in the noun. Thus the noun reflects also what occurs on the bed, the act of lying or, more specifically, cohabitation. Hebrew is frequently periphrastic. Thus, for example, in modern Hebrew, pederasty and sodomy are expressed by *miškab zākār* ("lying with a male"), the same expression found at Judges 21:11–12 in reference to the female inhabitants of Jabesh-gilead: "And this is the thing that you shall do: you shall utterly destroy every man and every woman who has lain with a man. And they found among the inhabitants of Jabesh-gilead four hundred young virgins who had not known a man by lying with him." In verse 11, the New American Standard Bible compresses into idiomatic English the phrase *every woman who has lain with a man*—a Hebrew periphrasis that includes two expressions for intercourse: *yādaᶜ* and *miškab-zākār* (*kol-ʾiššâ yōdaᶜat miškab-zākār*). The phraseology in verse 12 is similar. If the loss of a woman's virginity is expressed by the phrase *miškab zākār* and it is granted that sexual intercourse is expressed by the synonyms *to lie with* and *to know*, surely it must be conceded that the expression *miškab ᵓiššâ* is without ambiguity. A semantic field of terms of equal value clarifies any specific term in question. Baruch Levine is certainly correct when he says (1989: 123) that *miškab ᵓiššâ* "means literally 'after the manner of lying with a woman' by the introduction of the male member." The term *miškāb* in construct with either *zākār* or *ᵓiššâ* is a circumlocution for sexual intercourse.

Tôʿēbâ

Ascribing a restrictive meaning to *tôʿēbâ* so as to make it mean the same thing in all contexts results in misunderstanding and misinterpretation. Nevertheless, Boswell (1980: 100–102) limits the term to Jewish ritual impurity and cultic prostitution:

> The Hebrew word "toevah" . . . does not usually signify something intrin-sically evil, like rape or theft (discussed elsewhere in Leviticus), but some-thing which is ritually unclean for Jews, like eating pork or engaging in intercourse during menstruation, both of which are prohibited in these same chapters. It is used throughout the Old Testament to designate those Jewish sins which involve ethnic contamination or idolatry. . . . The dis-tinction between intrinsic wrong and ritual impurity is even more finely drawn by the Greek translation, which distinguishes in "toevah" itself the separate categories of violations of law or justice (*anomia*, ἀνομία) and infringements of ritual purity or monotheistic worship (*bdelygma*, βδέλυγμα). The Levitical proscriptions of homosexual behavior fall in the latter category. In the Greek, then, the Levitical enactments against homo-sexual behavior characterize it unequivocally as ceremonially unclean rather than inherently evil.

Boswell concludes (p. 101 n. 34) "that the condemnations in Leviticus were in fact aimed at curbing temple prostitution in particular rather than homosexual behavior in general. This was not the usual under-standing of the later Jewish tradition, but it is suggested by the LXX, upon which Christian moralists drew." By restricting *tôʿēbâ* to "Jewish sins" and more particularly to cultic prostitution and ritual impurity,

Boswell suggests that the stipulation at Leviticus 18:22 has validity only for ancient Israel and, therefore, has no relation to homosexuality in the modern sense.

Boswell's thesis is supported by many contemporary writers who argue that because verse 21 speaks of Molech worship, an idolatrous practice, and because *tôʿēbâ* is associated with idolatry elsewhere in Scripture, same-gender sexual relations proscribed at Leviticus 18:22 must be cultic in origin and practice. Thus Tom Horner (1978: 73) asserts that the law does not refer to homosexuality in general but only to cultic prostitution. He cites as his authority Norman Snaith, who says that *tôʿēbâ* usually "has to do with idolatrous actions, actions committed within the cultus of other gods. This links up with the previous verse if we see there a reference to children dedicated to temple prostitution. Thus homosexuality here is condemned on account of its association with idolatry." The inference to be drawn from this is that modern homosexual practice, which occurs outside the context of idolatry, is not covered by the biblical law. Two important issues are raised by these authors: (1) was it the intent of the levitical legislator and other biblical writers to limit the prohibition against homosexuality to specifically "Jewish sins" involving pollution or idolatry? and (2) in relation to the meaning of *tôʿēbâ*, do the Septuagint terms *anomia* (ἀνομία) and *bdelygma* (βδέλυγμα) reflect a distinction between intrinsic wrong and ritual impurity as claimed by Boswell?

Is Tôʿēbâ "Jewish Sin"?

Boswell includes homosexuality among "Jewish sins [such as eating pork and having sex with a menstruant] . . . which involve ethnic contamination or idolatry," and he makes a distinction between "intrinsic wrong and ritual impurity" based on the language of the Septuagint. These generalizations are inaccurate on two counts.

First, they imply that eschewing pork and avoiding sex during menstruation were especially Jewish practices. Such is not the case. As anthropologists have shown, a menstruous woman is avoided in many societies. Pollution concepts are observed throughout the world both in ancient and modern times, for example, among the Tamil peoples of India (Ferro-Luzzi 1974: 113) and the Nuer in Africa (Burton 1974: 517). The pig was considered unclean by almost everyone in the ancient Near East, sometimes as food but especially in relation to cultic activities. The pig (Egyptian *rri*, "sow"; also *šʒi* and *šʒw*) was domesticated in Egypt as early as 3500 B.C.; in the Fertile Crescent pig domestication can be traced to its beginnings in the Zagros Mountains between 6500 B.C. and 6000 B.C. and in Israel between 5000 B.C. and 4000 B.C. (Flannery 1983: 172, 180).

In Babylonia, the pig (Akkadian *šaḫû*) was a physically and cultically unclean animal. The *Chicago Assyrian Dictionary's* descriptions (Š 104) of several ancient views of the pig characterize it as unclean and hence an abomination (item 4 is from Moyer 1969: 59):

1. The pig is not fit for a temple—it is not intelligent, is not allowed to tread on paved [walks], an abomination to all the gods.
2. The pig is impure; it defiles everything behind it, makes the streets stink, besmirches the houses.
3. If [a man when going to the temple] eats beef or pork, he is not pure.
4. If a pig . . . approaches any of them [the implements of wood or clay that you have] and the kitchen servant does not discard it, but gives the god to eat from an unclean [vessel].

Whoever causes the impurity is destroyed together with his wives and children, a collective punishment for violating purity-impurity rules that sheds light on Israel's *kareth* penalty. In ancient Israel the pig was forbidden as food most likely because of its reputation elsewhere and because it was used in pagan magical rites, especially in offerings to chthonic deities (Milgrom 1991: 649). The concern for pollution in Israel was shared by its neighbors. Eating pork and having sex with a menstruant have nothing to do with ethnic contamination or Jewish sins.

Associated Terms

A semantic field of terms relating to the idea of abomination may be constructed from several ancient Near Eastern sources. For example, it is suggested that abomination and taboo are reflected in the Sumerian term NÍG-GIG, equal to Akkadian *ikkibu* (cf. Van Der Toorn 1985: 43). According to M. J. Geller (1990: 105 n. 3), who studied the Sumerian data, "the association between Hebrew *tōʿēbāh* and the semantically related terms *ikkibu*, *asakku*, and *anzillu* is supported by standard definitions: *CAD* I/J 55ff. translates *ikkibu* as something 'abhorrent' or 'sin'; *CAD* A/2 gives 'taboo' for *asakku* . . . and 'abomination' for *anzillu*." These terms are not used in relation to homosexuality in Akkadian or Sumerian, nor is there any idea about intrinsic wrong versus cultic impurity. Ancient Near Eastern peoples did not make Boswell's distinction, nor did the Israelites. David Greenberg, in his monumental work on homosexuality (1988: 195–96), concurs:

> Boswell's distinction between acts that are truly evil and those that are mere ritual violations is completely extraneous to the authors of Leviticus, for whom everything prohibited by Yahweh is totally wrong. That intercourse with a menstruating woman is also classified as an abomination along with homosexuality is an indication not, as Boswell suggests, that the latter offense was considered trivial, but rather that the former was considered extremely grave. However silly they may seem to contemporary rationalists, menstrual taboos are taken very seriously in many primitive societies. Late biblical Palestine was one of them.

Tôʿēbâ in the Septuagint

Second, no distinction is made between intrinsic wrong and ritual impurity in the Septuagint's rendering of tôʿēbâ. The Septuagint uses nineteen Greek terms in translating tôʿēbâ, including akathartos (ἀκάθαρτος, "uncleanness"; Prov. 3:32; 16:5; 17:15; 20:10), akatharsia (ἀκαθαρσία, "uncleanness"; Prov. 6:16; 24:9), and asebeia (ἀσέβεια, "godlessness, impiety"; only Ezek. 14:6), but the predominant Septuagint terms for tôʿēbâ are bdelygma (βδέλυγμα, "abomination, abhorrence, detestable thing"; sixty-eight times) and anomia (ἀνομία, "lawlessness"; twenty-eight times). Since the last two terms are those upon which Boswell bases his thesis, I restrict my analysis to them.

Anomia. Of the twenty-eight occurrences of anomia for tôʿēbâ, all but one (Jer. 16:18) are in Ezekiel. In every instance, as we might expect from the prophet Ezekiel, who as a priest is totally steeped in the language of the cultus, anomia is used in relation to the pollution generated from sexual deviations, idolatry, or other violations of God's statutes and ordinances. The Septuagint of Jeremiah 16:18 reflects the same usage: "And I will first doubly repay their iniquity and their sin, because they have polluted my land; they have filled my inheritance with the carcasses of their detestable idols and with their abominations (anomia)." Notice that idolatry and the abominations are separate crimes; this is not a hendiadys, a grammatical construction that forms a unit in which one word is used to qualify the other (cf. Speiser 1964: 5 n. 2). The common denominator between idolatry and the abominations is that both generate impurity that contaminates the land and the sanctuary where God dwells. The terms anomia and bdelygma are used interchangeably in the Septuagint to express this.

The evidence from Ezekiel is compelling. The term *anomia* is linked inextricably with the defilement caused by sin. It is *anomia*, not as lawlessness in general but as pollution-generating conduct that causes God to be far from his sanctuary (Ezek. 8:6). Idolatry and the presentation of improper incense—crimes both worthy of the *kareth* penalty (see Exod. 30:38 and Ezek. 14:8)—are *anomia* (8:9, 13). Association with the Tammuz cultus (8:14) and sun worship (8:16) are among the abominations that defile God's sanctuary (9:4–7). In the restoration, Ezekiel foresees the removal of abominations in compliance with God's statutes and ordinances (11:18, 21—using the same phraseology as Lev. 18:5). Punishment for abominations is by dispersion among the nations (Ezek. 12:16; 16:58). The Greek translators of Ezekiel 16 use the term *anomia* seven times, all for sexual violations (vv. 2, 36, 43, 47, 51 [twice], 58). It is not accidental that Sodom is mentioned in this context (v. 56) under *tôʿēbâ/anomia* because of the sexual nature of the crimes there, in addition to their arrogance and inhospitality: "Thus they were haughty and committed abominations before me. Therefore I removed them when I saw it" (16:50).

The sexual nature of *tôʿēbâ/anomia* is also seen at Ezekiel 16:58, where it stands parallel to *zimmâ*, a general term for sexual lewdness. That *tôʿēbâ/anomia* is not restricted to sexual crimes is evident from a careful reading of Ezekiel 18, where, in addition to defiling a neighbor's wife (Ezek. 18:6, 11; cf. Lev. 18:20) and having sex with a woman during her menstrual impurity (Ezek. 18:6; Lev. 18:19), it applies as well to robbery, usury, oppression of the poor and needy, idolatry, etc. (Ezek. 18:1–13, 20, 24). The remaining occurrences of *anomia* for *tôʿēbâ* in Ezekiel all reflect the prophet's concern for the effect of defilement (*ṭumʾâ*, טֻמְאָה): "Do not defile yourselves with the idols of Egypt" (20:7; see 20:4); Jerusalem is a city that makes idols "for defilement" (22:3; see 22:2); murder and adultery are paired with cultic violations that pollute (23:36b–39):

> Then declare to them their abominations. For they have committed adultery, and blood is on their hands. Thus they have committed adultery with their idols and even caused their sons, whom they bore to me, to pass through the fire to them as food [Molech worship]. Again, they have done this to me: they have defiled my sanctuary on the same day and have profaned my sabbaths. For when they had slaughtered their children for their idols, they entered my sanctuary on the same day to profane it; and lo, thus they did within my house.

At Ezekiel 43:8 the prophet writes, "they have defiled my holy name by their abominations," by harlotry. And finally we see at Ezekiel 44:6b–7, "enough of all your abominations, O house of Israel, when you brought in foreigners, uncircumcised in heart and uncircumcised in flesh, to be in my sanctuary to profane it, even my house, when you offered my food, the fat and the blood; for they made my covenant void—this in addition to all your abominations." In this last instance, the Levites in charge of guard duty failed to exercise their responsibility to protect the holy things from unauthorized contact (Milgrom 1970: 11). In all these verses, the term *anomia* translates *tô'ēbâ*. Boswell's suggestion that Greek *anomia* means something like "intrinsic wrong" is unequivocally incorrect according to the Septuagint in Ezekiel. It stands for sins that are ritually defiling.

Bdelygma. Do the Septuagint translators employ the term *bdelygma* to contrast *anomia*? An investigation of *tô'ēbâ/bdelygma* brings no surprises: twelve times it reflects pollution that is generated by sin. Again in Ezekiel, violations against God's statutes and ordinances (5:7) are called abominations (5:9) that threaten the removal of God's presence from his people: " 'So as I live,' declares the Lord GOD, 'surely, because you have defiled my sanctuary with all your detestable idols and with all your abominations, therefore I will also withdraw, and my eye shall have no pity and I will not spare' " (5:11). Dispersion among the nations is God's punishment for *bdelygma* (6:9, 11; 7:3–4, 8–9, 20). At Ezekiel 16:22, the Septuagint uses *bdelygma* for *tô'ēbâ* in a chapter where, it will be recalled, *tô'ēbâ* is rendered by *anomia* seven times. In the restoration, the people of God will be ashamed of their *bdelygma* (36:31), when the Lord "will save you from all your uncleanness" (36:29). A final unit (33:26–29) uses *bdelygma* for *tô'ēbâ* twice:

> "You rely on your sword, you commit abominations, and each of you defiles his neighbor's wife. Should you then possess the land?" Thus you shall say to them, "Thus says the Lord GOD, 'As I live, surely those who are in the waste places will fall by the sword, and whoever is in the open field I will give to the beasts to be devoured, and those who are in the strongholds and in the caves will die of pestilence. And I shall make the land a desolation and a waste, and the pride of her power will cease; and the mountains of Israel will be desolate, so that no one will pass through. Then they will know that I am the LORD, when I make the land a desolation and a waste because of all their abominations which they have committed.' "

The twelve occurrences of *tô'ēbâ/bdelygma* in Ezekiel confirm that in the Septuagint's rendering of this book, there is no distinction between *anomia* and *bdelygma* in translating *tô'ēbâ*. They do not distinguish intrinsic wrong from ritual impurity. How, then, does this data compare to the use of *tôʿēbâ* in Leviticus?

Tôʿēbâ in Leviticus. Most of the 113 uses of *tôʿēbâ* in the Hebrew Bible appear in Ezekiel and the Deuteronomic sources. It is remarkable that this term, which is so intimately related to pollution concepts, is used only six times in Leviticus. It is furthermore remarkable that it is used in the singular exclusively of homosexuality twice (Lev. 18:22; 20:13). In the plural it is used only to summarize the sexual sins registered in Leviticus 18 (vv. 26–27, 29–30). *Anomia* is not used to translate *tôʿēbâ* in Leviticus; five times *bdelygma* appears in the singular or plural, and there is one occurrence of the verb *bdelyssomai* (βδελύσσομαι; Lev. 18:30). The preference for *bdelygma* in Leviticus clearly places the locus of *tôʿēbâ* within the realm of impurity. It is intimately associated in the singular with homosexuality, and it is used to summarize all the sexual violations cited in Leviticus 18.

Terms Associated with Tôʿēbâ in Leviticus 18. Before bringing this section to a close, a brief look at three terms associated with *tôʿēbâ* in Leviticus 18 is instructive: *zimmâ* (זִמָּה, "plan, device, wickedness"; 18:17), *ḥālal* (חָלַל, "to profane, desecrate"; 18:21), and *tebel* (תֶּבֶל, "confusion, violation of nature, or the divine order"; 18:23). Like *tôʿēbâ*, these terms all show that the impurity generated by improper sexual acts is deliberate, defiling, and a violation of the natural order for sexual relations. The impurity generated by them is not merely ritual, as Boswell says, but rather moral. And because the impurity is sexual and deliberate, it is of the most dangerous kind. If words, like people, can be known by the company they keep, *tôʿēbâ* belongs to the direst category and cannot be classified as a mere synonym for idolatry. The levitical writer reserved *tôʿēbâ* for sexual crimes punishable by *kareth*.

The noun *zimmâ* is derived from the verb *zāmam* (זָמַם, "to plan, think, reflect"), and the idea of deliberate intention is implied in the noun. The etymology may be connected with Ethiopic *zamana* ("to fornicate"; S. Steingrimsson, *TDOT* 4:88). Of the twenty-nine occurrences of *zimmâ* in the Old Testament, four are in Leviticus (18:17; 19:29; 20:14 [twice]), all in reference to sexual deviations. Ezekiel uses *zimmâ* thirteen times, predictably and consistently of sexual violations (Ezek. 16:27, 43, 58; 22:9, 11; 23:21, 27, 29, 35, 44, 48, 49; 24:13), recalling the use of the term in Leviticus 18 and 20. In the allegory of Ezekiel 16, *zimmâ* is parallel to *tôʿēbâ* and *zānâ* (זָנָה, "to fornicate"; the Septuagint has *porneia* [πορνεία], at 16:25). At Ezekiel 22:26, the pollution of the land is due to the failure of the priests to implement their job description according to Leviticus 10:10: "Her priests have done violence to my law and have profaned (*ḥālal*) my holy things; they have made no distinction between the holy and the profane, and they have not taught the difference between the unclean and the clean; and they hide their eyes from my sabbaths, and I am profaned among them" (see also Ezek. 22:8).

The verb *ḥālal* (חָלַל) in the piel and hiphil always means "to profane" or "to desecrate" and is used, for example, with reference to the divine name in the case of Molech service (Lev. 18:21; 20:3) and swearing falsely (19:12), for inappropriate contact of the priests with corpses (21:11; 22:4), and for defiling the sanctuary through impurity (21:23). An impassable line is drawn between the holy and the impure in biblical law. Desecration of sacred objects or the divine name is punishable by *kareth*. God's anger is stirred up against all acts of desecration because of their contaminating influence. To commit an act that would be described by the verb *ḥālal* is to smudge or blur the line between the holy and the impure, to have utter disregard for the separateness demanded by the realm of the holy.

The noun *tebel* occurs only twice in the Bible, both times in chapters where homosexuality is mentioned: once for bestiality (Lev. 18:23) and once for incest with a daughter-in-law (Lev. 20:12). It is derived from the verb *bālal* (בָּלַל, "to mix, confuse, mingle"). The abomination (*tôʿēbâ*) of homosexuality in Leviticus 20:13 is sandwiched between *tebel* in verse 12 and *zimmâ* in verse 14. The Septuagint uses two different terms for *tebel*: the noun *myseros* (μυσερός, "loathsome, detestable, abominable thing") in Leviticus 18:23 and the verb *asebeō* (ἀσεβέω, "to act impiously") in 20:12. All three terms belong to a semantic field reflecting the sexual act. In his diatribe against Jerusalem (Ezek. 22:10–11), Ezekiel makes reference to laws at Leviticus 18:8–9, 11, 16, 19–20; 20:10–12, 17–18 (which also uses *ḥesed* [חֶסֶד, "shame, reproach"] for sex with a sister): "In you they have uncovered their father's nakedness; in you they have humbled her who was unclean in her menstrual impurity. And one has committed abomination (*tôʿēbôt*) with his neighbor's wife, and another has lewdly (*zimmâ*) defiled (*ṭāmēʾ*) his daughter-in-law. And another in you has humbled his sister, his father's daughter." It is noteworthy that Ezekiel must have understood *tebel* and *zimmâ* as synonymous, since he replaces *tebel* in Leviticus 20:12 with *zimmâ* at Ezekiel 23:11. All the terms associated with *tôʿēbâ* are also associated with impurity (*ṭāmēʾ*).

The early rabbis formed a semantic field of negative terms that included *tôʿēbâ*, through a method known as *notarikon* (i.e., shorthand) in which the letters of a certain word are said to represent the initial letters of other words. For example, the consonants of *nimreṣet* (נִמְרֶצֶת, "grievous") in 1 Kings 2:8 were said to refer to *nōʾēp* (נֹאֵף, "adulterer"), *môʾābî* (מוֹאָבִי, "Moabite"), *rōṣēaḥ* (רֹצֵחַ, "murderer"), *ṣōrēr* (צֹרֵר, "enemy"), and *tôʿēbâ* (תּוֹעֵבָה, "abomination") (Louis Jacobs, *EJ* 8:371).

Lesbianism

There is no explicit prohibition in the Bible regarding lesbianism. Does the law therefore permit sexual relations between women? All the stipulations in Leviticus 18 (except for the case of a woman who gives her body to an animal in a cross-species sexual act; v. 23) are in the masculine gender. Intention is a major part of the law, and the male is presumed to be the initiator of sexual intercourse. Ancient Israel was a male-dominated society, which is probably why the laws are phrased as they are. Legal codes throughout the ancient Near East reflect the same type of male-dominated phraseology (e.g., the common expression in Mesopotamian case law: "If a man (*šumma awīlum*) . . ."). Scholars offer various explanations for the biblical lacuna regarding lesbian legislation. According to Jacob Milgrom (1993: 11), "lesbians existed and flourished, as attested in an old (pre-Israelite) Babylonian text and in the work of the lesbian poet Sappho. . . . But there is a fundamental difference between the homosexual acts of men and women. In lesbianism there is no spilling of seed. Thus life is not symbolically lost, and therefore lesbianism is not prohibited in the Bible." (Gordon Wenham 1983 argues a similar thesis.) This view rests on the following syllogism: The spilling of semen implies loss of life. Semen is spilled in male homosexual acts. Therefore male homosexual acts are forbidden because they cause loss of life. And again: The spilling of semen implies loss of life. There is no spilling of semen in lesbian acts. Therefore lesbian acts are not forbidden.

The notion that semen contains life is found in various parts of the world. For example, among Hindus, the drinking of semen is recommended as a cure for impotence since the principle of life is in the semen (O'Flaherty 1976: 340). The only biblical reference to life being symbolized by a body fluid is Leviticus 17:11 where blood is called the seat of life and therefore the medium of atonement. But nowhere does the Bible state that semen symbolizes life; in fact, semen is a source of impurity (Lev. 15). In the first human birth, it is not semen that is the agent of life but God himself (Gen. 4:1). In Hindu practice, the idea of life in the semen can be accepted because body products are drunk or eaten for purposes of purification (cow's urine, milk, ghee, curds, dung). However, the magical effect of all body fluids is rejected in biblical religion, and under no circumstances are blood or any other body fluid to be consumed by humans. Scripture always accounts for the loss of life, but there is no indication that this takes place with the loss of semen. In the homicidal shedding of blood, both man and beast are culpable (Gen. 9:5–6). Homosexuality is not prohibited because life is lost in the extravaginal ejaculation of semen but because it is contrary to the natural order. The biblical legislator should not, therefore, be made to appear to support lesbianism because no semen is involved in the sexual union of two females.

A rationale for the prohibition against male homosexuality (and in my view lesbianism) must be sought in the levitical writer's concept of impurity and order as I shall demonstrate in chapter 8. If the order of creation defines the sexual relationship, neither male homosexuality nor lesbianism can meet the criterion of procreation. In the ancient Near East, children played an important role in beliefs about afterlife and in more temporal matters. Thus levirate marriage was practiced for the purpose of raising up progeny through a deceased brother's widow; and when it was flouted by a willful act to eliminate the name of the deceased, as in the case of Onan (Gen. 38), death by divine intervention ensued. In this instance, the unauthorized disposition of semen is specifically associated with failing to produce offspring to preserve the name of his brother. It would be a mistake, however, to think that this incident is only about semen. In a larger sense, Onan violated the established custom of Hebrew society and usurped the divine right of determining whose name was to be preserved. He was struck dead on this basis, not because he violated a life-principle of semen. Implicit in the Onan story is the idea that God alone is sovereign over life, and any infringement on his rights results in severe reprisal. Only God can determine who shall be barren and who shall conceive. Semen, stripped of all magical powers and the sacredness with which it was esteemed in Hindu society and other cultures (Douglas 1966: 125), plays a role in a larger complex of ideas relating to Israelite beliefs in kin, cult, land, and afterlife.

There are no examples of lesbianism in the Bible (just as there are no examples of homosexuality), despite some weak attempts to show that Ruth and Naomi had a sexual relationship (Horner 1978: 40). If lesbianism was practiced in the Near East, perhaps it was not legislated against in the Bible because it did not fit the category of sexual intercourse that, by definition, implied penetration by the male member. By the time the New Testament was written, the Greek island of Lesbos was famous for its sexual activity between women, as were the cities of Corinth and Rome. References to sexual relations between women are found in the later Greek literature and the New Testament (Rom. 1:26). Given the importance of progeny throughout the ancient Near East (in part to achieve felicity in the afterlife); given the necessity for structuring Israelite society through pollution rules at the time the laws of Leviticus 18 were written (i.e., when external enforcement of morality and ethics could not be effected by a centralized government); given the role of pollution rules for the purpose of maintaining the land of promise in a condition of holiness pleasing to Yahweh; given the prevalence of sexual practices (homosexuality, lesbianism, bestiality, incest, etc.) against the order of creation among people contemporaneous with the Israelite tribes upon their entrance into Canaan; and given the lack of evidence in the ancient Near East for basing sex unions on what moderns call "romantic love" or even companionship—it is probably not safe to conclude with Tikva Frymer-Kensky (1989: 92) that "in the case of homosexuality, men were more bound than women, since homosexuality was considered a major threat requiring the death penalty (whether real or threatened) and lesbian sex was not a matter of concern."

Certainly women were not immune from punishment with regard to sexual violations. The principle of intention informs all biblical law, extending even to animals. For example, in the law at Leviticus 20:16 both the woman and the animal are put to death (as are the man and the beast in Lev. 20:15). The same prohibition occurs at Leviticus 18:23 proscribing male and female relations with animals: both are sanctioned by being "cut off" (*kareth*). Of course, animals are not subject to the *kareth* penalty; they are simply put to death. If lesbianism was not forbidden among the ancient Hebrews (granting the necessity to argue from silence), one has to wonder why male and female sex acts with animals carried the same penalties while male homosexuality and lesbianism did not. Both were violations against the divine order in creation, the male-female roles in continuing the creation. Same-gender sexual relations usurp the divine right to create life through sexual union. If this analysis is correct, it is not surprising that later rabbinic thought, following the hermeneutics of Rabbi Hillel and Rabbi Ishmael current at the time, placed lesbianism as well as male homosexuality under divine sanction. As noted by Baruch Levine (1989: 123): "There has been considerable speculation as to why lesbianism is not explicitly forbidden in the Torah. In due course, rabbinic interpretation added this prohibition, as well" (citing Maimonides' *Book of Holiness* 135).

Conclusion

We may come now to some conclusions. First, from study of Ezekiel, it is apparent that Boswell's position with respect to *tô'ēbâ* must be rejected. There is no distinction between the Septuagint terms *anomia* and *bdelygma* in translating *tôʿēbâ*. The more general term *anomia* may have been influenced by *bdelygma* (the more common word for *tôʿēbâ*), thus giving to *anomia* the color of cultic impurity, but there is no evidence for a line finely drawn between *anomia* as a category of violations of law or justice and *bdelygma* as infringements of ritual purity or monotheistic worship. The Greek terms are used synonymously in the Septuagint.

Second, when *tôʿēbâ* is used with respect to idolatry, the sexual nature of the idolatrous activity is stressed. The sexual nature of *tôʿēbâ* is explicit in Leviticus 18, but it would be incorrect to suggest that *tôʿēbâ* was used only of sexual violations in other places. For example, in Deuteronomy it is used of prohibited food (14:3), idolatry (12:31; 13:15), magic (18:12), and injustice (24:16), but not of sexual offenses. According to Jacob Milgrom (*EJ* 2:97), "common to all these usages is the notion of irregularity, that which offends the accepted order, ritual, or moral."

Third, the term *tôʿēbâ* has a narrower meaning in Leviticus. It was known and could have been used, for example, of the food prohibitions in Leviticus 11, but it was not. There the terms *ṭāmēʾ* (טָמֵא, "to be or become impure") and *šeqeṣ* (שֶׁקֶץ, "detestable thing") are used to describe the condition or category of impurity, whereas in Leviticus 18, *tôʿēbâ* describes a human action that results in impurity. English versions do not make this distinction: the New Jewish Publication Society Version renders *šeqeṣ* as "abomination" and *tôʿēbâ* as "abhorrence," while the Revised Standard Version renders both terms as "abomination." The term *šeqeṣ* belongs properly to the general category of impurity (cf. Assyrian *shiktzu*, "impurity, blemish"). That *tôʿēbâ* is strictly related to the sphere of pollution concepts in the priestly literature is evident in virtually every passage where it is used. This is further supported by its association in priestly sources with the *kareth* penalty that serves to sanction those crimes that profane the land or God's sanctuary. Practices subsumed under the category of *tôʿēbâ* threaten the removal of God's presence from Israel. Therefore all inhabitants of the land, native Israelites and resident aliens alike, are subject to the *kareth* penalty following *tôʿēbâ* violations (Lev. 18:26). The term *tôʿēbâ* in Leviticus refers only to sexual sins, all of which generate impurity.

Finally, it is impossible to restrict homosexuality to cultic prostitution or an idolatrous practice based on the uses of the term *tôʿēbâ* in either the Hebrew Bible or the Septuagint. Examination of the terms in Leviticus 18:22 precludes the interpretation that cultic prostitution or idolatry are related to this verse. When *tôʿēbâ* is associated with idolatry, one may surmise that such idolatrous acts had a sexual component, perhaps even a homosexual element, depending on the extent that Leviticus 18 influenced later writers. I agree with Bailey (1975: 30), who writes: "It is hardly open to doubt that both the laws in Leviticus [i.e., 18:22; 20:13] relate to ordinary homosexual acts between men, and not to ritual or other acts performed in the name of religion." (A rationale for the prohibition of the sexual relations in Leviticus 18 will be given in the next chapter.)

The proximity of the proscription against homosexuality to Molech worship in Leviticus 18 does not weaken my case, and in this I have to disagree with the view expounded by Norman Snaith and supported by Tom Horner. The Molech cultus, although its definition remains incomplete, consisted of a sexual element and is therefore categorized as *tô‛ēbâ*; it is the sexual aspect of the cultus that places it in the list of crimes in Leviticus 18, not its idolatrous element. Giving one's seed to Molech may have involved cultic prostitution of some kind, dedicating a child to the idol, or even child sacrifice. The inclusion of Molech worship in Leviticus 18 might seem odd at first, since it is the only stipulation that deals with false worship. But if we see this chapter as a unit analogous to the Hittite suzerainty treaty, then the common denominator is the sexual nature of all the stipulations—not idolatry. Therefore, it is improper method to compare the homosexuality of verse 22 with the Molech worship of verse 21 and conclude that both are idolatrous practices. The idolatry of Molech worship is incidental to the sexual nature of this crime in this context. The biblical writer's awareness of the several aspects of Molech worship enables him to place it in this list. The sex crimes of Leviticus 18, with the possible exception of Molech worship, were not cultic in nature. The stipulations were placed upon all Israelites, who, as the people of Yahweh, were to conduct themselves in a pure, moral manner pleasing to their suzerain, in sharp contrast to the behavior exemplified by their neighbors.

Having come to a proper understanding of the legal vocabulary on homosexuality, we may conclude that all same-gender sexual relations are categorically forbidden by the Hebrew terms. The biblical writer leaves no room for compromise. The language is emphatic. The term *zākār* includes all males and all acts, and by inference lesbianism is also included. Under this language, even consensual sexual relations between adults of the same gender must be ruled out. We find no ambiguity in the expression *miškĕbê ʾiššâ*; it denotes sexual intercourse in general without reference to specific positions. The inference is clear: only heterosexual intercourse is normal and normative. Finally, the term *tô‛ēbâ* shows no distinction between intrinsic wrong and ritual impurity as suggested by Boswell. Neither can *tô‛ēbâ* be restricted to Jewish sins of a strictly cultic variety. An argument to limit the law against homosexual practices to the ancient Israelite cultus cannot be supported, or else the Canaanites and Egyptians would not be condemned for such conduct. In *tôʿēbâ* we find an inherent sexual component. The reference is to a deliberate act against the divine law resulting in impurity. Even when idolatry is associated with this term, it appears that some sexual violation is implied. All the violations of Leviticus 18 are sexual aberrations. The unity of the chapter demands that all be considered together. The term *tebel* suggests that homosexuality, bestiality, and incest are contrary to the divine order. The writer of Leviticus 18 subsumes all under the rubric of *tôʿēbâ*. With these thoughts in mind, let us turn our attention to the issue of impurity in Israel.

8

Impurity in Israel

Do not defile yourselves by any of these things; for by all these the nations which I am casting out before you have become defiled. For the land has become defiled, therefore I have visited its punishment upon it, so the land has spewed out its inhabitants. But as for you, you are to keep my statutes and my judgments, and shall not do any of these abominations, neither the native, nor the alien who sojourns among you; (for the men of the land who have been before you have done all these abominations, and the land has become defiled); so that the land may not spew you out should you defile it, as it has spewed out the nation which has been before you.

—Leviticus 18:24–28

In the closing verses of Leviticus 18, the legislator gives the rationale for the stipulations of the chapter and invokes the penalty for violating them. He clearly states that Israelites must avoid certain sexual aberrations, among which is listed homosexuality (v. 22), for two reasons: (1) forbidden sexual relations cause pollution on the personal level: "Do not defile yourselves by any of these things," a condition that the Canaanites, the offspring of Ham, generated and for which they were dispossessed of the land (v. 24); and (2) the land itself is polluted by sexual deviations and receives God's judgment, leading ultimately to the expulsion of its inhabitants (v. 25). Personal impurity and environmental pollution are explicit results of illicit sex. A third consequence of these forbidden relations, derived from the priestly writer's statements beyond Leviticus 18, is that they impact the realm of the holy. In particular, Israel's sanctuary where Yahweh resides is contaminated thereby, and even the very name of Yahweh is defiled by these acts (Lev. 20:3). This third aspect of the effect of impurity is especially dangerous because the presence of Yahweh will be removed should the accumulation of sins continue (Ezek. 5:11). For the priestly writer, no greater tragedy could be imagined than the removal of God's presence. To ensure Yahweh's continued presence in Israel, the highest standard of sexual conduct is required. While the incentive to comply with the sexual code is provided by imposing the threat of the *kareth* penalty (see the next chapter), it is necessary now to turn our attention to the rationale for impurity and to the means by which purification was effected in ancient Israel.

What precisely is meant by "impurity" or "pollution," and how did it affect the person committing the violation? What was the effect on the land and the sanctuary? Was it physical or symbolic? How does impurity in the levitical system reflect an ethical component? Was impurity demonic or magical in origin, or was it strictly the product of human action? Once a sexual violation had occurred, what resources were available for removing the impurity generated thereby? Were expulsion from the land, the *kareth* penalty, and even death at the hands of the community deemed inevitable punishments for sexual deviance? How was the homosexual reconciled to God and the community? Why were the particular sexual relationships cited in Leviticus 18 proscribed—what single rationale can be postulated for their being placed together in this list? These and other important questions will be answered as we explore the priestly writer's concept of impurity. At the end of our study, it will be clear why same-gender sexual relations were forbidden in ancient Israel.

According to Leviticus 10:10, it is part of a priest's job description to differentiate "between the holy and the profane, and between the unclean and the clean." The particular goal of Leviticus 18 is to establish holiness and purity in sexual relations at the personal and national levels. A complete analysis of biblical impurity would take us too far afield; I shall, therefore, restrict our study to the defilement associated with the laws of Leviticus 18. Homosexual acts are among those that cause impurity, and impurity is incompatible with holiness. To better understand the biblical view of homosexuality, we need to examine (1) the idea of impurity from several interdisciplinary perspectives, (2) the semantic field of impurity in the Bible, and (3) the idea of purification and the means of removing the impurity generated by sexual offenses. I will demonstrate that homosexual acts were deliberate violations of God's laws and as such were not covered by the sacrificial system (Num. 15:30–31); nevertheless a provision of the most merciful magnitude was made for reconciling the homosexual to God (see chap. 10 on the role of sacrifice in the removal of impurity).

Interdisciplinary Approaches to Impurity

The idea of impurity has been studied extensively in Jewish tradition, since a large part of the Talmud is dedicated to this subject. Islamic tradition has historically placed great importance on impurity rules as well, often reflecting customs prevalent in pre-Islamic Arabia. On the other hand, Christians have not exhibited much scholarly interest in impurity, despite the role of this concept in the biblical sources, especially with regard to sexual morality. In recent years, social scientists have given their attention to the role of impurity concepts in diverse societies, both ancient and modern, in an effort to understand how impurity rules influence behavior and help to provide structure and order in society. The results of their labors are useful for biblical research. Some understanding of the various approaches to impurity is necessary before we discuss impurity in relation to homosexuality in the Bible. After defining impurity, we shall consider in order the sociological, psychological, anthropological, and moral approaches to understanding impurity.

Definition of Impurity

Generally speaking, impurity concerns the distinction between the sacred and profane and may be defined in terms of either its sources or its means of removal. Persons, animals, objects, and places may be categorized as impure under certain conditions, and different categories of impurity reflect greater or lesser degrees of severity. For instance, space and time may be designated either sacred or profane with a view toward structuring society. According to Mircea Eliade (1959: 20), "there is, then, a sacred space, and hence a strong, significant space; there are other spaces that are not sacred and so are without structure or consistency, amorphous. Nor is this all. For religious man, this spatial non-homogeneity finds expression in the experience of an opposition between space that is sacred . . . and all other space, the formless expanse surrounding it." In many ritualistic cultures, the "camp" or settlement where the tribe dwells is sacred, while the area outside the settlement is profane and dangerous. Rules to define impurity are meant to enforce a strict border between these two realms. In a similar fashion, time dedicated to sacred purposes is distinguished from ordinary time, while the passage of time is a requirement accompanying purification rituals. Violations of sacred space and sacred time carry severe sanctions.

Sociology

A major contribution to the understanding of impurity concepts was made by sociologist Émile Durkheim in *The Elementary Forms of the Religious Life* (1915). He emphasizes the social significance of the sacrificial system and impurity rules and defines both negative and positive cults. The negative cultus is dominated by interdictions or rules that define the barrier between the sacred and the profane:

> A man cannot enter into intimate relations with sacred things except after ridding himself of all that is profane in him. He cannot lead a religious life of even a slight intensity unless he commences by withdrawing more or less completely from the temporal life. So the negative cult is in one sense a means in view of an end: it is a condition of access to the positive cult. It does not confine itself to protecting sacred beings from vulgar contact; it acts upon the worshipper himself and modifies his condition positively. The man who has submitted himself to its prescribed interdictions is not the same afterwards as he was before. (1915: 348)

The abstinence demanded in Leviticus 18 is clearly a function of the negative cultus. Abstinence, however, as a means of controlling profane conduct does not give the complete picture of religious life. A positive relationship to the holy is required as well. Durkheim defines the positive cultus as a "special system of rites": "Men have never thought that their duties towards religious forces might be reduced to a simple abstinence from all commerce; they have always believed that they upheld positive and bilateral relations with them, whose regulations and organization is the function of a group of ritual practices" (p. 366). The levitical sacrificial system, in particular the means of cleansing from impurity, belongs to the positive cultus.

Psychology

The social model proposed by Durkheim has features in common with the psychological model presented in Rudolf Otto's *Idea of the Holy* (1923). For Otto, holiness is beyond moral goodness. It concerns the "numinous," which produces a "creature-feeling," a response of subjugation to an absolute and objective power outside the self (p. 10). Like the social-symbolism theory advanced by Durkheim, the psychological model of Otto is useful in understanding the idea of impurity in the Bible. An important part of my thesis is that the levitical writer is not concerned with sterile rituals or mere entrenched legalism as some commentators suppose. Rather, the legal stipulations and sacrificial rituals reflect a profound understanding of the human psyche on the questions of guilt and forgiveness. The psychological component is as evident in the law of homosexuality as the sociological aspect.

Anthropology

At the turn of the century, Arnold Van Gennep was the first anthropologist to demonstrate the significance of ceremonies and pollution rules for ordering society. The relationship of the individual to society is of great importance (1960: 189): "Sometimes the individual stands alone and apart from all groups; sometimes, as a member of one particular group, he is separated from the members of others. Two primary divisions are characteristic of all societies irrespective of time and place: the sexual separation between men and women, and the magico-religious separation between the profane and the sacred." If pollution rules of other societies do not make sense to us, it may be because we have cast off much of the ritual observance that might help to structure our world. The trend away from ritual in modern Western society has resulted in the fragmentation of our institutions and alienation from one another. As Mary Douglas observes (1973: 19–20), ritual regulations provide form and structure to society and help to standardize conduct that maintains order in society.

The anthropological efforts associated with Claude Levi-Strauss, reflected in his important book *Structural Anthropology* (1963), have influenced a generation of investigators. Structuralists attempt to understand social institutions and the natural world as a systematic ordering of categories and events. A major contribution in this regard was made by Mary Douglas in *Purity and Danger* (1966). Based on her study of the abominations of Leviticus 11, she explains (p. 53) holiness on the ground of order:

> Holiness requires that individuals shall conform to the class to which they belong. And holiness requires that different classes of things shall not be confused. Another set of precepts refines on this last point. Holiness means keeping distinct the categories of creation. It therefore involves correct definition, discrimination and order. Under this head all the rules of sexual morality exemplify the holy. Incest and adultery (Leviticus 18:6–20) are against holiness, in the simple sense of right order.

Douglas's insight is important to our model of a rationale for the sex laws in Leviticus 18. She also makes a pioneering effort in identifying the social boundaries and effects of pollution (p. 122):

> Four kinds of social pollution seem worth distinguishing. The first is danger pressing on external boundaries; the second, danger from transgressing the internal lines of the system; the third, danger in the margins of the lines. The fourth is danger from internal contradiction, when some of the basic postulates are denied by other basic postulates, so that at certain points the system seems to be at war with itself.

These categories provide a framework against which the moral and ethical view of biblical impurity can be examined.

Ethics

Pollution rules may buttress morality, and they are especially important in tribal societies that lack the means to enforce order. The general rule is intoned by Mary Douglas (1966: 132): "When the sense of outrage is adequately equipped with practical sanctions in the social order, pollution is not likely to arise. Where, humanly speaking, the outrage is likely to go unpunished, pollution beliefs tend to be called in to supplement the lack of other sanctions." In the Bible, pollution rules ultimately enhance the covenantal relationship between Israel and Yahweh. Thus the national identity of Israel and the covenant between God and the people is central to the sacrificial rituals and therefore to the discussion of impurity. According to Douglas Davies, the covenant relationship is important because it emphasizes that transgression has two aspects, "one relating to the offender who was thrown out of proper relationship both with God and his fellow men, and the other to God the offended one, whose integrity of holiness might be brought into question if his covenant partners were permitted to do whatsoever they willed" (1977: 392). For the priestly writer, as I demonstrate below, this covenant is extended to Israel in particular. However, the entire human race is subject to God's order of creation:

> Accordingly, we may think of the holiness of the nation in terms of these ordered social relationships, an orderliness and perfectness which mirrored the perfection of God so that just as the goodness of the creation in Gen 1, which is also a Priestly document, lies in its ordered state as opposed to the state of chaos, so the social life of Israel is only "good" when its social network of relationships is ordered. This process of ordering involves the question of ethics and morality, in that one function of sacrifice in Israel is the maintenance of the moral life of the nation in a balanced condition. (Davies 1977: 390)

The world of the holy is ordered and in harmony with God. The world of the impure reflects disorder and chaos and therefore poses a threat to the realm of the holy.

The Biblical Language of Impurity

No single approach adequately explains the biblical rules of impurity. Each of the above approaches has made some contribution to our understanding of this subject. But none can suffice apart from a study of the language of impurity in the Bible.

The primary Hebrew term for impurity is *ṭāmēʾ* (טָמֵא), which occurs frequently with other words that describe what is unclean, unfit, or sinful. The verb *ṭāmēʾ* ("to be or become unclean, defile") appears 160 times in the Bible, the adjective *ṭāmēʾ* ("unclean") 85 times, and the noun *ṭumʾâ* (טֻמְאָה, "uncleanness, impurity") 35 times. One-half of all the occurrences of the root *ṭmʾ* are found in Leviticus: the verb 88 times, the adjective 44 times, and the noun 17 times.

In the Septuagint, two terms dominate the semantic field of words used to render the root *ṭmʾ*. The noun *akatharsia* (ἀκαθαρσία, "uncleanness") occurs 49 times in the Hebrew Bible, 23 of them in Leviticus. It is possible to see a general development in the meaning of this term, from an early usage in which uncleanness was thought of in a material way. Later, "clean becomes a moral rather than a cultic or ritual term, and the deity itself is regarded as a moral force" (Friedrich Hauck, *TDNT*

3:415). In the same way, a material-moral evolution is ascribed to the verb *miainō* (μιαίνω, "to spot, stain, defile"), the dominant term for the verb *ṭāmēʾ* in Leviticus and Ezekiel, and the noun *miasma* (μίασμα, "defilement").

The material interpretation of impurity is said to belong to an early stage of religion, while the moral meaning supposedly characterizes a later development. One should not, however, lean too heavily upon the evolutionary idea proposed for these terms, for, as we have learned from interdisciplinary approaches to pollution concepts, internal lines of structure reflecting standards of morality and ethics are not inconsistent with remote antiquity. The noun *miasma* occurs only seven times in the Septuagint and in Leviticus only at 7:18 for forbidden flesh. In Greek sources, the material nature of *miasma* is apparent: "It clings to the doer, but can be transferred from him to the countries, sanctuaries and images of the circle which tolerates him in its midst, also to unjust judges and witnesses who prevent expiation" (Friedrich Hauck, *TDNT* 4:646). Both a material and moral aspect of the root *ṭmʾ* seems to be reflected in the Septuagint's choices of *akatharsia* and *miainō*. Cultic contamination and moral impurity are implicit in the term *ṭāmēʾ*.

The borders of the semantic field of impurity in the Bible are set by the four terms found in Leviticus 10:10: *qōdeš* (קֹדֶשׁ, "holy"), *ṭāhôr* (טָהוֹר, "pure"), *ḥōl* (חֹל, "profane, common"), and *ṭāmēʾ* (טָמֵא, "impure"). The categories and conditions described by these terms function in complex dynamic relationships. Each term defines a category or condition that should be kept in isolation from the others, but each sphere might intrude upon another through human misconduct or severe natural impurity. The resultant contact (not necessarily direct, since severe impurity can affect the realm of the holy from afar) presents a situation that demands correction from the individual, the community, and the priests, lest the boundaries become indistinct and order yield to chaos.

While it is essential to see these terms in their horizontal plane or spatial relation (emphasizing time and place), to picture them in a vertical dimension is helpful as well. There is a descending hierarchical order: holy-pure-common-impure. Arranging the terms in this way suggests degrees of gradation. The realm of the holy is furthermore divided into regular holiness and superlative holiness. Because the categories or conditions represented by these terms are dynamic, it is possible to move between them. For example, a common utensil used by the priests within the sanctuary must be elevated to the status of holy and, hence, pure. The same utensil would be lowered to the status of impure if brought into the presence of a corpse. And if it were properly cleansed, it could be reelevated to holy status, depending on its composition (i.e., made of metal and not clay). Thus a sliding scale places holiness and impurity at opposite ends.

Of course, within the boundaries of these four terms a number of other words are used by the priestly writer to further define impurity. For example, in Leviticus the noun *šiqqûṣ* (שִׁקּוּץ, "detested thing") is often translated "abomination" with reference to impure categories of animals prohibited for food. We have already seen that the term *tôʿēbâ* is associated only with sexual impurity in Leviticus, while it is used in a wider sense elsewhere in Scripture and the Dead Sea Scrolls, especially of idolatrous practices. *Niddâ* (נִדָּה, "sexual impurity") is often used in the Bible with reference to sexual intercourse with a menstruant, but also in a wider sense (e.g., the *niddâ* water used to purify corpse contamination). So also *piggûl* (פִּגּוּל), a term referring to sacrificial flesh that is unfit to eat. The mixing of categories is suggested by the term *tebel* (תֶּבֶל, "violation of nature or the divine order") in Leviticus, and so it too is brought into the field of impurity. To desecrate or remove from the status of the holy is expressed by the term *ḥālal* (חָלַל). Even the divine name is subject to desecration (Lev. 20:3)! The list could be easily expanded, but these terms suffice to show how vitally important the idea of impurity was to the levitical writer.

Beyond the borders of the biblical semantic field of terms for impurity, neighboring semantic fields may be studied in other ancient Near Eastern literature to help elucidate the biblical idea of impurity. I shall make use of the non-Israelite data in detail later in this chapter and in our discussion of purification from impurity. Now let us turn our attention to the biblical rationale for sexual impurity.

Sex and Impurity: A Rationale

Keeping in mind the value of the several approaches to understanding impurity rules and our brief analysis of the language of impurity, let us now attempt to construct a rationale for the laws of Leviticus 18. The rationale must fit all the sex crimes mentioned in the chapter: incest (vv. 6–18), sex with a menstruant (v. 19), adultery (v. 20), giving one's seed to Molech (v. 21), homosexuality (v. 22), and bestiality (v. 23). Ancient Israel was a kinship society, in which the individual was subordinated to the group. In such societies incest prohibitions are universal and serve to structure society at a simple yet profound level.

Claude Levi-Strauss in *Structural Anthropology* (1963) defines kinship societies as nontechnological and hence lacking in the formal and powerful organs of statecraft that provide for law and order through abstract enforcement mechanisms such as courts, police departments, decrees from centralized government, etc. The basic unit of such a society is the nuclear family or the extended family. Modern technological societies also maintain fundamental kinship rules to the degree that they respect institutions such as marriage and the family, but they do not qualify in the strictest sense as kinship societies, for by definition the latter lack the power structures to enforce sanctions. Fundamental to the observance of rules that restrict sexual relationships in the family is the principle of order in society.

The structure of kinship societies, according to Levi-Strauss, rests on four relationships or "unit[s] of kinship" (1963: 46): brother, sister, father, son. It provides three types of family relations: "A relation of consanguinity, a relation of affinity, and a relation of descent—in other words, a relation between siblings, a relation between spouses, and a relation between parent and child. . . . The primitive and irreducible character of the basic unit of kinship, as we have defined it, is actually a direct result of the universal presence of an incest taboo. This is really saying that in human society a man must obtain a woman from another man who gives him a daughter or a sister." Because sexual temptations lie close at hand in families, severe sanctions are found throughout the world to enforce incest rules. The priestly regulations on incest in Leviticus 18 and 20 provide the incentive to maintain family order in Israelite society. The motivation is predicated on the idea of impurity as a dynamic force potentially destructive to the people of Israel.

How then does the prohibition against homosexuality relate to the laws concerning incest? The rationale for the law against same-gender sexual contact rests on two principles from the creation account in Genesis 1:27–28: (1) all humanity (*hāʾādām*, הָאָדָם) is created in the image of God as male (*zākār*, זָכָר) and female (*nĕqēbâ*, וּנְקֵבָה) and as such are unique and separate from the rest of creation; and (2) as male and female, humanity is commanded to "be fruitful and multiply, and fill the earth, and subdue it." These principles describe the order or structure of humanity in two relationships: to God and to society. All the laws of Leviticus 18 may be understood as violations of these principles.

The incest laws prohibit relations at the structural level of society where they might be engaged in through "natural" means, that is, between male and female. Such laws curb the appetite for sex and subordinate it to the need for communal order. Two other outlets for sexual gratification are possible: between males, and between humans and animals.

It is not accidental that the law against homosexuality is placed in proximity to the laws on incest and bestiality. That they belong to one category is recognized by Harry Hoffner (1973), for all prohibit a sexual relation that is against the principle of order: incest violates the order of kinship, homosexuality violates the order of gender (Gen. 1:27), and bestiality violates the order of species. On the sixth day of creation, God made the animals after their kind and proclaimed his work good (1:25). The expression *after their kind* separates the animals from humans. Accordingly, humans are created not "after their kind" but "in the image and likeness of God" (1:26). The human male and female are made for each other (Hoekema 1986).

The point is reiterated in Genesis 2. When the creation is finished but for woman, God says: "It is not good for the man (*hāʾādām*, הָאָדָם) to be alone; I will make him a helper suitable for him (*ʿēzer kĕnegdô*, עֵזֶר כְּנֶגְדּוֹ)" (2:18). That there was no helper (i.e., counterpart) for the man is made clear by the following verses, where we are told that God fashioned the animals and birds and brought them to the man for naming, which he did, but no counterpart was found for him (2:20). Thereupon, God created woman, not from the earth as he did the beasts, thus to emphasize the division between the species, but from the man himself. So God constructed the woman from the man's rib and brought her to him. This caused the first man to proclaim: "This is now bone of my bones, and flesh of my flesh; she shall be called woman (*ʾiššâ*, אִשָּׁה), because she was taken out of man (*ʾîš*, אִישׁ). For this cause a man shall leave his father and his mother, and shall cleave to his wife; and they shall become one flesh" (2:23–24). The union between a man and a woman thus recreates the natural order of creation. Man was an entity before woman was created, but incomplete, not good, incapable of reproducing like the animals around him, hence threatened with extinction. Together, the man and woman comprise a completed unit, and they can perpetuate the human species. They are able to fulfill the command to "be fruitful and multiply and fill the earth" (1:28; 9:7).

It should now be clear why incest, homosexuality, and bestiality are placed together in Leviticus 18. The rationale for proscribing all three is found not only in the pollution rules, but also in their disregard of the purpose of creation. Unnatural acts, that is, cross-species and same-gender sexual relations, ultimately deny the creative work of God and offend the design of the human species, which is patterned after the image of God. Furthermore, these acts cannot fulfill the obligation to be fruitful and multiply. For the same reason sexual intercourse with a woman during her menses is forbidden: she cannot conceive during that time. Similarly, Molech worship, the giving of "seed" (or children, if child sacrifice is represented by this practice) is forbidden because the command to be fruitful and multiply is flouted: the progeny, a life given by God, has been destroyed.

Adultery too is forbidden because it violates the principle of union between a man and a woman in marriage. Furthermore, sleeping around for the married individual implies a mixing of "seed," which is forbidden under the term *tebel*. For this reason, one who is divorced and has another wife cannot leave the second wife and return to the first. This situation is proscribed by biblical law because it defiles the land and thereby qualifies as an abomination (*tôʿēbâ*, Deut. 24:1–4). Like the other sexual sins in the chapter, adultery is out of order.

Finally, the case of sex with a menstruant may seem more difficult to explain as a an offense against the divine order. No rationale is certain other than the simple explanation that blood and semen were not to be mixed (once again a case of *tebel*). Many cultures place a taboo on sex during the menstrual cycle, fundamentally because of purity-impurity rules. Because blood was somehow equated with life, it may be that sex was forbidden during this time because "life" was flowing from the woman's body; hence, an association with the impurity caused by death may have been made. It is also possible that the law protects the privacy of the woman during her menses because she experiences pain and the sex act would not be enjoyable to her. Scripture gives no rationale for this law apart from the issue of impurity and the danger that is generated by the act.

In the creation story, it is humanity as "male and female" together that reflects God's greatest work. Sex in the Bible is not intrinsically sinful. According to the rabbis, "were it not for the evil inclination (*yēṣer*), no man would build a home and marry" (*Genesis Rabbah* 9.7). Procreation is an important part of the male-female relationship, but it is not the entire essence of it, for Eve is Adam's "counterpart" in much more than only the sexual sense. The term *ʿēzer* (עֵזֶר) implies a certain psychological and emotional wholeness for the male of the species when he is with his female companion, just as humans are whole in a spiritual sense when the image of God is realized in them. Without her partnership, something essential is missing from the life of man in the natural order of things.

In the next section, we will look closely at the concept of impurity in the Bible from the perspective of specialists. With the exception of the dead and certain animals categorically forbidden as food (see Lev. 11), the condition of impurity was temporary, lasting for a specified period of time, and could be removed either by ritual washing or sacrificial means. Certainly, the laws of impurity were postulated on the principle of contagion. This principle does not function mechanically or magically but is governed by its ethical component. Since homosexuality was a source of impurity, let us now examine the impact it had on Israel's sanctuary.

Impurity and Israel's Sanctuary

Too often the idea of impurity is restricted to purely cultic or ritual contexts, while its moral components are ignored. In the Bible, sin generates impurity, which in turn pollutes God's sanctuary, even sometimes desecrating his holy name. Sin, defined as missing God's standard of moral behavior or (in the legal sense) violating God's stipulations, had an effect both on the individual and on Israelite society. Not only was the sanctuary Israel's center of worship but it was also the political center of Israel's camp. As the center of worship, it was the holy place where Yahweh's presence was manifest. As the center of the theocracy, it provided an organizational structure for the Israelites during their wilderness wandering. The levitical laws portray a time in Israel's history when the institutions of statehood did not exist. Pollution rules created a means by which Israelite society could be made seamless in its confrontation with pagan cults and contemporary taboos. It was a fundamental principle of the levitical law that whenever a violation occurred the sanctuary was contaminated. The dynamic force of impurity set off a chain of events that posed a threat to the continuing existence of ancient Israel's society, for with the pollution of the sanctuary God himself might forsake his dwelling and abandon the Israelites to their doom.

Who was responsible for setting off this chain reaction? Some scholars ascribe the contagion of impurity to magical or demonic influences:

> Becoming impure as the result of an offense against the deity introduced a kind of demonic contagion into the community. The more horrendous the offense, the greater the threat to the purity of the sanctuary and the surrounding community by the presence of the offender, who was a carrier of impurity. This person required purification if the community was to be restored to its ritual state, which, in turn, was a precondition set

down by the resident deity for his continued presence among the people. (Levine 1974: 75)

Baruch Levine furthermore states (p. 90) that the purification or expiation rituals in the Bible "contained a magical component, related primarily to the particular utilization of sacrificial blood." This view portrays the contagion of impurity not as a force released by the conduct of humans, but as a force that exists quite apart from them.

Other biblical scholars reject the magical and demonic influences in the religion of Israel (Kaufmann 1972: 70). Jacob Milgrom has produced some of the most insightful work in this regard. He emphasizes the ethical dimension in the relation of impurity to holiness, maintaining that the severity of the impurity resulting from sin "varies in direct relation to the depth of its penetration into the sanctuary" (1990: 446). Impurity derives not from demons or from nonhuman forces but from humans alone. This view presumes an active role for individual responsibility and the freedom of choice in the face of God's commandments. The degree of impurity generated by certain types of conduct was made coincident with the mental attitude of the offender. When an individual sinned inadvertently, only the outer altar of the tabernacle was defiled. When the community sinned unintentionally, the inner altar was defiled. But deliberate sins contaminated the holy of holies, the most sacred spot on earth for the ancient Israelites. The effect of sin on the sanctuary is illustrated by Milgrom (1990: 496):

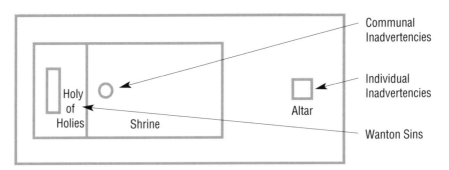

Milgrom remarks that "this diagram provides graphic illustration of the priestly notion of impurity as a dynamic force, magnetic and malefic to the sphere of the sacred, attacking it not just by direct contact but from a distance. The outer altar is polluted, although the nonpriest may not even enter it; and, finally, the adytum [i.e., holy of holies] is polluted, although no man, not even the priest, may enter. Yet despite the fact that Israelites have had no access, the sancta must be purged 'of the impurities of the Israelites' (Lev. 16:16)" (p. 446). This model protected Israel as a people from the misconduct of every individual, whether Israelite or resident alien. Violations of God's covenantal law were dangerous to the entire society. Individuals who committed crimes were punished individually (as in the case of murder), unless the pollution rules were infringed upon; then the offender's family or community could be punished collectively (as in the case of a Molech worshiper; Lev. 20:1–5). Their polluting effect on the sanctuary could be removed only through the sacrificial provision. Thus, for example, to cleanse the sanctuary on the Day of Atonement, two special goats were required. One was sacrificed and the blood was applied to the sacred outer altar and to the ark of the covenant in the holy of holies. The second goat, the familiar "scapegoat," symbolically carried Israel's transgressions into the wilderness. In this ritual of the goats, the material-moral effects of impurity are combined. (See chap. 10 for further examination of the Day of Atonement ritual and its significance for ancient Israel, including the person who deliberately committed homosexual acts.)

We know that homosexual conduct was considered a deliberate act since it warranted the *kareth* penalty. The homosexual placed his entire family and community in the path of divine wrath, threatening the extinction of all, because his deliberate act polluted the sanctuary, indeed the very holy of holies, the place where God's presence was deemed to be especially evident. Beyond the sanctuary, homosexuality polluted the land, for Leviticus 18 clearly states that no difference could be traced between the result of Israelite homosexual acts and those committed by the Canaanites who inhabited Palestine before the Israelites. It cost the Canaanites their heritage in real estate, and it would cost the Israelites similarly despite their covenantal selection as the heirs of Canaanite soil: "Do not defile yourselves by any of these things; for by all these the nations which I am casting out before you have become defiled. For the land has become defiled, therefore I have visited its punishment upon it, so the land has spewed out its inhabitants" (Lev. 18:24–25). The verb *ṭāmēʾ* occurs six times at the end of Leviticus 18. Like a sponge, the land could absorb only so much impurity before becoming oversaturated. In that state, the land required cleansing by removal of the source of impurity through expulsion of its inhabitants. According to Helmer Ringgren (*TDOT* 5:332), "sin and uncleanness is often treated as identical in the Old Testament because they both damage the whole community. They can be regarded as expressions of the hostile reality that permeates life, attempting again and again to penetrate the sphere of what is divine and good. There is, so to speak, a sphere of evil and death that continually threatens man's life: it is called uncleanness, sin, chaos."

Conclusion

The laws of Leviticus 18 are motivated by the generation of impurity that affects explicitly the individual, the land, and the sanctuary of the Lord. This impurity places the individual, the community, and the nation in jeopardy. The rationale for the laws is found in the creation account from the hand of the priestly writer. The motivation for avoiding homosexual practices in Israel is not idolatry or the association of homosexual practices with temple prostitution or cultic worship. Rather, homosexuality, as well as all the sexual acts listed in Leviticus 18, is an affront to the order of society based on impurity rules; and ultimately it violates the order of creation. Same-gender sexual relations are forbidden because they desecrate the image of God in human beings and they cannot fulfill the positive command to be fruitful and multiply. Sexual misconduct places the entire community in tension. How then can this tension be avoided? Two solutions are offered in the law: a negative solution in the form of sanctions and a positive solution available through the sacrificial system. Let us consider the sanctions first.

9

Sanctions for Homosexuality

For whoever does any of these abominations, those persons who do so shall be cut off from among their people. Thus you are to keep my charge, that you do not practice any of the abominable customs which have been practiced before you, so as not to defile yourselves with them; I am the LORD your God.

—Leviticus 18:29–30

I n the last chapter we saw that the biblical writer's view of impurity provided a rationale for the sexual stipulations of Leviticus 18. Impurity was viewed as having an ethical and moral component as well as a ritual role. Homosexual conduct was a threat to Israel's well-being because it violated social and religious order. Sexual relations incapable of carrying out the design of the divine image in humanity or the purpose of procreation were a source of impurity, incompatible with holiness. Jews and Christians have endorsed a variety of penalties for homosexuality, including live burial, burning, castration, death, excommunication, exile, monetary fines, flogging, mutilation, penance, and stoning (Bailey 1975: 179). In the Old Testament, those who engaged in homosexual activities were subject to either the death penalty or the *kareth* penalty. An investigation of these two penalties for homosexual acts reveals in greater detail the rationale for prohibiting same-gender sexual contact. The severity of the penalty matches the seriousness of the crime in biblical law.

As we address the penalties for homosexuality in detail, let us not forget that biblical law, despite its close relationship to aspects of ancient Near Eastern law, was a self-contained unit with its own set of presuppositions. We have seen some of the similarities and differences in our study of the law earlier in this book. Now it is necessary to emphasize the uniqueness of Israel's legal code against its contemporary environment. Only then will these penalties become clear.

Mesopotamian and Biblical Law

Homosexual conduct was not sanctioned as strictly in non-Israelite societies as in Hebrew society because of the latter's theological underpinnings. According to Moshe Greenberg (*IDB* 1:737), the law collections of the ancient Near East are "the product of a secular jurisprudence which recognized the state and the king as the promulgators and ultimate sanction of law. . . . Sexual crimes, not having the nature of sins against God, are less severely punished." This secular orientation, focusing on government and the relation of the individual to society, overshadowed the development of religion, the relationship of the individual and society to the universe. This situation is described by Ephraim Speiser (1967: 320–21, 562):

> Mesopotamian law, as we know it from many sources that span [a] score of centuries, was strictly secular. It concerns itself with private and public property, trade and commerce, agriculture and land tenure, professions and wages, and the general administration of justice. It is not a religious pronouncement. . . . In the case of Mesopotamia, religion failed to keep pace with secular advances, in that the religious concepts did not promote spiritual security. Since no Mesopotamian god was truly omnipotent, the gods as a body were likewise unsure of themselves. They were arbitrary and capricious, not just. Hence in his relations with nature the Mesopotamian lacked the solace of genuine ethical standards. Religion and government were not in balance.

The peoples of the ancient Near East lived in a kind of existential relativism. A plethora of junior and senior gods demanded attention at the family shrine or the city temple. Throughout the Fertile Crescent, nature religions dominated the public conscience. These religions existed not in the modern sense as organized systems of thought but as popular beliefs focused in two directions. Earth and sky, with their dynamic seasonal and yearly changes, were immortalized and personified as gods and goddesses. At a given moment, the ancient Semite was subject to the forces of nature and to whatever deities were imagined to reside in them. Thus Baal, Rider on the Clouds, expressed himself in the power of the thunderstorm. Mot was the death of vegetation during the hot, dry summer. Among the many gods and goddesses, no absolute authority could claim obedience and worship. (See Jacobsen 1976 for an introduction to Mesopotamian religion; for the contrast with Israelite beliefs, see Kaufmann 1972.)

Unlike this Mesopotamian relativism, Israelite society was based on the principle of divine authority. Yahweh, as the only true God, was all powerful, the absolute and ultimate source and sanction of law, justice, ethics, and morality. This meant that crimes committed against society were seen as crimes against Yahweh as well. This view that humanity was made in the image of God is evident in the biblical perspective on homicide: "And surely I will require your lifeblood; from every beast I will require it. And from every man, from every man's brother I will require the life of man. Whoever sheds man's blood, by man his blood shall be shed, for in the image of God he made man" (Gen. 9:5–6). Life was held in such sanctity that the principle of "life for life" applied not only to persons who committed homicide but even to animals that killed a human being.

This principle is carefully applied in biblical law. A good example can be found in the law of the goring ox, which demonstrates both the exception and the rule (Exod. 21:28–32):

And if an ox gores a man or a woman to death, the ox shall surely be stoned and its flesh shall not be eaten; but the owner of the ox shall go unpunished. If, however, an ox was previously in the habit of goring, and its owner has been warned, yet he does not confine it, and it kills a man or a woman, the ox shall be stoned and its owner also shall be put to death. If a ransom is demanded of him, then he shall give for the redemption of his life whatever is demanded of him. Whether it gores a son or a daughter, it shall be done to him according to the same rule. If the ox gores a male or female slave, the owner shall give his or her master thirty shekels of silver, and the ox shall be stoned.

In this law of homicide, we have the only example in the Bible where a monetary fine is substituted for a life. According to Moshe Greenberg (1991: 339), "a ransom may be accepted only for a homicide not committed personally and with intent to harm. For murder, however, there is only the death penalty." The killer ox must be put to death; it has committed murder. The law presumes that the flesh of the ox is unfit for consumption, ostensibly because it is impure by contact with death.

The principle of intention underlies all biblical law. If the ox acts on its own, it is subject to death. The owner bears responsibility only when he has been made aware of the evil nature of his animal. Then, if he fails to confine it and the ox gores someone, his negligence places the death sentence on him—a human life has been sacrificed. Out of mercy, he may be only fined since he did not actually commit the crime himself. Since there is no way to measure the owner's intention, no way to tell whether he trained his ox to be a killer, he is free to go. Nevertheless, the ox must die. There is, however, no hint that the compensation paid is in any way equal to the life of the slain. The law simply reiterates the principle established in Genesis 9: the murderer—whether human or animal—who takes the life of a human, must give "life for life."

Only a life compensates for a life, but this principle applies in a special way to human life, as we see from the penalty enjoined when an ox kills another ox: "And if one man's ox hurts another's so that it dies, then they shall sell the live ox and divide its price equally; and also they shall divide the dead ox. Or if it is known that the ox was previously in the habit of goring, yet its owner has not confined it, he shall surely pay ox for ox, and the dead animal shall become his" (Exod. 21:35–36). Presumably, the dead ox in either of these incidents may be used for food; there is no impurity involved. In both cases, there is no life-for-life principle for the ox, because animals are not made in God's image. They have an important place in creation and should not be abused by their supervisors, but their value is limited to draft labor and to food.

How do the laws of the ancient Near East compare to this biblical law? A similar situation is portrayed in the laws of Eshnunna (§§53–55; *ANET* 163):

> If an ox gores an(other) ox and causes (its) death, both ox owners shall divide (among themselves) the price of the live ox and also the meat of the dead ox. If an ox is known to gore habitually and the authorities have brought the fact to the knowledge of its owner, but he does not have his ox dehorned, it gores a man and causes (his) death, then the owner of the ox shall pay two-thirds of a mina of silver. If it gores a slave and causes (his) death, he shall pay 15 shekels of silver.

This law is plainly the exact counterpart of Exodus 21:35. In Eshnunna, the ox is not guilty of homicide; it is not killed to compensate for the loss of human life; there is no capital punishment for negligent homicide in Mesopotamia; the owner is liable only for a fine payable to the family of the victim, according to the latter's class status. The homicidal animal is executed even for the death of a slave in the Bible, whereas no harm befalls the animal for killing a slave according to Mesopotamian law. There is no theological motivation in the Mesopotamian law; it is strictly economic. Life may be compensated monetarily because it is not considered sacred, modeled on the divine image.

Other ancient Near Eastern laws reflect this principle. Three centuries after the laws of Eshnunna, the law of Hammurapi restates the case of the goring ox (§§250–52; *ANET* 176):

> If an ox, when it was walking along the street, gored a seignior to death, that case is not subject to claim. If a seignior's ox was a gorer and his city council made it known to him that it was a gorer, but he did not pad its horns (or) tie up his ox, and that ox gored to death a member of the aristocracy, he shall give one-half mina of silver. If it was a seignior's slave, he shall give one-third mina of silver.

No life is required for the life of the victim in Babylon; monetary compensation is satisfaction. Noting the differences between the Hebrew and Mesopotamian laws and based on the requirement that the ox be treated as a criminal in the biblical law, Godfrey Driver and John Miles (1952–55: 1.444) suggest that "the Hebrew point of view, therefore, is much more primitive than the Babylonian; and it is submitted that the Hebrew lawgiver cannot have borrowed anything from paragraphs 250–2 of the Babylonian Laws." But it seems otherwise to me. The Hebrew law is not more primitive. It is founded on a different principle: the life of a human being is inviolable because humanity is made in the image of God.

How is this principle applied to homosexuality? Homosexuality cannot be understood unless it is placed in the context of the writer's view of the sanctity of life, and the underlying principle is that humanity is created in the image of God. When the law requires the death penalty or the *kareth* penalty for homosexual conduct, it is meant to serve not only as a punishment but as a sanction. By "sanction," I mean a specified penalty or moral pressure that acts to insure compliance or conformity. Two sanctions for homosexuality are imposed because of the severe degree of impurity generated by the homosexual act. Both penalties have a history of interpretation, some of it controversial. Let us examine the death penalty first.

The Death Penalty

According to Leviticus 20:13, both partners in the homosexual act are sentenced to death. The language in this verse parallels that of Leviticus 18:22, including references to zākār (זָכָר), miškěbê ʾiššâ (מִשְׁכְּבֵי אִשָּׁה), and tôʿēbâ (תּוֹעֵבָה). As noted above, the casuistic style of the verse contrasts to the apodictic style of Leviticus 18:22. The introduction of capital punishment is the new feature of Leviticus 20:13, expressed by the verb môt yûmātû (מוֹת יוּמָתוּ, "they shall certainly be put to death"). The added expression *their bloodguiltiness is upon them* is the customary way of invoking the death penalty. Based on the principle of intention in biblical law, in this case both partners have acted deliberately against the law and defiled themselves, the sanctuary, and the land.

We are not explicitly told by whom the death penalty is imposed. There are basically two possibilities: death by humans or death by God (Milgrom 1970). According to the rabbis, when the imperfect form of the verb *mwt* (i.e., יָמוּת, yāmût) is used in the qal conjugation, "shall be put to death" means at the hands of God (Mishnah, tractate *Sanhedrin* 9.6). Correctly maintaining that the verb in the hophal conjugation (יוּמָת, yûmāt) always means death by humans, Jacob Milgrom (1970: 6) lists eight categories that come under the penalty of death by humans in the so-called priestly source:

1. Sabbath violation (Exod. 31:14–15; 35:2; Num. 15:35)
2. illicit sex (Lev. 19:20; 20:10–13, 15–16)
3. Molech worship (Lev. 20:2)
4. blasphemy (Lev. 24:16)
5. abuse of parents (Lev. 20:9)
6. the proscribed person (Lev. 27:29)
7. playing the medium (Lev. 20:27)
8. ascending Mount Sinai (Exod. 19:12)

Of special interest to us, of course, is the appearance of Leviticus 20:13 in this list and the absence of Leviticus 18:22.

Death for homosexual acts probably was by stoning, as in the case of the Molech worshiper, the Sabbath breaker, the blasphemer, or the medium. In the instance of contact with the holy mountain, death is by stoning or piercing, in either case so that "no hand shall touch him" (Exod. 19:13). That is why the Sabbath breaker is executed "outside the camp" (Num. 15:35). We may expect that the other executions listed here were carried out in a similar manner. Death itself is a source of severe contamination or impurity, designated by the rabbis as a "father of uncleanness" (Mishnah, tractate *ʾOholot* 1.1). Stoning was a means of execution whereby the offender would not have to be touched by the crowd of executioners and the impurity consequent upon contact with a corpse would not befall the community. Even so, it is possible that ritual purification would have to be performed before the executioners reentered the camp of Israel because direct contact is not necessary in order to become defiled. Failure to perform the prescribed rituals for corpse contamination placed the individual in jeopardy; he was open to the *kareth* penalty explicitly because his impurity was still on him, and he had defiled the sanctuary of the Lord (Num. 19:13, 20). Contamination of the sanctuary also threatened the community. Thus the death penalty of Leviticus 20:13 agrees with the *kareth* penalty of Leviticus 18:29 as regards motivation: the homosexual act poses a grave threat to Israelite society, a threat to the individual, his progeny, the land, the sanctuary, and God's continued presence and consequent blessing—because it is a source of impurity.

No cases of execution for homosexuality are recorded in the Bible, so we have no evidence that the death penalty was actually carried out. Some scholars maintain that the Mesopotamian laws represented by the code of Hammurapi and earlier collections were not enforced. For example, Leo Oppenheim (1977: 158) says that the code of Hammurapi "does not show any direct relationship to the legal practices of the time. Its contents are rather to be considered in many essential respects a traditional literary expression of the king's social responsibilities and of his awareness of the discrepancies between existing and desirable conditions." While this comment may accurately represent the situation in Mesopotamia, it is doubtful that it fairly describes biblical law. I suggest instead that Israel's law, integrated with its faith, was a means of structuring and maintaining sociological and theological order in Hebrew society. It had a practical, not merely a literary or forensic function. We do have reports that executions took place for other violations (e.g., Sabbath breaking in Exod. 31:12–17 and Num. 15:32–36). It is plausible that the homosexual, if apprehended, would have been summarily executed by the community in the manner described in detail for the Molech worshiper (Lev. 20:2–5):

> Any man from the sons of Israel or from the aliens sojourning in Israel, who gives any of his offspring to Molech, shall surely be put to death (*yûmāt*, יוּמָת); the people of the land shall stone him with stones. I will also set my face against that man and will cut him off from among his people, because he has given some of his offspring to Molech, so as to defile

my sanctuary and to profane my holy name. If the people of the land, however, should ever disregard that man when he gives any of his offspring to Molech, so as not to put him to death, then I myself will set my face against that man and against his family; and I will cut off from among their people both him and all those who play the harlot after him, by playing the harlot after Molech.

Of course, two other options were open to the community should they elect not to put the homosexual to death; they could close their eyes to the practice of homosexuality and by doing nothing either (1) wait for God to take action by imposing the *kareth* penalty or (2) wait for the Day of Atonement to arrive so that the necessary rituals might be carried out to neutralize the effects of the impurity generated by the illicit sex, in the meantime exposing themselves to God's wrath. Given these options, it is certainly plausible that the death penalty was carried out in ancient Israel for homosexual conduct.

The Kareth Penalty

Let us suppose that the homosexual act was committed in secret and that the community could not execute the violators because it was unaware of the crime. A law of consenting adults did not exist in ancient Israel. Such a law presumes that two individuals can act to carry out their private sexual desires without having an impact on society. According to biblical law, however, homosexual conduct—whether performed in secret or in public—was a source of impurity. If the community would not act in the case of the Molech worshiper, then God might impose the *kareth* penalty. Similarly, if the community could not act, either out of ignorance that a homosexual act had been committed or if insufficient witnesses were available to sustain the evidence, the administration of justice fell into divine hands. God could execute the *kareth* penalty or he could allow the sinners to be reconciled to both the community and himself. Reconciliation is the subject of the next chapter. Here we consider the nature of the *kareth* penalty and its effectiveness as a sanction against homosexuality.

The meaning of the *kareth* penalty has been debated for centuries. The major opinions on *kareth* may be clustered into two groups, those that follow rabbinic tradition and those advocated by modern, essentially non-Jewish, scholarship. Most rabbinic sources agree that being "cut off" was a divine punishment, but there is little agreement upon the exact form of the penalty:

1. He shall die childless and prematurely (Rashi in Babylonian Talmud, tractate *Šabbat* 25a).
2. He shall die before he reaches the age of sixty or with a sudden death (Babylonian Talmud, tractate *Moʿed Qaṭan* 28a).
3. He shall die in his youth, and his soul shall not share in the resurrection (Ramban in Babylonian Talmud, tractate *Šebuʿot* 13a).
4. At his death his soul too shall die, and he will not enjoy the spiritual life of the hereafter (Maimonides, *Yad, Hilchot T'shubâ* 8.1; Sifra, tractate *Emoraim* 14.4).
5. His name shall be completely cut off and disappear through the extinction of his descendants (Ibn Ezra in Tosepta, tractate *Sanhedrin* 20–21).

Against the rabbinic view of *kareth* as a divine penalty, a number of modern scholars define *kareth* as a strictly human punishment: either excommunication or death. Gerhard von Rad explains (1962: 264 n. 182) that "in cases where Jahweh had not reserved to himself a special settlement for good or for ill, order was restored by either execution or the excommunication of the offender." In the Holiness Code and in the priestly writings,

> we still find ancient ban formulae which quite certainly were formerly practiced in cultic life in a very concrete form. "Cutting off (כרת) from the midst of the people of Israel" is particularly frequently mentioned. . . . The fate of a sacrally expelled person was terrible (Gen. 4:13f.), for as the bearer of a curse it was impossible for him to find shelter in another community; he was refused admission to all other groups, and, because at that time no one could dispense with relationships to supernatural powers, he was forced into the arms of the unlawful cults of magic.

Another group of scholars either ignores the *kareth* penalty or attempts to side with both views, as does Julian Morgenstern (1931–32: 47): "The legislators have in mind not so much the regular implication of the punishment of 'cutting off,' viz. eventual, but nevertheless premature death at the hands of Yahwe, but rather what is . . . the secondary implication or corollary of the punishment of 'cutting off,' viz. the much more immediate and practical punishment of excommunication."

The Septuagint data is categorically against the idea of *kareth* as excommunication or as death at the hand of humans: it was a divine penalty of annihilation. The Qumran evidence also overwhelmingly supports the view that *kareth* was a divine curse of extinction. In addition, the Qumran sectarians projected *kareth* onto an eschatological event in which the wicked will be utterly destroyed without remnant and consumed by fire, while the victorious sons of light will have an everlasting inheritance and an eternal hope, anticipating in this respect the later views of the rabbis (Wold 1978: 253).

According to the Mishnah (*Keritot* 1.1), the language of *kareth* in the Hebrew Bible is applied to some thirty-six crimes, including sexual crimes, sacrilege, idolatry, blasphemy, and dietary violations. To reflect the association of homosexuality with the crimes for which *kareth* was imposed, they may be outlined as follows:

1. violations against sacred time
   a. failure to observe Passover at its proper time (Num. 9:13)
   b. eating leaven on Passover and the Feast of Unleavened Bread (Exod. 12:15, 19)
   c. working on the Sabbath (Exod. 31:14)
   d. working or eating on the Day of Atonement (Lev. 23:29–30)
2. violations against sacred substance
   a. eating blood (Lev. 7:27; 17:10, 14)
   b. eating sacrificial fat (Lev. 7:25)
   c. compounding and/or misusing the oil of installation (Exod. 30:33)
   d. eating the well-being sacrifices on the third day (Lev. 7:18; 19:8)
   e. eating the sacred offerings while ritually impure by either a layperson (Lev. 7:20–21) or priest (Lev. 22:3, 9)
   f. duplicating and/or misusing the sanctuary incense (Exod. 30:38)
   g. unauthorized contact with sacred property (Num. 4:19–20)
3. failure to perform required rituals
   a. neglect of circumcision (Gen. 17:14)
   b. failure to be cleansed from corpse contamination (Num. 19:13, 20)
4. illicit worship
   a. slaughtering outside the sacred precinct (Lev. 17:4)
   b. sacrificing outside the sacred precinct (Lev. 17:9)
   c. worshiping Molech (Lev. 20:1–5)
   d. consulting the dead (Lev. 20:6)
   e. idolatry (Ezek. 14:8)
5. illicit sexual relations (Lev. 18:29)
6. blasphemy (Num. 15:30–31)

In previous research, I analyzed the *kareth* penalty linguistically with respect to the semantic field of synonymous and antithetical terms in the Bible and the ancient Near East and identified a curse formula with parallels in Akkadian, West Semitic, and Hittite sources (Wold 1978). The collective linguistic data suggests that *kareth* was a conditional divine curse of extinction, obliterating the sinner (and progeny) from any role in the drama of Israel's history. The individual may die prematurely, remain childless, be destroyed collectively with his family, etc. The means, however, are not explicit in the Bible.

The effect of *kareth* upon the Israelite mind must have been far-reaching, for it touched on matters of proper burial and on the hope for felicity in the afterlife (material support for a belief in afterlife in ancient Israel comes from burial customs; Meyers 1971). Several medieval rabbinic scholars, especially Maimonides (*Mishneh Torah*, tractate *Hilchot Sanhedrin* 15.10–11) and Nahmanides (1974: 278), associated *kareth* with belief in afterlife, which is also supported by Egyptian (*sbj n k3.f*: "to go to one's Ka") and Akkadian (*ana* GIDIM *kimtisu isniq*: "he shall be gathered to his family [ghosts]") sources. Several biblical expressions antithetical to *kareth* parallel these ancient Near Eastern phrases: *wayyēʾāsep ʾel-ʿāmmāw* (וַיֵּאָסֶף אֶל־עַמָּיו, "and he was gathered to his people"; Gen. 25:8) and *tābôʾ ʾel-ʾăbotêkā* (תָּבוֹא אֶל אֲבוֹתֶיךָ, "you shall go to your fathers"; Gen. 15:15).

Conclusion

The biblical *kareth* penalty is at home in the kin-cult-land-afterlife complex postulated by Herbert Brichto in 1973. In short, *kareth* is a conditional divine curse of extinction. It may occur simultaneously with or subsequent to death, whether the latter is prematurely wrought by God or humans. It is imposed for deliberate violations against the priestly pollution concept and for trespasses against the fixed boundary between the sacred and the profane. As such, it is removed from the realm of human jurisdiction since offenses against God are, in the priestly writer's estimation, punishable only by God. The sinner served with the *kareth* sentence may be acquitted by God, pending repentance and proper observance of the Day of Atonement. The deliberate act is viewed by the priestly writer as defiling to the sanctuary and is an offense against the divine presence. For this defilement, the deliberate sinner may be cut off at any time by God's wrath, but the Day of Atonement is testimony to a profound principle of priestly theology, namely, that the sword of God's wrath is always wrapped in the mantle of his mercy—even the vilest offender may be forgiven. Thus the only sin that cannot be forgiven is the unrepented sin (Wold 1978: 254).

According to the sanctions imposed for homosexual conduct in the Bible, any homosexual act might involve death at the hand of humans or the *kareth* penalty or both. Thus the desire to commit a homosexual act in ancient Israel had to be weighed against the serious consequences of both corporal and eternal punishment. If homosexual relationships were practiced in ancient Israel, they would have been in direct conflict with the kin-cult-land-afterlife beliefs that held that society together. The severity of the *kareth* penalty must have served as a strong motivation to observe God's rules for moral conduct, precluding the likelihood of wholesale homosexual practice in Israel.

My analysis of the penalties for homosexuality has been limited to the biblical language. It is worth pointing out that in the modern discussions on homosexuality in the Bible, only the death penalty is mentioned. The *kareth* penalty is completely ignored, an omission that comes at great expense to the full biblical view of homosexuality. In order to fully understand the means by which the high-handed sinner is reconciled to God, homosexuality must be understood as a deliberate crime against the holiness of God, for which the most severe penalty is invoked. A day of grace was afforded even the deliberate sinner, a provision to which the homosexual offender might appeal for reconciliation and through which the impurity generated by his act might be removed from Israel's sanctuary and the land.

10

Reconciling the Homosexual

And this shall be a permanent statute for you: in the seventh month, on the tenth day of the month, you shall humble your souls, and not do any work, whether the native, or the alien who sojourns among you; for it is on this day that atonement shall be made for you to cleanse you; you shall be clean from all your sins before the LORD. It is to be a sabbath of solemn rest for you, that you may humble your souls; it is a permanent statute. So the priest who is anointed and ordained to serve as priest in his father's place shall make atonement: he shall thus put on the linen garments, the holy garments, and make atonement for the holy sanctuary; and he shall make atonement for the tent of meeting and for the altar. He shall also make atonement for the priests and for all the people of the assembly. Now you shall have this as a permanent statue, to make atonement for the sons of Israel for all their sins once every year.

—Leviticus 16:29–34

The Day of Atonement served as the only means of reconciling one who had committed homosexual acts under Israelite authority. The regulations for this day applied equally to native Israelites and to resident aliens. All manner of work was to cease and a fast was to be observed. Failure to comply placed the recalcitrant offender under the penalty of *kareth* (Lev. 23:29). The rationale for the Day of Atonement is concise: individual and corporate sin, whether unintentional or deliberate, contaminated Israel's sanctuary in varying degrees. Homosexual acts belonged to the category of deliberate sins and contaminated the most holy area of the sanctuary. It was only on the Day of Atonement, once each year, that the entire sanctuary was cleansed by the ritual of the sin or purgation offering (*ḥaṭṭāʾt*, חַטָּאת). This cleansing was necessary inasmuch as the sanctuary was the place where God had chosen to quintessentially manifest his presence. Impurity generated by moral lapses or high-handed violations of God's laws threatened ancient Israel with the removal of his presence. Holiness and impurity are antithetical in biblical law.

Sanctuary pollution occurred in various ways through physical impurity (Lev. 12–15), unintentional sins against God (Lev. 4), and intentional violations (Num. 15:30–31). Deliberate sins were not covered by the individual's purification offering. The expiatory sacrifices covered only offenses against God; crimes against humans were adjudicated by the human court and executed by humans. The purification of the sanctuary on the Day of Atonement had no effect on the status of the homosexual before God without that person's corresponding confession and repentance. The arrogant, unrepentant offender remained subject to the divine penalty of being cut off.

The priestly ideal was that Israel would honor the covenant relationship with Yahweh and emulate his holiness. In reality, it was understood that failures—even blatant violations of God's laws—to meet this high standard would occur and that, consequently, provisions must be made for removing the impure effects of sin and for reconciling the alienated sinner to God and to the community. The sacrificial system, in particular the purification offering or *ḥaṭṭāʾt*, served this end, based on the general principle that blood was the seat of life: "For the life of the flesh is in the blood, and I have given it to you on the altar to make atonement for your souls; for it is the blood by reason of the life that makes atonement" (Lev. 17:11). To see how this principle could be a source of hope for one who had fallen into the sin of homosexuality, we will discuss four topics: (1) intention and atonement, (2) purification and atonement, (3) expiation and atonement, and (4) forgiveness.

The priestly theology of atonement is dominated by the verb *kipper* (כִּפֶּר). Cognates for *kipper* in Arabic and Akkadian suggest the respective meanings "to cover" or "to wipe." The basic idea may be represented by the motion of scrubbing a surface with a product like wax or detergent. Since our focus is on the deliberate sinner, it should be pointed out that the application of the blood was only to sacred objects, never to individuals. Only the sanctuary was cleansed by the blood of the slain goat on the Day of Atonement. On this day alone, a second live *ḥaṭṭāʾt* goat—the so-called scapegoat—was also part of the ritual. The sins of the people were symbolically transferred to this animal, which served as a substitute or ransom (Lev. 16:21–22). It is clear that this event takes away the sin of even the gravest offender, for Leviticus 16:34 reiterates that the Day of Atonement is for all the sins of the Israelites.

In this chapter we explore several important aspects of the Day of Atonement as they relate to pardon for deliberate sin. The principles established here serve as a foundation for understanding the cleansing that the apostle Paul addresses to the homosexual in 1 Corinthians 6:11. The ritual involving the two *ḥaṭṭāʾt* goats on the Day of Atonement accomplished three bold purposes: (1) the sanctuary was cleansed in order to ensure the continued presence of the Lord there; (2) the anger of God was appeased toward the sinner; and (3) the sinner could be relieved of guilt and reconciled to God. The sacrificial system was of no avail unless the offender acknowledged that individual sin was the cause of divine disfavor and sought to correct behavior inconsistent with God's performative and prohibitive commandments. Especially threatening to the economy of ancient Israel were deliberate acts against prohibitive commands like Leviticus 18:22, for these defiled not only the sanctuary but the land as well. As Jacob Milgrom writes (1991: 230): "The violation of prohibitive commandments generates impurity, which can be lethal to the community of Israel unless it is purified—by the *ḥaṭṭāʾt*, the purification offering."

Intention and Atonement

The principle of intention is fundamental to understanding the biblical view of homosexuality. This principle implies premeditation and, therefore, responsibility for one's actions. Since homosexual conduct falls into the category of deliberate sin, it will be better appreciated after studying the sacrificial system as it relates to consciousness of sin. Four categories of intention are identifiable in Scripture:

1. *Mere intention* is represented by the term *yēṣer* (יֵצֶר). This Hebrew word includes the idea of choice and may be translated as "purpose" or "intention." The idea is expressed directly in Genesis 6:5: "Then the LORD saw that the wickedness of man was great on the earth, and that every intent (*yēṣer*) of the thoughts of his heart was only evil continually." In modern English, the term *orientation* is close to the meaning of *yēṣer*; it may be good or evil.
2. *Unintention* is noted by the term (*bišgāgâ*, בִּשְׁגָגָה). Sinners in this category are aware of the requirements of the law but inadvertently fall short of fulfilling them. Upon experiencing the pangs of conscience regarding their error, they are required to bring a guilt offering and make restitution as necessary (Lev. 5:14–16).
3. *Ignorance* is expressed by *lōʾ yādaʿ* (לֹא יָדַע, lit. "he does not know"). In this case the offender is unaware of the requirement of the law and violates it. The error is deemed unintentional and is covered by the guilt offering (Lev. 5:17–19) and the purification offering (Num. 15:27–29). The community may also err unintentionally, and their sin is atoned for by the purification sacrifice (Num. 15:22–26).
4. *Defiance* is denoted by the noun *pešaʿ* (פֶּשַׁע, "transgression") and the expression *bĕyād rāmâ* (בְּיָד רָמָה, "with a high hand"). Deliberate offenders are guilty of blasphemy and subject to the outpouring of God's wrath through the penalty of being cut off. Their guilt remains on them; there is no sacrificial option for them.

Bernard Jackson (1971: 207) makes two noteworthy points about intention in biblical law: "First, there is no evidence that liability for mere intention was ever applied in a human court. Second, and equally significant, the idea did exist that merely to intend a wrong was itself wrong. It was a principle employed in God's justice, but not, at this period, in the jurisprudence of man. However, its potentialities in human jurisprudence were later realized." This point is illustrated in the teaching of Jesus with reference to adultery: "You have heard that it was said: 'Do not commit adultery.' But I tell you that anyone who looks at a woman lustfully has already committed adultery with her in his heart" (Matt. 5:27–28 NIV).

The principle of intention in biblical law contradicts the opinions of certain modern writers who classify homosexuality as a psychological, genetic, or hereditary condition. D. Sherwin Bailey (1975: xi), for example, makes a distinction between perversion and inversion. Perversion denotes an act for which a person has full responsibility, such as a heterosexual engaging in homosexual practices. Inversion, however, is an authentic homosexual condition for which a person cannot be held responsible. Bailey explains (p. x): "Strictly speaking, the Bible and Christian tradition know nothing of homosexuality; both are concerned solely with the commission of homosexual acts. . . . Homosexuality is not, as commonly supposed, a kind of *conduct*; it simply denotes in male or female a *condition* characterized by an emotional and physico-sexual propensity towards others of the same sex." Bailey argues further (p. xi) that "it must be made quite clear that the genuine invert is not necessarily given to homosexual practices, and may exercise as careful a control over his or her physical impulses as the heterosexual." Bailey must mean that the invert can remain celibate by choice, but he does not say this. He would establish the homosexual invert as a normal category of creation, since normal conditions are not morally reprehensible.

In the priestly model, normal conditions may be defiling, though not morally reprehensible. As such, they are dangerous and must be cared for in the appropriate manner. A case in point is bodily discharges, which are deemed unclean (Lev. 15). The lawgiver puts uncleanness in perspective: "You shall keep the sons of Israel separated from their uncleanness, lest they die in their uncleanness by their defiling my tabernacle that is among them" (v. 31).

The high-handed sin of homosexuality generates severe impurity requiring purification of the adytum, or most holy chamber, in the priestly tabernacle. Intentional sins are the most defiling.

Purification and Atonement

Scholars who see purification as the main purpose of the Day of Atonement rituals concentrate their attention on the need to cleanse the sanctuary from impurity. Jacob Milgrom has established himself as the chief exponent of this view. His systematic approach to the function of the *ḥaṭṭāʾt* (חַטָּאת), the purification offering, is predicated on his analysis of impurity as a graduated force that penetrates the sanctuary. To date, his view of this sacrifice has not been discussed in relation to homosexuality, an unfortunate circumstance given the importance of his work. A brief summary of Milgrom's thesis follows.

Milgrom (1983: 67) restricts the meaning of the *ḥaṭṭāʾt* to "purification offering" on contextual, morphological, and etymological grounds. Two kinds of *ḥaṭṭāʾt* are described. In one, the animal's blood is daubed on the outer, sacrificial altar, and its meat becomes the perquisite of the officiating priest (Lev. 4:30; 6:18). In the other, the animal's blood is daubed on the inner, incense altar and sprinkled before the veil, while the remains (except for the suet) are burned on the ash heap outside the camp (Lev. 4:6–8, 11–12). A differentiation between the two is made not on the basis of the manner in which they are disposed but rather on the degree of impurity that they cleanse. Let Milgrom speak for himself (1983: 73):

> The eaten *ḥaṭṭāʾt* purges the outer altar. The altar is the first of the *sancta* met upon entering the sanctuary and represents the minimal incursion of impurity caused by inadvertent sins of the individual. At this lowest level, the impurity is not transferrable to the *ḥaṭṭāʾt* and, hence, it is eaten by the priests for their services. The burnt *ḥaṭṭāʾt*, however, represents the higher degrees of impurity caused by inadvertences of the high priest and community, and at its worst, by presumptuous sins. This impurity is powerful enough to penetrate into the shrine and adytum [i.e., the holy of holies] and is dangerously contagious. In being purged by the *ḥaṭṭāʾt* blood it is likely to infect the carcass itself which therefore has to be burned. Indeed, it is striking that only in the case of the burnt *ḥaṭṭāʾt* does the text prescribe that the high priest must bathe *after* the ritual (Lev. 16:23–24). The reason, in my opinion, is obvious: in purging the *pešāʿîm*, the rebellious, presumptuous sins (v. 16), he may have become infected and must wash at once.

Not everyone agrees with Milgrom's position. Baruch Levine (1974: 108) identifies two types of *ḥaṭṭāʾt* as well: one was offered by the priests and served an apotropaic function, warding off evil and safeguarding the sanctuary and the priesthood from contamination (Lev. 4:1–21); the other was presented by the people and effected expiation for sin (4:22–35). According to Levine, the *ḥaṭṭāʾt* "actually represents the coalescence of two originally distinct rites; the one a rite of riddance and the other a gift of expiation." The "gift of expiation" is meant to appease the realm of the demonic, mentioned explicitly in the reference to the scapegoat on the Day of Atonement.

Of these two main views regarding the *ḥaṭṭāʾt*, Milgrom's is to be favored. The magical aspect of warding off evil cannot be found in the *ḥaṭṭāʾt* ceremony as Levine argues. Nor does the scapegoat appease the demonic realm. There is no demonic realm in the priestly writer's estimation.

Expiation and Atonement

The idea of expiation focuses on removal of sin from the sinner. As already mentioned, the sins of the people are symbolically transferred to the live goat. Its departure to the wilderness signifies the removal of iniquity from the people and the land where they dwell. In this matter, I follow the view of the rabbis in the Mishnah, tractate *Šebuʿot* 1.6:

> And for uncleanness that occurs in the temple and to its holy sacrifices through wantonness, [the] goat whose blood is sprinkled within [the holy of holies on the Day of Atonement] and the Day of Atonement effect atonement, and for [all] other transgressions [spoken of] in the law, light or grave, premeditated or inadvertent, aware or unaware, transgressions of positive commands or transgressions of negative commands, sins whose penalty is excision (*kareth*) or sins punishable by death imposed by the court, the scapegoat makes atonement.

An important axiom of the reconciliation process must be understood. Grant that deliberate sin contaminated the sanctuary in the strongest degree. Grant also that the sanctuary is cleansed by the blood of the slain *ḥaṭṭāʾt* and that the scapegoat carries off the sins of the people. How do deliberate sinners qualify for the removal of their sin since the benefits of the *ḥaṭṭāʾt* are prohibited to them (Num. 15:30–31)? What could one who performed homosexual acts do to be cleansed and forgiven?

The clue to this dilemma is given by Milgrom is his study of the guilt offering *ʾāšām* (אָשָׁם). The key is to be found in the case of the false oath that is intentional, yet atonement is effected through the sacrifice of a ram of expiation (Num. 5:8; Lev. 6:7). In order for the sacrifice to achieve its desired result, the deliberate sinner must make a confession; the involuntary sinner need only suffer remorse. In Milgrom's view, the articulation of deliberate sin commutes it to involuntary status. Then and only then can it be expiated by the sacrifice. Once again, let Milgrom speak for himself on the law at Numbers 15:30–31 (1983: 57):

> It should not be taken to mean, as many critics aver, that only involuntary wrongdoers are eligible for sacrificial atonement. . . . A more correct understanding of this priestly postulate would be that sacrificial atonement is barred to the *unrepentant* sinner . . . but not to the deliberate sinner who has mitigated his offense by his repentance. Confession (*htwdh*),

then, is a prerequisite for the ultimate expiation of deliberate sin; it means to "acknowledge" the sin by identifying it and accepting blame.

This view recapitulates that of Rabbi Simon ben Lakish who comments: "Great is repentance which converts intentional sins into unintentional ones" (Babylonian Talmud, tractate *Yoma*ᵓ 86b). Confession and repentance are thus critical factors in avoiding divine retribution for deliberate sin. One final step remains for the reconciliation of the homosexual to be complete, and that is the matter of divine forgiveness.

Forgiveness

Forgiveness may be defined as "the act of God by which he graciously takes away the obstacles or barriers which separate man from his presence, thus opening the way to reconciliation and fellowship" (Warren A. Quanbeck, *IDB* 2:314). Of the many terms used for forgiveness in the Hebrew Bible, the most important for our purpose are *sālaḥ* (סָלַח, "to forgive, pardon") and *kipper* (כִּפֶּר, "to cover, rub off, wipe away, atone"), since they occur in a standard formula used only in connection with the expiatory sacrifices *ḥaṭṭāᵓt* and *ᵓāšām* (Milgrom 1983): "The priest shall make atonement (*kipper*) for him/them, and he/they shall be forgiven (*sālaḥ*)." The formula occurs thirteen times (Lev. 4:20, 26, 31, 35; 5:10, 13, 16, 18; 19:22; Num. 15:25–26, 28).

The term *kipper* is used in the priestly literature exclusively for the activity of the priest in performing the sacrificial rituals. The emphasis is on what he does with respect to the application of the blood to the sanctuary and in the disposal of the sacrificial animal. Since the need for forgiveness implies wrongdoing, it is evident that the *ḥaṭṭāᵓt* does more than purify the sanctuary. When God's conditions are met, the benefits of atonement accrue to the guilty individual or the errant congregation in the form of forgiveness, expressed by *sālaḥ* in the hiphal passive. In the economy of ancient Israel, forgiveness could not be granted without the prior shedding of the blood of a pure sacrificial animal.

The passive tense of *sālaḥ* shows that forgiveness is not the work of the individual but is the sole prerogative of God. Sinners who defiled themselves and the sanctuary were not forgiven automatically through the blood sacrifice but were dependent on the grace of God. This point is made by Noam Zohar (1988: 617–18) with reference to Leviticus 17:11: "Finally, the stress on God as the chief actor ('I have assigned it to you') and on the atonement being attained 'before God' reflects the central sensibility, that atonement (and purification of the sanctuary) is achieved not by a manipulative blood-ritual, but by God's forgiving response to the disowned impurity brought before him."

The homosexual, like every other deliberate sinner who deserved the death penalty and/or *kareth*, could find no relief for guilt apart from the blood of the *ḥaṭṭāʾt*. But wait! None of the texts that include the formula for forgiveness, whether of the *ḥaṭṭāʾt* or the *ʾāšām*, apply to the deliberate sinner; they all refer to sins committed unintentionally. Does this imply that there is no forgiveness for the deliberate sinner? Indeed it does—but with this exception: they might carry their guilt for an entire year, but on one day, the Day of Atonement, through faith in the efficacy of the *ḥaṭṭāʾt* they could find forgiveness by repenting and confessing their sin. Only in this way could homosexual offenders find reconciliation. The provision for reconciliation was made by God; sinners who failed to participate in the mercy of God condemned themselves.

Conclusion

A systematic approach to the subject of homosexuality in the context of the sacrificial system cannot be overemphasized. For the levitical legislator, not only did that system provide a means of social order for the ancient Israelites but the sanctuary and the expiatory sacrifices served as the center of a moral and ethical system. Compliance with the commandments of God maintained the sanctuary (and the land) in a pure condition and assured God's continued presence there.

How merciful was that system? From our study of it, we derive a profound theological truth: the only sin that cannot be forgiven is the sin that is not confessed. Imagine living under the priestly law and having deliberately committed a heinous crime. Imagine feeling the alienation from God that followed such an act. Imagine knowing that none of the means of reconciliation apply to you, the intentional sinner. Imagine knowing that you have put the entire community at risk by virtue of the impurity you have generated. Imagine the fear of being put to death or causing your entire family to suffer extinction for what you have done.

Imagine the stain on your conscience by having to live with your sin every day. Then imagine what a great relief it must have been to trust in the activities on your behalf of the high priest on the Day of Atonement. Imagine the sense of awe at the power of the *ḥaṭṭāʾt* blood to cleanse the sanctuary and give the assurance that God was near. Imagine the freedom from a guilty conscience as the priest symbolically transfers your sins to the head of the scapegoat by laying his hands on it and sending it away into the desert. Imagine falling prostrate in contrite repentance before the presence of the one true God near the outer altar of the sanctuary, openly confessing your sin, acknowledging the sovereignty of God in your life, and submitting yourself to the rule of his law in your heart. Then imagine standing upright again, standing tall, free of the burden of sin you had carried, knowing by faith that God has forgiven you and you have been reconciled to him. Such is the mercy of God!

The homosexual subject to Israelite law could find his way back to God in these terms. The Day of Atonement was his salvation. The covenant of God was with his people. But what of the peoples to whom this covenant was not addressed? What of the nations who did not come under the canopy of God's covenant of mercy and grace? Did God have one law for Israel and nothing for the Gentiles? Is not God sovereign over all? If so, did not the Gentiles also from time to time fall short of God's standards of holiness? Were there not homosexuals among them? What provisions were made for them? How could they be reconciled to God?

With these questions we turn our attention to the New Testament. The same concern for order that we have seen in the Hebrew Bible prevails there. Sin still generates impurity, and the sinner still deserves death. Sin still causes chaos in the individual's life and disorder in the community, exposing both to God's wrath. As in the Old Testament, the homosexual act is condemned and the homosexual is excluded from the kingdom of God. And finally, as we shall see in detail, provisions are made for the reconciliation of the homosexual. The sword of God's wrath is always wrapped in the mantle of his mercy.

PART 3

Homosexuality
in the New Testament

11

Christ and the Homosexual

Do not think that I came to abolish the Law or the Prophets; I did not come to abolish, but to fulfill. For truly I say to you, until heaven and earth pass away, not the smallest letter or stroke shall pass away from the Law, until all is accomplished. Whoever then annuls one of the least of these commandments, and so teaches others, shall be called least in the kingdom of heaven; but whoever keeps and teaches them, he shall be called great in the kingdom of heaven.

—Matthew 5:17–19

T he image of homosexuality in the New Testament is carved from the block of Old Testament teaching on the subject. The basic shape of the Old Testament representation of homosexuality consists of the following perspectives:

1. The order of creation stipulates that humanity is made to reflect the divine image (Gen. 1:26–27).
2. The first and archetypal sexual relationship described in Genesis between Adam and Eve was heterosexual and was accompanied by a blessing of fertility (Gen. 1:28).
3. Order and fertility were chief concerns of all peoples throughout the ancient Near East—the Hebrews shared these concerns with

their neighbors but infused these concerns with a strict belief in monotheism.

4. The paradigm for marriage is between heterosexuals: "For this cause a man shall leave his father and his mother, and shall cleave to his wife; and they shall become one flesh" (Gen. 2:24).
5. Order in society is predicated on order in the cosmos—the biblical idea of the Sabbath finds its rationale in the divine rest on the seventh day of creation (Gen. 2:3; Exod. 20:8).
6. All the references to homosexual acts in the Old Testament are negative—whether in narrative (Gen. 9:20–27; 19; Judg. 19) or law (Lev. 18; 20)—and carry heavy sanctions in the form of death or the threat of extinction.
7. The priestly sanctuary describes a graduated order of holiness for the community of Israel.
8. Physical impurities and violations against the performative and prohibitive commands of God contaminate the Israelite sanctuary and the land.
9. Sins are categorized as unintentional or deliberate, with the latter presenting the greatest threat to an individual, his or her family, the sanctuary, and society at large.
10. Deliberate sinners remain outside the umbrella of the expiatory sacrifices (Num. 15:30–31) and so continue in their sin and guilt until the Day of Atonement (Lev. 16), at which time they may confess their sins, repent, put their faith in the effectiveness of the *ḥaṭṭāʾt* rituals to cleanse the sanctuary (slain sacrifice) and their conscience (scapegoat), be forgiven by God, and thus be reconciled to the Lord and to the community.

The New Testament teaching on homosexuality does not stray from these basic principles, but rather expands on them. The principle that sin is judged on the basis of individual responsibility is reinforced. The idea that sin causes impurity and provokes the wrath of God is continued. The ideal of order in creation and society as based on the principle of law is reiterated. The heterosexual relationship as the standard for sexual relations and family structure is upheld. Homosexual conduct is categorically forbidden and attached with severe sanctions. But in the end, even the homosexual who has deliberately violated God's laws and codes of conduct may be cleansed from sin, reconciled to God, and reinstated into the community. No postulate of Old Testament law with respect to homosexuality is contradicted by New Testament teaching.

The *de novo* contributions of the New Testament to our understanding of homosexuality in the Bible are twofold. Of greatest importance is the introduction of the role of Jesus Christ, both his person and his work. In second position stands the message of God's revelation, addressed to Israel in the Old Testament, which now takes on universal dimensions in the New Testament. These two themes are intertwined and form the warp and woof of the discussion that follows.

Since so much rests on understanding the person of Christ, the first chapter of this section explicates his roles in creation and redemption. This chapter prepares the reader to understand more fully Paul's arguments against homosexual conduct on the basis of natural order (Rom. 1) and his very clear and precise language on the reconciliation of homosexuals and their entrance into the kingdom of God (1 Cor. 6). I hope to establish that the Jesus of Scripture is not the same Jesus of the modern homosexual movement. Although he did not speak directly to homosexual conduct, he could not have condoned it nor was he, as some gay apologists claim, prone to homosexual inclinations himself. To the contrary, an examination of Scripture demonstrates that Jesus supported both the order of creation and the requirements of the law. Furthermore, his role as redeemer is proof positive that he could not have favored a homosexual lifestyle.

Christ and Creation

All views of Jesus and homosexuality must rest on a proper understanding of his identity according to Scripture. The need to appreciate the role of Jesus Christ as creator is obvious. By affirming this role, we confirm these aspects of his divine nature: that he existed before the creation and therefore was not subject to the limitations of it; that as the agent of creation, the design and order established in nature, even in sexual matters, were instituted by him; that deviations from the divine order are inconsistent with his arrangement and oppose his purposes; that severe sanctions are imposed upon people who do not measure up to the divine standards.

The order set up in nature is, in the general sense, perceivable by people everywhere and in every generation. In that sense the creator places his imprimatur within every human heart with respect to moral axioms. This—what we call conscience—rests on what theologians call general revelation. The apostle Paul refers to it when he writes of everyone: "That which is known about God is evident within them; for God made it evident to them" (Rom. 1:19). He goes on to state in the next verse that the ground for this knowledge is based on creation: "For since the creation of the world his invisible attributes, his eternal power and divine nature, have been clearly seen, being understood through what has been made, so that they are without excuse" (v. 20). The natural creation points to a knowledge of God.

Of supreme importance in this regard is the biblical view that human beings are created in the image of God: "Then God said, 'Let us make man in our image, according to our likeness.' . . . And God created man in his own image, in the image of God he created him; male and female he created them" (Gen. 1:26–27). Exactly what image can this text be speaking of, since Scripture affirms that God is invisible? I submit that it is the image of the preexistent Christ who served as the agent of creation (see also Helyer 1994: 237). As John writes: "No man has seen God at any time; the only begotten God, who is in the bosom of the Father, he has explained him" (John 1:18). The point is made by the apostle Paul concerning Christ: "He is the image (eikōn, εἰκών) of the invisible God, the firstborn of all creation. For by him all things were created, both in the heavens and on earth, visible and invisible, whether thrones or dominions or rulers or authorities—all things have been created by him and for him. And he is before all things, and in him all things hold together" (Col. 1:15–17). At the beginning of creation, when God decided to make human beings, he made them in the very image that the incarnate Jesus would one day take on. The exact pattern for humanity of the image of God in creation is, therefore, Jesus himself.

This point is reiterated by Paul in his letter to the Philippians. He exhorts his readers to have the mind of Christ with regard to humility, for Christ provided the perfect example: "Although he existed in the form of God, [he] did not regard equality with God a thing to be grasped, but emptied himself, taking the form of a bond-servant, and being made in the likeness of men. And being found in appearance as a man, he humbled himself by becoming obedient to the point of death, even death on a cross" (Phil. 2:6–8). One cannot miss the import of the creative terms in this passage: "form" (morphē, μορφή) equates to Hebrew "image" (ṣelem, צֶלֶם), and "the likeness of men" (homoiō-mati anthrōpōn, ὁμοιώματι ἀνθρώπων) to Hebrew "likeness" (dĕmût, דְּמוּת). In the order of creation, human beings are to emulate the likeness of Christ, for he is their blueprint.

The creative role of the preexistent Christ can be established from a variety of other texts. Perhaps the most familiar passage is at the beginning of John's Gospel with reference to Jesus as the divine Word or logos (λόγος): "In the beginning was the Word, and the Word was with God, and the Word was God. He was in the beginning with God.

All things came into being by him; and apart from him nothing came into being that has come into being" (John 1:1–3). Having taken on the form of humanity, Jesus embodied the glory of God (1:14).

A more complete picture of the identity of Christ may be obtained by studying the name of God and its application to Jesus. There is one name for God in the Old Testament: *yhwh* (יהוה, probably pronounced "Yahweh"). This name is a form of the verb "to be," expressed in the first person by "I am." When God appears to Moses at Sinai, Moses is instructed to say that "I AM" sent him to the Israelites as their leader (Exod. 3:14). Jesus uses the same expression of himself in controversy with certain Jews who had questioned his identity: " 'Truly, truly, I say to you, before Abraham was born, I AM.' Therefore they picked up stones to throw at him" (John 8:58–59). The quick response of his audience to stone Jesus indicates that they accused him of blasphemy.

One more example will suffice to show that Jesus was not a mere human but God incarnate. Paul concludes the passage in his letter to the Philippians quoted above by referring to the resurrected Christ in the following terms: "Therefore also God highly exalted him, and bestowed on him the name which is above every name, that at the name of Jesus every knee should bow, of those who are in heaven, and on earth, and under the earth, and that every tongue should confess that Jesus Christ is Lord [*kyrios*, κύριος = Yahweh], to the glory of God the Father" (Phil. 2:9–11). Which name? The name *Yahweh*. Paul clearly alludes to a speech of Yahweh recorded by the prophet Isaiah (45:18–25). Isaiah reports the identity of Yahweh (translated "LORD" in English versions) as creator and redeemer, as the one true God and Savior. The universal appeal of Yahweh follows: "Turn to me and be saved, all you ends of the earth; for I am God, and there is no other. By myself I have sworn, my mouth has uttered in all integrity a word that will not be revoked: Before me every knee will bow; by me every tongue will swear" (Isa. 45:22–23 NIV). Here the deity of the resurrected Christ is affirmed. He was reinstated to his former position or essence in the "form" of God.

If one accepts the instruction of Scripture, the identity of Jesus as creator in the name of Yahweh must be granted as well. Since the order of creation is clearly patterned on the divine image as fully expressed in the person of Christ and since the model of human conduct according to creation is heterosexual, it follows then that homosexual conduct is alien to the person of Christ. Moreover, homosexuality expressly abrogates the law, which, by reasonable inference given the identity of the preexistent Christ, was authored by him and which he came to fulfill.

Christl and the Law

I n his book *Jonathan Loved David*, in the chapter entitled "Jesus and
Sexuality," Tom Horner argues that the "the Gospels are rather comprehensive in their treatment of what is really important; and what
is really important is not so much a set of legalistic rules but a body of
spiritual truths" (1978: 111). Horner represents a wide spectrum of gay
apologists who emphasize the contrast between love and law. Based
on an idea of love that is foreign to Scripture, Horner suggests that "it
is impossible to conceive of Jesus as displaying hostility toward anyone
because of his or her sexual preferences" and that Jesus' high regard for
women "goes hand in hand with a tolerance for homosexuality" (p. 121).
Misrepresenting the work of W. D. Davies, he concludes that Jesus was
a "Man for All People," the "supreme Prophet of Love" (p. 126).

Of love, yes, but also of law. Love without law is a non sequitur.
The relationship of Jesus to the Hebrew Scriptures in general and to
the law in particular is an essential element in the biblical view of
homosexuality. As the epigraph of this chapter shows, Jesus saw himself as one who fulfills the law. To what extent, then, did Christ uphold
the law, and what did Paul mean by referring to Jesus as the "end"
(*telos*, τέλος) of the law (Rom. 10:4)? Let us consider first Jesus' own
view of the law and then look at Paul's teaching about the status of
the law for the Roman church. Both have implications for homosexuals today.

Contrary to what Horner and company assert, when Jesus refers to
specific commandments in the Sermon on the Mount, he does not abrogate the law. I have already emphasized the importance that intention
plays in the law. Jesus emphasizes the intention when he says of the law
on adultery that "every one who looks on a woman to lust for her has
committed adultery with her already in his heart" (Matt. 5:28). The law
forbids sexual relations with a married person, but Jesus goes to the
heart of the law and addresses the underlying motivation for the violation. Eliminate the intent (lust), and the law will be obeyed. Once again,
on marital issues, Jesus upholds the law in a stricter fashion than the
teachers of his day. Based on Deuteronomy 24:1–4, followers of Hillel
argued that a man could divorce his wife for a matter as small as burning the toast, for "any unpleasant thing" (Babylonian Talmud, tractate
Gittin 90a). Jesus gives a more conservative interpretation of this law
by limiting the reasons for divorce to adultery (Matt. 5:32). His disap-
proval of the abuse of the divorce law and simultaneous affirmation of

the institution of marriage are founded on the theological principle that men and women are made in the image of God. As God is inseparable, so also are a man and woman in marriage; the sexual union is symbolic of a spiritual union. Jesus' view of the law supports his role as creator. The order of law compliments the order of creation.

One might argue at this point that what Jesus meant with respect to law was only the Decalogue or the so-called moral code. I have insisted that the ceremonial law, also called the ritual law, is impregnated with moral and ethical principles. These principles are timeless. Let us consider the issue of impurity.

Jesus speaks plainly about sexual impurity as a product of the human heart, and in so doing he may have alluded to homosexuality:

> For from within, out of the heart of men, proceed the evil thoughts [recall the use of *yēṣer* at Gen. 6:5] and fornications (*porneiai*, πορνεῖαι), thefts, murders, adulteries (*moicheiai*, μοιχεῖαι), deeds of coveting and wickedness, as well as deceit, sensuality (*aselgeia*, ἀσέλγεια), envy, slander, pride and foolishness. All these evil things proceed from within and defile the man. (Mark 7:21–23)

All the terms for which I have given Greek equivalents refer to sexual deviations from the norm that Jesus advocated. Two of these terms reappear in Paul's list in 1 Corinthians 6:9: fornications (*porneiai*) and adulteries (*moicheiai*). The remaining sexual term, *aselgeia*, suggests the idea of "license" or "debauchery," a condition marking those subject to the *kareth* penalty in the Old Testament. More particularly, *aselgeia* reflects utter abandon to defiant and deliberate sin. Homosexual acts fall into this category. Given the use of this term elsewhere, it is possible that Jesus had homosexuality in mind when he used it. Let's have a closer look.

In the Septuagint, *aselgeia* appears only twice, at 3 Maccabees 2:26 and Wisdom of Solomon 14:26. The latter passage is of particular interest since *aselgeia* occurs there in a list of vices that may include homosexuality: "Defiling of souls, confusion of sex, disorder in marriage, adultery, and wantonness (*aselgeia*)."

The term *aselgeia* belongs to a semantic field describing unauthorized sexual conduct that is defiling. A few examples will suffice. Ezekiel associates *asebeia* (ἀσέβεια) with the sexual crimes of incest outlawed by Leviticus 18. In Ezekiel 14:6 *asebeia* is combined with the *tôʿēbôt* of Israel and, not surprisingly, the *kareth* penalty (see also 16:43, 58; 22:11; 23:27, 29, 35, 48–49; 33:9, 14). In the face of Israel's sexual crimes and the complaint that God is unfair in requiring his strict sexual code, Ezekiel offers hope through repentance:

"But the house of Israel says, 'The way of the Lord is not right.' Are my ways not right, O house of Israel?

"Is it not your ways that are not right? Therefore I will judge you, O house of Israel, each according to his conduct," declares the Lord GOD. "Repent and turn away from all your transgressions (*asebeion*), so that iniquity may not become a stumbling block to you. Cast away from you all your transgressions (*asebeias*) which you have committed, and make yourselves a new heart and a new spirit! For why will you die, O house of Israel?" (Ezek. 18:29–31)

In these verses *asebeiōn* (ἀσεβειῶν) translates *pĕšāʿîm* (פְּשָׁעִים. "deliberate sins"), of the high-handed variety, for which *kareth* is imposed and for which only the Day of Atonement is efficacious. Ezekiel preserves the requirement of the law that deliberate sins require confession and repentance before atonement is possible.

Aselgeia characterized Sodom and Gomorrah and the pagan world generally (Otto Bauernfeind, *TDNT* 1:490). Since we have already established that the Sodom story is about homosexual conduct, it is noteworthy that both *asebeia* and *aselgeia* are found in 2 Peter 2:6–10a in the context of homosexuality. The passage is worth quoting in full:

And if he condemned the cities of Sodom and Gomorrah to destruction by reducing them to ashes, having made them an example to those who would live ungodly (*asebein*, ἀσεβεῖν) thereafter; and if he rescued righteous Lot, oppressed by the sensual conduct (*aselgeia anastrophēs*, ἀσελγείᾳ ἀναστροφῆς) of unprincipled men (for by what he saw and heard that righteous man, while living among them, felt his righteous soul tormented day after day with their lawless deeds), then the Lord knows how to rescue the godly from temptation, and to keep the unrighteous under punishment for the day of judgment, and especially those who indulge the flesh in its corrupt desires (*epithymia miasmou*, ἐπιθυμίᾳ μιασμοῦ) and despise authority.

A general designation for *aselgeia* such as "license" or debauchery" is not enough to carry the sexual weight of this term. It would appear that Peter thought of *aselgeia* as a term for homosexuality. That he may have had in mind the pollution concept of the levitical writer is hidden in the term *miasma* (μίασμα), with which the translators of the Septuagint rendered the idea of impurity.

The sense of sexual excess is found also in Romans 13:13; Galatians 5:19; 2 Corinthians 12:21; 1 Peter 4:3; and 2 Peter 2:2, 18. At Romans 13:13, *aselgeia* appears parallel to *koitai* (κοῖται, "beds"), translated by the New American Standard Bible as "sexual promiscuity," an obvious euphemism for illicit sexual intercourse (we will see the term again in *arsenokoitēs* in the discussion of 1 Cor. 6:9–11). The sexual license implied by *aselgeia* is characteristic of the Gentiles, but for the Christian transformed by Christ's atonement, such practices are no longer done. That the individual's will and desires are subordinated to the will of God is made clear by the apostle Peter: "For the time already past is sufficient for you to have carried out the desire of the Gentiles, having pursued a course of sensuality (*aselgeiais*, ἀσελγείαις), lusts, drunkenness, carousals, drinking parties and abominable idolatries" (1 Pet. 4:3). The transition from being controlled by one's own lust to conforming to the will of God is further discussed in chapter 13.

The term *koitē* (κοίτη) occurs in the Septuagint of Leviticus 18 with reference to sexual excesses, in particular the emission of semen in the act of intercourse, including homosexual acts. One should not fail to recognize the association with impurity, either in the words of Jesus or in the language of Peter.

Paul also combines *aselgeia* with two other terms for sexual impurity in 2 Corinthians 12:21, where he laments the fate of those who have "not repented of the impurity (*akatharsia*, ἀκαθαρσίᾳ), immorality (*porneia*, πορνείᾳ) and sensuality (*aselgeia*, ἀσελγείᾳ) which they have practiced." As we have already seen in chapter 7, *akatharsia* is the Septuagint's translation for Hebrew *ṭumʾâ* (טֻמְאָה, "impurity") in the levitical prohibition against homosexuality. Paul understood fully the intentional nature of these sexual violations and the need for repentance before reconciliation could be effected. The pattern for reconciliation set in the levitical law is upheld.

A final example is drawn from Paul's letter to the Ephesians, where he appeals to believers not to practice the behavior pattern of the Gentiles. In this admonition, one can hear the echo of the levitical writer warning Israel against the sexual mores of the Canaanites and Egyptians in Leviticus 18:

> This I say therefore, and affirm together with the Lord, that you walk no longer just as the Gentiles also walk, in the futility of their mind, being darkened in their understanding, excluded from the life of God, because of the ignorance that is in them, because of the hardness of their heart; and they, having become callous, have given themselves over to sensuality (*aselgeia*), for the practice of every kind of impurity (*akarthasias*) with greediness. (Eph. 4:17–19)

This paragraph is as close a parallel as can be found to Paul's description of homosexuals in the first chapter of his letter to the Romans.

This short excursus into the use of *aselgeia* demonstrates its close affinity to impurity and homosexuality. Peter used the term expressly of the practices of the Sodomites. We may accept a similar connotation for the use of this term by Jesus, Peter's tutor. There is no reason to think otherwise. No proof exists for excluding homosexual nuances from this term. Certainly we can say that Jesus affirmed the requirements of the law. How then can it be said that he was the "end" (*telos*) of the law? A mistake at this point might cause one to conclude that the law is of no further value. A correct interpretation sustains the continued value of the moral and ethical principles inherent in the law.

I follow at this point the exegesis of Steven Bechtler (1994: 298) with regard to Paul's use of *telos* at Romans 10:4. The meaning of this term is significant for our understanding not only of homosexuality in the Bible but also of the relationship between Jews and Christians, between Israel and the church. The reader will do well to consult the details of Bechtler's view. In sum, he argues that "outside of Rom 10:4, and apart from the three occurrences in which *telos* follows a preposition in an adverbial expression and the two in which it means 'tax,' *telos* is found seven times in Paul's correspondence, never unequivocally denoting 'termination' or 'cessation' " (p. 299). Christ is rather the goal or completion of the process of revelation set out in the law, the culmination of it. At issue is the question of righteousness and how it is achieved.

I showed in the discussion of the *ḥaṭṭāʾt* on the Day of Atonement that reconciliation of the homosexual on that day is not automatic. A wooden or mechanistic observance of the law was never accepted by God. The deliberate sinner must confess and repent of sin. The requirement is to bring "offerings in righteousness" (Mal. 3:3). Bechtler concludes correctly (p. 302):

> In Rom 3:31 Paul explicitly denies that Torah is abolished "through faith" and insists that "on the contrary, we establish the law" (*alla nomon histanomen*, ἀλλὰ νόμον ἱστάνομεν). Furthermore, for Paul, Torah continues to function as a witness to Christ (3:21) and as Scripture, which he cites repeatedly to buttress his exposition of the gospel. Finally, Torah retains its role, in principle, as that which is "fulfilled" in the ethical life of the believer (8:4; 12:10); this is true no matter how infrequently Paul enjoins obedience to specific commandments of Torah.

I have affirmed that Jesus lived up to the requirements of the law, as expected given his identity. I have also affirmed that the law is not abrogated by the gospel but is in fact suggested by the gospel. As Paul writes to the Galatians, the law is not contrary to the promises of God but is rather "our tutor to lead us to Christ, that we may be justified by faith" (Gal. 3:24). We must consider now how it is that redemption is made available to the homosexual through Christ.

Christt and Redemption

$\mathbf{T}$he redemptive work of Christ is meaningless unless we grant to him the identity I propose in this chapter. If he was not who he said he was, there is no significance to his death on the cross and no power in his resurrection. C. S. Lewis (1952: 56) writes eloquently on this point:

> A man who was merely a man and said the sort of things Jesus said would not be a great moral teacher. He would either be a lunatic—on a level with the man who says he is a poached egg—or else he would be the Devil of Hell. You must make your choice. Either this man was, and is, the Son of God: or else a madman or something worse. You can shut Him up for a fool, you can spit at Him and kill Him as a demon; or you can fall at His feet and call Him Lord and God. But let us not come with any patronizing nonsense about His being a great human teacher. He has not left that open to us. He did not intend to.

Jesus' mission was clear. He stated it himself: "For the Son of Man has come to seek and to save that which was lost" (Luke 19:10). Again he said: "For even the Son of Man did not come to be served, but to serve, and to give his life a ransom for many *(lytron anti pollōn,* λύτρον ἀντὶ πολλῶν)" (Mark 10:45). The focus of Jesus' life is his death, for it is at the cross that he addressed the human dilemma of sin and separation from God. The law was limited to Israel; the Gentiles were not savvy to its demands but fell into sin as well. The law was particular; the righteousness by faith in Christ universal. Paul stated it thus: "For what the Law could not do, weak as it was through the flesh, God did: sending his own Son in the likeness of sinful flesh and as an offering for sin [i.e., *ḥaṭṭāʾt*], he condemned sin in the flesh, in order that the requirement of the Law might be fulfilled in us, who do not walk according to the flesh, but according to the Spirit" (Rom. 8:3–4).

Since the mission of Christ was to effect the ransom of humanity, it is important that we focus on the meaning of the expression *ransom for many (lytron anti pollōn,* λύτρον ἀντὶ πολλῶν) in Mark 10:45.

Ransom

The term *lytron* (λύτρον, "ransom") is used in the New Testament only in reference to Jesus' death (see also Matt. 20:28). In the Septuagint, it belongs to the same semantic field as the term *kipper*, which is found in the expiatory sacrifices (cf. Lev. 4–5). A parallel to the ransom expression is found in Mark 14:24 and Matthew 26:28, where Jesus says: "This is my blood of the covenant, which is to be shed on behalf of many."

The term *lytron* was used outside the New Testament for the payment of a sum to release prisoners from their bondage. In New Testament terms, the blood of Christ is the payment for the many to be set free from sin. More specifically, as *ḥaṭṭāʾt* blood, its purpose is fundamentally that of cleansing and appeasing, preparing the way for the sinner to find reconciliation. In the case of the deliberate sinner (i.e., the homosexual), following our study of the Day of Atonement, this could only occur through repentance and confession and through faith in the efficacy of the blood sacrifice. In the sacrificial system described in Leviticus, the *ḥaṭṭāʾt* always received priority over the other sacrifices, expressly because it cleansed the sanctuary and appeased the wrath of God. Even the order of sacrifices is significant! This was clearly understood by rabbinical exegetes: "The blood of the *ḥaṭṭāʾt* precedes the blood of the *ʿolâ* ('burnt offering') because it appeases" (Mishnah, tractate *Zebaḥim* 10.2). "Rabbi Simeon said: To what may the *ḥaṭṭāʾt* be compared? To a paraclete, who enters in to appease [the judge]. Once the paraclete has accomplished appeasement, then the gift [i.e., the *ʿolâ*] is brought in" (Tosepta, tractate *Para* 1.1). The significance of the order of sacrifices is discussed by Jacob Milgrom (1991: 488).

On the Day of Atonement, the sins of the Israelites were transferred to the scapegoat, which was then sent into the wilderness. To the Corinthian church, comprised in part of former homosexuals, Paul writes to explain the *ḥaṭṭāʾt* function of the death of Christ (2 Cor. 5:14–21):

1. The death of Christ is substitutionary: "one died for all, therefore all died" (v. 14); "he [God] made him [Christ] who knew no sin to be sin on our behalf, that we might become the righteousness of God in him" (v. 21).
2. The death of Christ is transforming: "therefore if any man is in Christ, he is a new creature; the old things passed away; behold, new things have come" (v. 17).
3. The death of Christ is reconciling: "[God] reconciled us to himself through Christ, and gave us the ministry of reconciliation" (v. 18).
4. The death of Christ is far-reaching, encompassing even deliberate sin: "not counting their trespasses against them" (v. 19).

Paul concludes this passage with an emotional appeal: "Therefore, we are ambassadors for Christ, as though God were entreating through us; we beg you on behalf of Christ, be reconciled to God" (v. 20).

A number of passages in the New Testament emphasize the effectiveness of the blood of Christ to cleanse from sin and to appease the wrath of God. In Romans 3:25, Christ is called a propitiatory sacrifice. Paul affirms that "having now been justified by his blood, we shall be saved from the wrath of God through him" (Rom. 5:9). To the Ephesians, Paul writes that "we have redemption (*apolytrōsin*, ἀπολύτρωσιν) through his blood" (Eph. 1:7) and "you who formerly were far off have been brought near by the blood of Christ" (2:13).

The fullest explanation in the entire New Testament regarding Christ as the *ḥaṭṭāʾt* is found in Hebrews 9:11–28. This passage is explicated by our understanding of the Day of Atonement. The law required that "all things are cleansed with blood, and without shedding of blood there is no forgiveness" (v. 22). What the high priest accomplished for Israel in the sanctuary on a temporal level, Christ accomplished on a cosmic level (vv. 11, 23–24). The former sacrifices had to be repeated; Christ's sacrifice was once for all (vv. 12–14, 25–26). On the basis of Christ's blood the new covenant is inaugurated.

Substitution

The second term in the expression *ransom for many* is the preposition *anti* (ἀντί, "on behalf of"). Some scholars translate this term of substitution as "to the advantage of," but there is no real difference in the meaning. As one commentator notes: "For, even if the ἀντί be translated 'to the advantage of,' the death of Jesus means that there happens to Him what would have had to happen to the many. Hence He takes their place" (Friedrich Büchsel, *TDNT* 4:343). The idea of substitution is clearly part of the Day of Atonement ritual with regard to the scapegoat *ḥaṭṭāʾt*.

Beneficiaries

Finally, we must consider who are the "many" (*pollōn*, πολλῶν) for whom Christ died. The Greek word *pollōn* is best explained as an allusion to the "many" (*rabbîm*, רַבִּים) of Isaiah 52–53, where the term *rabbîm* occurs for Gentiles: the servant will sprinkle "many nations" (*gôyim rabbîm*, גּוֹיִם רַבִּים; 52:15), bear the sin "of many" (*lārabbîm*, לָרַבִּים; 53:11), and receive an inheritance "with the many" (*bārabbîm*, בָּרַבִּים; 53:12). This is supported by the New Testament interpretations of the Isaiah servant songs. The messianic role of the servant is to be a "light to the Gentiles." Thus, as a child, Jesus was seen to be "a light of revelation to the Gentiles, and the glory of . . . Israel" (Luke 2:32; see Isa. 42:6; 49:6). Allusions to the servant in the Book of Acts are recorded at 3:13, 26; 4:27, 30, while the first explicit identification with Jesus is in Acts 8:35. Jesus said: "I am the light of the world; he who follows me shall not walk in the darkness, but shall have the light of life" (John 8:12). The language of the prophet Isaiah is appropriated for the mission of the early church: "For thus the Lord commanded us, 'I have placed you as a light for the Gentiles, that you should bring salvation to the end of the earth' " (Acts 13:47, citing Isa. 49:6). Through believing in the work of Christ on their behalf, the Gentiles could enjoy the same covenantal blessings that God had promised to his people Israel (see Rom. 9–11).

The kingdom of God is thus comprised of Jews and Gentiles, all subject to the authority of Christ because of his identity as Yahweh, the sovereign God, who accomplished salvation for all through his incarnation, death, and resurrection. According to the apostle Paul, admission into the kingdom is the same for all (Rom. 10:9–13):

> If you confess with your mouth Jesus as Lord [*kyrios*, κύριος = Yahweh], and believe in your heart that God raised him from the dead, you shall be saved; for with the heart man believes, resulting in righteousness, and with the mouth he confesses, resulting in salvation. For the Scripture says, "Whoever believes in him will not be disappointed." For there is no distinction between Jew and Greek; for the same Lord is Lord of all, abounding in riches for all who call upon him; for "Whoever will call upon the name of the LORD will be saved."

These words imply that there is no difference between homosexual and heterosexual, since all have sinned, and sin brings the penalty of death, "but the free gift of God is eternal life in Christ Jesus our Lord" (Rom. 6:23). The wrath of God toward sin is turned away from sinners who by faith embrace the blood of Christ as atonement for their sin (3:21–31). Even the deliberate homosexual act can be forgiven pending the sinner's confession and repentance. Forgiveness, as on the Day of Atonement, is still the act of God in response to the blood of Christ and the contrite attitude of the sinner.

Conclusion

In this chapter, I affirmed that the Day of Atonement serves as a paradigm for the deliberate sinner—including the homosexual—to find reconciliation with God. The functions of the expiatory sacrifices on that day find their parallel in the sacrifice of Christ to reconcile the world to himself. According to Scripture, Christ was not mere human but was God in the flesh. According to New Testament teaching, he was involved in the work of creation. He fulfilled the law and completed his mission in accordance with the work of redeeming humankind from sin. He is the *ḥaṭṭāʾt* sacrifice par excellence.

Turning now to the passages on homosexuality in Paul's letters, it must be remembered that the controlling feature in Paul's thought is the reconciliation of the world to God in Christ.

12

Nature and Homosexuality

> *Therefore God gave them over in the lusts of their hearts to impurity, that their bodies might be dishonored among them. For they exchanged the truth of God for a lie, and worshiped and served the creature rather than the Creator, who is blessed forever. Amen.*
>
> *For this reason God gave them over to degrading passions; for their women exchanged the natural function for that which is unnatural, and in the same way also the men abandoned the natural function of the woman and burned in their desire towards one another, men with men committing indecent acts and receiving in their own persons the due penalty of their error.*
>
> —Romans 1:24–27

An examination of the term *nature* in the first chapter of Romans confirms that the apostle's thought is consistent with the levitical writer's view on homosexuality. The practice of same-gender sexual relations violates the natural order of creation and flouts the image of God in humanity. Homosexual relations deny validity to the opposite gender and thereby devalue the male-female bond established in creation. They also run counter to the procreative purpose of sexual intercourse upon which the human species depends for survival.

Only by abandoning Paul's commitment to the Torah can one avoid this conclusion, as James De Young writes (1988: 440): "The only model of sexual expression contemplated in Scripture is that which is patterned after the creation model of Genesis 1–2. This is the pattern that our Lord (Matt. 5:19) and his disciples taught or commanded. . . . Revisionist interpretations would do well to come under the authority of Scripture."

Paul and the Order of Creation

The context of Romans 1 indicates that Paul's view of the word *nature* cannot be classified with modern scientific descriptions of it. Of key importance to Paul's indictment of humanity in this chapter is his view that the word *nature* is defined by revelation. Four postulates must be kept in mind as we consider this topic.

First, the order of creation serves to reveal the invisible attributes of God, namely, his eternal power and divinity (*theiotēs*, θειότης; 1:20). This postulate eliminates the possibility of reductionist views of nature and ensures that positive and normative moral principles are linked to the order of creation. Thus nature cannot be defined simply as what is. For Paul, it consists of what ought to be.

Second, in keeping with our understanding of the Old Testament law, the principle of intention underlies Paul's thought. The verbs (italicized below) he uses indicate human responsibility for alienation from the Creator: "though they knew God, they *did not honor* him as God, or give thanks" (v. 21); "[they] *exchanged* the glory of the incorruptible God for an image in the form of corruptible man" (v. 23); "they *exchanged* the truth of God for a lie" (v. 25); "their women *exchanged* the natural function for that which is unnatural" (v. 26); "men *abandoned* the natural function of the woman" (v. 27). The response of God to give them over to their lusts and degrading passions is directly proportionate to their rejection of the divine revelation in nature (v. 26).

This postulate is key to understanding Paul's anthropology in Romans 1. As a student of the famed Gamaliel ha-Zaken (the "elder"), a grandson of Hillel, Paul was no doubt schooled in rabbinic traditions. A midrash may help to understand his view of humans in the order of creation. It is recorded that when God created the world, he produced on the second day angels with their natural inclination to do good. He then created beasts who lived only by their instinctual desires. Unhappy with this situation, he then created humankind: "If the angels follow my will," said God, "it is only on account of their inability to act in the opposite direction. I shall, therefore, create man, who will be a combination of both angel and beast, so that he will be able to follow either the good or the evil inclination" (Schechter 1961: 81). The generation of the flood was judged because they abandoned the knowledge of God's ways: "The name of God was profaned by its transfer to abominations (or idols), and violence and vice became the order of the day" (p. 83, citing *Mekilta* §67b).

In rabbinic thought, human conduct determines whether God remains present with them. For example, those who speak lies are banished from his presence (Babylonian Talmud, tractate *Sanhedrin* 102b). This is a scriptural principle: "But your iniquities have separated you from your God; your sins have hidden his face from you so that he will not hear" (Isa. 59:2 NIV). Paul acknowledged homosexual acts as a deliberate affront to God's design for humanity.

Third, Paul affirms the levitical principle that moral deviations from the divine order result in impurity (*akatharsia*, ἀκαθαρσία; Rom. 1:24). This impurity is offensive to God and generates his wrath (v. 18). Furthermore, the deleterious effects of it are carried in the body of the offender (v. 27). For Paul, the body represents the sanctuary or the temple: sexual immorality must be avoided because it defiles the sanctuary: "Or do you not know that your body is a temple of the Holy Spirit who is in you, whom you have from God, and that you are not your own?" (1 Cor. 6:19).

The imagery of the body as the sanctuary derives from the fourth postulate. A new order of creation is established by the work of Christ in reconciling the world to God: "Therefore if any man is in Christ, he is a new creature" (2 Cor. 5:17). The gospel reveals the righteousness of God (Rom. 1:17) in Christ, whose blood effects a new order (Col. 1:20). Making known the reconciliation to God, through the *ḥaṭṭāʾt* sacrifice of Christ, is the primary goal of Paul's ministry (2 Cor. 5:20–21). The effect is individual moral conduct in harmony with the order of God's holiness, that is, the requirements of the law (Rom. 8:3–4). This point is made explicitly at Colossians 1:22: "Yet he has now reconciled you in his fleshly body through death, in order to present you before him holy and blameless and beyond reproach." The indictment of homosexuals in Romans 1 must be seen in the larger context of Paul's concern for reconciliation.

Stephen Pope coined the term *revealed natural law* to define Paul's view of nature. This is an apt description. Pope interprets as follows (1997: 104):

It focuses on Christ as the prime exemplar and ontological basis for what it is to be human. The ability to understand genuine human flourishing has become obscured by sin, and the one and only way to attain it is through grace-inspired conversion and discipleship, both of which require adherence to the moral and religious dictates clearly enunciated in the New Testament. . . . Reason, elevated by grace and inspired by faith, hope, and charity, can comprehend the basic intelligibility of the moral law, the sublation of natural moral goodness within the Christian moral life, and the value of Christian moral precepts for the common good of even secular societies. Yet because of its corrupted condition after the Fall, human reason, unaided by revelation and a teaching church, cannot grasp the natural law.

This view gives pride of place to Scripture above science and reason as the ultimate guide to sexual ethics. Bearing it in mind, let us turn to an analysis of the debate about the meaning of nature in Romans 1.

The Debate about the Meaning of *Nature*

Modern Errors in Interpretation

John Boswell comments on Romans 1 at some length, arguing in the first place that the subject of homosexuality is ancillary to the passage. Thus he maintains that the context emphasizes the Romans' rejection of monotheism and that Paul's reference to homosexuality is "simply a mundane analogy to this theological sin; it is patently not the crux of his argument. Once the point has been made, the subject of homosexuality is quickly dropped and the major argument resumed" (1980: 108–9).

Boswell introduces his second point as follows (p. 109):

What is even more important, the persons Paul condemns are manifestly not homosexual: what he derogates are homosexual acts committed by apparently heterosexual persons. The whole point of Romans 1, in fact, is to stigmatize persons who have rejected their calling, gotten off the true path they were once on. It would completely undermine the thrust of the argument if the persons in question were not "naturally" inclined to the opposite sex in the same way they were "naturally" inclined to monotheism. What caused the Romans to sin was not that they lacked what Paul considered proper inclinations but that they had them.

Based on his definition of gay persons as those who have a "permanent sexual preference," Boswell argues that it was not such persons whom Paul addressed. Boswell insists that there is "no clear condemnation of homosexual acts in the verses in question" (p. 110).

As his third point, Boswell continues with an analysis of the expression *against nature*. In his view, the term *nature* in Romans 1:26 "should be understood as the personal nature of the pagans in question" (p. 111). In this way, Boswell restricts the term *nature* to a possessive adjective modifying pagans, an ethnic term describing the character of the Gentiles. He cites as support the *Testament of Naphtali* 3.3.4–5, despite its uncertain date: "The Gentiles, deceived and having abandoned the Lord, changed their order. . . . [Be not therefore] like Sodom, which changed the order of its nature. Likewise also the Watchers changed the order of their nature" (p. 111).

Finally, remarking on the phrase *against nature*, Boswell cites Romans 11:24 to show that the term does not have a moral connotation. The context pictures Gentiles in relation to Israel in terms of a horticultural analogy: "For if you were cut off from what is by nature (*kata physin*, κατὰ φύσιν) a wild olive tree, and were grafted contrary to nature (*para physin*, παρὰ φύσιν) into a cultivated olive tree, how much more shall these who are the natural branches be grafted into their own olive tree?" Boswell comments: "Since God himself is here described as acting 'against nature,' it is inconceivable that this phrase necessarily connotes moral turpitude. Rather, it signifies behavior which is unexpected, unusual, or different from what would occur in the normal order of things: 'beyond nature,' perhaps, but not 'immoral' " (p. 112).

Reviews of Boswell's work range from generally praiseworthy (Adams 1981) to highly negative (Neuhaus 1995; Olsen 1981; J. Wright 1984). Each of the four points mentioned above require correction.

First, the departure from monotheism does not nullify the reference to homosexuality. Rather, homosexuality is a result of the departure from God's order in creation. If this were not so, why would Paul, a seasoned debater, use a weak analogy to establish the most important doctrine in Judeo-Christianity? The point of the first chapter of Romans is an appeal for righteous conduct in order to avert God's wrath toward deliberate sinners. In Romans, conduct—whether generated from conscience or obedience to the law—is the issue. All humanity is under the rule of sin. God's wrath is especially associated with the presence of impurity, which alienates the world from him.

In the second place, Scripture knows of no distinction between morally neutral homosexual inverts and immoral heterosexuals who commit homosexual acts. Paul, a firm supporter of the law, was no doubt aware that Leviticus 18:22 categorically included under divine punishment all acts between members of the same sex.

Third, according to Paul, nature is the created order of male and female in the image of God, regulated by conscience and the law. The reference to the *Testament of Naphtali* actually supports the interpretation of nature as a reflection of gender and species according to the creation. The Sodomites changed the order of creation with respect to gender, and the Watchers (probably a reference to the Nephilim of Gen. 6:1–4) changed the order of the species as well, commingling angelic and human flesh.

Fourth, employing the analogy of tree grafting similar to John 15:4–6, Paul addresses in Romans 11:11–24 the theological issue of the temporary rejection of Israel and the salvation of the Gentiles; whereas in Romans 1, he addresses human sinfulness, an inescapably moral subject. It is hermeneutically unsound to ignore the context of specific expressions.

Errors similar to Boswell's are made by Pim Pronk (1993), who argues that since "Paul does not equate creation (= normative creation order) and nature, the word 'unnatural' in Romans 1 cannot without qualification be taken as referring to Genesis 1" (p. 277). He concludes: "Paul indeed regards the normal as the natural and the natural as God-created nature, but the idea that the natural or normal is normative because it expresses the creation order is not his line of reasoning" (p. 278).

Pronk ends with the wrong conclusion because he starts from a wrong assumption. He assumes that nature has no moral overtones in 1 Corinthians 11:14 and, by some long leap of logic, no moral implication in Romans 1. Immediately prior to his conclusion, he acknowledges that Paul uses the term *nature* (*physis*, φύσις) differently in the few places where he employs it. Thus he gives to *physis* at 1 Corinthians 11:14 a normative meaning where hairstyle is the subject (p. 276). There Paul develops a midrash or commentary on the creation story, emphasizing especially the hierarchy of order in the universe (God-Christ-man-woman) to make a point about women covering their head in prayer. The natural order is stressed in the commentary, and reference is made to the woman's covering "because of the angels," probably an allusion to Genesis 6:1–4 (see also Jude 7). While the issue of hairstyle is not indigenous to the creation story, the message about order is, otherwise Paul's argument would bear no weight. The creation order as "revealed natural law" is a concept unknown to Pronk. The methodological error in his work is clear: he imports his view of *physis* from 1 Corinthians 11, supports it from silence in Romans 1, and then asserts that *nature* has no moral implications (i.e., it is not normative) in the latter. The flaw in reasoning is that he states as fact what he has not proved.

Neither Pronk nor Boswell come to grips with the term *asebeia* in Romans 1:18, which, as we saw in the last chapter, has homosexual overtones. As long as Paul's thought is alienated from the levitical system, errors will continue to be made with respect to his view of homosexuality in Romans 1. Order is an intrinsic part of the levitical system, just as creation is inseparable from the divine norm. From a biblical perspective, time and space, involving creation and individual acts, fall into history that is teleological; that is, linear, not cyclical. As Walther Eichrodt says (1961–67: 2.101):

> The creature can discover its destiny only in constant interaction with the will of God, at whose hands it experiences at the same time both limitation and renewal. It is no mere accident . . . that both the Yahwist and the Priestly writers make the *creation the starting point of history*—a history determined on the one hand by the self-willed flight of the creature from that life-relationship with God which is essential to him, and on the other by God's activity, shaping history in an inexhaustible variety of ways in order to bring back to God those who are lost in alienation from him.

Finally, those who interpret Romans 1 along the lines of Boswell and Pronk ignore the importance of the image of God in the discussion. They ignore that Christ is the image of the godhead bodily and that he is the pattern from which humanity was made and the blueprint according to which regenerate humanity is being recreated. Homosexuality compromises that image; in order for this image to be restored, the atoning work of Christ must effect reconciliation between the homosexual and God. This point is key to Paul's theology of reconciliation.

Paul's Interpretation of "Nature"

The key passage for Paul's interpretation of the term *nature* is Romans 1:26–27:

> For this reason God gave them over to degrading passions (*pathē atimias*, πάθη ἀτιμίας); for their women exchanged the natural function (*physikēn chrēsin*, φυσικήν χρῆσιν) for that which is unnatural (*para physin*, παρὰ φύσιν), and the men abandoned the natural function (*physikēn chrēsin*, φυσικὴν χρῆσιν) of the woman and burned in their desire towards one another, men with men committing indecent acts (*aschēmosynēn*, ἀσχημοσύνην).

A natural function is assigned to both men and women, and it is clear from this passage that it is heterosexual. Shameful passions, described earlier as "lusts of their hearts" leading to the dishonoring of their bodies (v. 24), seem to have overpowered the natural function, causing both sexes to exchange or abandon it for homosexual relations. Such relations are deemed indecent acts of an unnatural type, "things which are not proper," the product of a depraved mind, that is, a mind "that has failed the test" (*adokimon noun*, ἀδόκιμον νοῦν; v. 28). Paul follows this description with a list of negative attributes that characterize those in this state (vv. 28–32) and concludes with a glance toward the sanctions imposed by the law: they are worthy of death (Lev. 20:13).

The crux of this passage is the meaning of the noun *physis* and the derived adjective *physikos*, translated as "nature" and "natural" respectively. These terms describe the normal heterosexual roles of male and female according to the order of creation. The expression *para physin* ("against nature") describes homosexual relations that are literally "paranormal." The opposite of *para physin* is *kata physin*: "according to nature" or the "normal condition."

These terms and expressions indicate that in the mind of Paul a certain pattern exists for humanity. A clue to this pattern is found in his use of the term *aschēmosynēn* to describe homosexual acts. A related term is *schēma* (σχῆμα), used in the New Testament by Paul only at Philippians 2:7 to describe the earthly "form, appearance, shape, or essence" of the incarnate Christ. It is noteworthy that Paul uses this term to depict the true and essential humanity of Jesus. Johannes Schneider (*TDNT* 7:956) writes that *schēma* "does not merely indicate the coming of Jesus, or His physical constitution, or the natural determination of His earthly life, or the shape of His moral character. It denotes the 'mode of manifestation.' The reference is to His whole nature and manner as man." It describes Christ as the perfect and complete human, the pattern for all humanity, the second Adam, who, by his resurrection establishes a new order (1 Cor. 15:20–28). Christ as the *schēma* becomes for Paul the litmus test for both Jews and Gentiles. Everyone is measured against the sinless Christ. Men who have sex with men do not emulate the image or *schēma* of Christ. Thus, in Romans 1:27, Paul very powerfully refers to their conduct as *aschēmosynēn*, acts that are literally *out of order*.

The excellent work of Richard Hays, who has marshaled a number of arguments against the methods and conclusions of Boswell, supports this conclusion. He maintains (1986: 196) that "in Paul's time the categorization of homosexual practices as *para physin* was a commonplace feature of polemical attacks against such behavior, particularly in the world of Hellenistic Judaism." I conclude this section with a passage from Hays that precisely encapsulates Paul's view of nature in Romans 1 (p. 194):

> Though he offers no explicit reflection on the concept of "nature," it is clear that in this passage Paul identifies "nature" with the created order. The understanding of "nature" in this conventional language does not rest on empirical observation of what actually exists; instead, it appeals to an intuitive conception of what ought to be, of the world as designed by God. Those who indulge in sexual practices *para physin* are defying the creator and demonstrating their own alienation from him.

Conclusion

Romans 1 will always be a key chapter in the discussion of homosexuality in the Bible. Revisionist interpretations, among other things, narrow the application of Paul's words to pederasty, restrict the meaning of the term *nature* to the condition of individual pagans, and deny the relevance of creation to Paul's thought. All of these arguments, in their various forms, fall short of the power of the gospel, which transformed Saul, the persecutor of Christians, into Paul, the servant of Christ. The sinful condition of humanity, illustrated (but not fully exhausted) by the example of homosexuality in Romans 1, serves as the point of departure for Paul's demonstration of the gospel as the means to change people from wanton slaves of their own lust to holy vessels for God's indwelling. Of this change, the apostle Paul had personal experience through faith in the risen Christ, and to this end the letter to the Romans is written.

Paul's description of homosexuality in Romans 1 leads to only one conclusion consistent with his theology: the gospel "is the power of God for salvation to every one who believes" (Rom. 1:16). It is clear that homosexuals are included in this category, as will be seen in our study of 1 Corinthians 6:9–11. In a critical review of Robin Scroggs's *New Testament and Homosexuality*, D. F. Wright accurately summarizes the proper attitude toward Paul's view of same-gender sex (1985: 120):

> Perhaps he was capable of seeing the connections . . . between the Old Testament's condemnation of homosexual acts, its sexual anthropology grounded in Genesis, in divine creation and contemporary sexual disorder in Mediterranean society. Perhaps he had the insight to embrace a con-

demnation of pederasty, respectable and disreputable alike, in a more comprehensive verdict that judged all homosexual behaviour, male and female, to be contrary to God-given nature. Perhaps—what a thought!—the New Testament may even have something directly to say about homosexuality today.

One could only conclude that Paul's proclamation of the gospel was nothing but empty words if he did not apply it in some way to the homosexual's need for transformation. What, if anything, does Paul say about key questions facing us today, such as: What is the role of homosexuals in the church? Shall the church accept them with open arms? If so, how should this be the case when, to use Paul's language in Romans 1, God so vehemently expressed his anger toward them. This is stressed three times: God "gave them over in the lusts of their hearts to impurity," "gave them over to degrading passions," and "gave them over to a depraved mind" (vv. 24, 26, 28). Since Paul already affirmed the universality of the gospel, is it not a contradiction to say that God has so abandoned homosexuals? How then, according to Paul, can one who is a homosexual be reconciled to God?

13

Homosexuals and the Kingdom of God

Do you not know that the unrighteous shall not inherit the kingdom of God? Do not be deceived; neither fornicators, nor idolaters, nor adulterers, nor effeminate, nor homosexuals, nor thieves, nor covetous, nor drunkards, nor revilers, nor swindlers, shall inherit the kingdom of God. And such were some of you; but you were washed, but you were sanctified, but you were justified in the name of the Lord Jesus Christ, and in the Spirit of our God.

—1 Corinthians 6:9–11

But we know that the law is good, if one uses it lawfully, realizing the fact that law is not made for a righteous man, but for those who are lawless and rebellious, for the ungodly and sinners, for the unholy and profane, for those who kill their fathers or mothers, for murderers and immoral men and homosexuals and kidnappers and liars and perjurers, and whatever else is contrary to sound teaching, according to the glorious gospel of the blessed God, with which I have been entrusted.

—1 Timothy 1:8–11

I n two controversial passages, the apostle Paul encapsulates his view of homosexuality and its connection to both the law of the Old Testament and the gospel of the New Testament. Before coming to the terms for homosexuality and reconciliation that are the focus of 1 Corinthians 6:9–11 and 1 Timothy 1:8–11, it should be observed that Paul places them in the larger context of the law and, hence, the Old Testament. The first passage is addressed to the believers at Corinth, a city where homosexuality was extensively practiced, as a reminder of the believer's position in Christ, for some members of the church there had compromised their faith, apparently in matters of doctrine as well as practice: "You yourselves wrong and defraud, and that your brethren" (1 Cor. 6:8). The second passage is intended to instruct the young pastor Timothy in sound doctrine so that he may give wise counsel to his flock.

The purpose in both passages is to sharply differentiate between the righteous (who enter the kingdom of God) and the unrighteous (who do not). Righteousness and unrighteousness are legal terms in Paul's writings. Fulfilling the requirements of the law marks the character of the believer in Christ, the one who walks "in the Spirit" as opposed to "in the flesh," as the apostle clearly says in another place: "For what the Law could not do, weak as it was through the flesh, God did: sending his own son in the likeness of sinful flesh and as an offering for sin, he condemned sin in the flesh, in order that the requirement of the Law might be fulfilled in us, who do not walk according to the flesh, but according to the Spirit" (Rom. 8:3–4). This fulfillment is not a utopian ideal for the apostle, as though it were to be achieved only in an eschatological or future kingdom of God. It is the normal daily experience of a person changed by God's grace and enlightened by his Spirit through faith in Jesus Christ, just as the apostle himself had been changed and enlightened. Paul, the man who had vehemently "persecute[d] the church of God beyond measure, and tried to destroy it" (Gal. 1:13), who was "formerly a blasphemer and a persecutor and a violent aggressor" (1 Tim. 1:13), could also say, "I have been crucified with Christ; and it is no longer I who live, but Christ lives in me; and the life which I now live in the flesh I live by faith in the son of God, who loved me, and delivered himself up for me" (Gal. 2:20). Herein is the essence of the changed apostle. Having experienced the mercy of God through Christ, he pursued good works (Titus 3:8, 14) in order to serve "as an example for those who would believe in him for eternal life" (1 Tim. 1:16).

Placed in this perspective, the issue surrounding a proper understanding of the biblical view of homosexuality is nothing short of everlasting life. That is why Paul's list of violations in 1 Corinthians 6:9 begins with an imperative: "Do not be deceived." The Greek suggests a concern to stop action already in progress, rather than forbidding the beginning of an action (Brooks and Winbery 1979: 116). Apparently the Corinthians had already been deceived on the subject of homosexuality and the other offenses in this list. Some of them may have returned to their former practices, so Paul writes to clarify their status as believers. In this chapter I will first examine the two Greek nouns Paul uses for homosexuality and than the three Greek verbs he uses for reconciliation.

Paul's Language of Homosexuality

At 1 Corinthians 6:9 two terms refer to homosexuals: *malakos* (μαλακός, "effeminate") and *arsenokoitēs* (ἀρσενοκοίτης, "homosexual"). Since these are the only terms Paul uses for "homosexual," they are worthy of close scrutiny.

The word *malakos* is used only three times in the New Testament (Matt. 11:8; Luke 7:25; 1 Cor. 6:9). The basic meaning, "soft," is clear when it is used of things. For example, Jesus asks the multitude about John the Baptist: "What did you go out into the wilderness to look at? A reed shaken by the wind? But what did you go out to see? A man dressed in soft (*malakois*) clothing? Behold, those who are splendidly clothed and live in luxury are found in royal palaces" (Luke 7:24–25; see also Matt. 11:8). *Malakos* is used of persons only once in the New Testament, at 1 Corinthians 6:9, and there it means "soft, effeminate, esp. of catamites, men and boys and who allow themselves to be misused homosexually" (BAGD 489). BAGD cites numerous examples from Greek literature where *malakos* is used in this way. The term *catamite*, derived from the name Ganymede, the boy in Greek mythology who was raped by Zeus, refers to the passive partner in the homosexual act.

The term *arsenokoitēs* is a compound that seems to have been used by Paul for the first time. The first part of the word, *arseno-*, means "male," while the second part of the word, *-koitai*, means "sexual intercourse." There is no ambiguity to either of these terms when used separately. It is a matter of some curiosity, therefore, as to why some writers on homo-

sexuality perceive such ambiguity when the apostle Paul creates from
these words a compound to accurately convey his meaning. Within the
context of 1 Corinthians, *arsenokoitēs* refers to the active partner in the
homosexual act (a view confirmed by Grosheide 1976: 140).

Today, there is strong opposition to this view. One of the leading
voices is that of John Boswell, who uses an entire appendix entitled "The
Lexicography of Saint Paul" to strip the homosexual meaning from
malakoi and *arsenokoitai*. After stating that "no modern translations of
these terms are very accurate" (1980: 339), Boswell (pp. 339–41) identifies what he sees as three lexical errors made in the literature on this
subject:

1. The word *malakos* is wrongly associated with homosexuality. In
   the ancient world gay men were not considered effeminate unless
   they had feminine characteristics. Patristic sources use a number
   of Greek terms for "effeminate" but not *malakos*; it was generally
   applied to masturbation or moral laxity.
2. *Malakos* is sometimes applied to obviously gay persons in classical literature. This is, however, no proof that it has "some inherent relationship to homosexuality," since in ancient literature
   many people, for many different reasons, were denigrated as
   malakoi. The most valid inference is that *malakos* has no specific
   link to homosexuality.
3. That *malakoi* and *arsenokoitai* at 1 Corinthians 6:9 represent the
   active and passive roles in homosexual intercourse cannot be lex-
   icographically supported. The context at 1 Timothy suggests that
   the association of *pornoi* and *arsenokoitai* concerns prostitution,
   male heterosexual, and, perhaps in one case, male homosexual.
   Assuming that *porneia* means prostitution, and given the thirty references to *pornos* and its derivatives in Paul's writing compared
   to its rare references to homosexuality, one may infer that Paul
   was more troubled by prostitution than homosexuality.

Boswell's objections suffer from substantial evidence, which I shall show
in the following discussion of *malakos* and *arsenokoitēs*.

Malakoi: The Passive Role

Exact meanings for terms like *malakos* are especially difficult to obtain
when the terms are found rarely and then in texts from which we are
greatly removed by time and culture. In this case, even the Septuagint,

which uses the adjectival form of *malakos* only three times, reveals little: Proverbs 25:15 (a gentle tongue that can break a bone); 26:22 (tender meat); and Job 41:3 (gentle words). In each case, it translates the Hebrew term *rak* (רך, "soft, delicate, tender"), which is elsewhere used of children who are frail and too weak to travel (Gen. 33:13) or metaphorically of someone who is timid and weak of heart (Deut. 20:8). In Deuteronomy 28:54–57, *rak* is used to describe the weakness and delicateness of both men and women.

The Septuagint and the Hebrew Bible reveal no places where *malakos* is used of homosexuality or in any sexual sense whatever. It simply describes someone who is weak, frail, delicate. A study of the noun *malakia* (μαλακία, "softness, weakness, ailment") in the New Testament, Septuagint, and Hebrew Bible yields the same result.

At best, until further data becomes available, the term *malakos* must go without the precise definition demanded by Boswell. There is no doubt that the term is negative, indicating an unrighteousness sufficient to exclude from the kingdom of God. *Malakos* was used in ancient times of passive homosexuals in Greece. Unfortunately, the term is not addressed in standard reference works such as the *Theological Dictionary of the New Testament*. BAGD admits the reference of *malakos* to homosexuals, and we have some direct evidence from sources like Lucian. On this basis, the burden of proof is on those who say that *malakos* does not or cannot refer to the passive homosexual role.

We are not, however, without further evidence for the effeminate role that the term *malakos* suggests. Classical Greek sources report passive or effeminate roles as well as aggressive active roles for homosexuals. Two classes of homosexuals are described in Greek literature: *eromenos* (ἐρόμενος) is the passive partner in the sexual act (another common word for this role is *pais*, παῖς, "boy, child"), and *erastēs* (ἐραστής) is the active partner, frequently portrayed in Greek art as chasing, capturing, subduing, and performing anal or intercrural intercourse with the *eromenos*. Kenneth Dover (1989: 79), an expert in this area of study, depicts a change in homosexual preferences for the effeminate:

Hellenistic poetry suggests that after the fourth century [B.C.] there was a certain shift of taste towards feminine characteristics in *eromenoi*. The adolescent Philinos in Theokritos 7.105, with whom Aratos is despairingly in love, is *malthakos*, "soft," "unmanly." . . . *Hapalos*, "supple," "tender," "soft" (Asklepiades 20, Meleagros 76), distinguishes adolescence from maturity, not simply female from male; there are other words, e.g., *habros* (Polystratos 1) and *trupheros* (Meleagros 61), which convey a suggestion of soft living, delicacy and fastidiousness, and thus indirectly a suggestion of effeminacy, without specifically indicating a female physique.

In the period of Greek society before the apostle Paul, female characteristics in a boy were a stimulus to homosexual desire. This was apparently not true for the earlier classical period in Greece, the fifth century B.C. and before, when *eromenoi* were portrayed as muscular and handsome and especially with broad shoulders and strong thighs, athletes of the first order. The shift toward homosexual interest in effeminate-looking males during the fourth century "derives some support from a consideration of the history of human shape, stance and movement in vase-painting" (Dover 1989: 69–70). These paintings show in explicit detail the homosexual acts involving effeminate males in the passive role. The Greeks practiced homosexuality, and they perceived of passive-effeminate and active-aggressor roles. None of the terms cited by Dover are used only of homosexuality, that is, they have no "inherent relationship to homosexuality," yet no one would deny that these terms describe the type of homosexual conduct pictured in Greek art. It is plausible, therefore, to accept the view that *malakos* was Paul's term for the passive partner in the homosexual relationship, the Classical Greek *eromenos*. That he chose the term *malakos* to express the idea of softness or effeminacy rather than any of several other Greek terms is simply a matter of style.

In an effort to negate the possibility that *malakoi* and *arsenokoitai* refer to homosexual conduct, Boswell presents another *a priori* argument that uses this syllogism: the word *pornoi* in 1 Timothy means "prostitution"; *arsenokoitai* appears with it in context; therefore, *arsenokoitai* means "prostitution." A neat package indeed. Taking a quantitative approach, like the failed approach we saw him use with respect to *yādaͨ* in the Sodom story, Boswell leads us to believe that Paul is more interested in prostitution, because he refers to it more frequently than he does homosexuality. Then, by a quantum leap in logic, *malakos*, formerly not associated with *arsenokoitai* in Boswell's mind, becomes "prostitution" or "whatever is meant by *porneia*" (p. 341). The semantic field of *porneia* deserves special study, but it cannot be restricted to prostitution. It is rather a more general term for sexual immorality under which *malakos* may be classed. Homosexuality is encompassed by it.

Arsenokoitai: The Active Role

The standard New Testament lexicon, BAGD (not cited by Boswell and company), translates *arsenokoitai* as "a male who practices homosexuality, pederast, sodomite" (p. 109). Boswell prefers to translate this term as "male prostitute" and so restricts it, but this cannot be accepted. Darrell Lance (1989: 147) follows in Boswell's footsteps, concluding that no certain meaning can be found for *arsenokoitai*: "In short, Boswell's work has raised such doubts about the meaning of *arsenokoitai* and by extension the preceding word *malakoi* that 1 Corinthians 6:9–11 and 1 Timothy 1:10 must be put in brackets for the time being in the ongoing discussion of the Bible and homosexuality." Neither of these authors apparently opened their Greek Bibles to the legal texts at Leviticus 18:22 and 20:13. In almost twenty pages of appendix on this subject, Boswell never mentions the Septuagint. Yet Paul's use of Septuagint quotations is well known. A glance at the Septuagint is quite revealing.

As we try to understand this term, we should remember that the Corinthians of Paul's day must have inherited many of the practices that had characterized their city from the preceding centuries. However, it is wrong to suppose that the Greek culture and Paul's culture of Judaism have everything in common. They come to the subject of homosexuality from completely different foundational beliefs. According to Dover (1989: 203), "the Greeks neither inherited nor developed a belief that a divine power had revealed to mankind a code of laws for the regulation of sexual behaviour; they had no religious institution possessed of the authority to enforce sexual prohibitions. . . . Fragmented as they were into tiny political units, they were constantly aware of the extent to which morals and manners are local." Paul, on the other hand, had the law as his heritage and a belief in the one God of Israel as his source of inspiration and revelation. When the question of homosexuality came up for him in the church at Corinth, we can accurately suppose that Paul's understanding would be influenced by the Old Testament homosexuality law. And it is on this basis that he uses the term *arsenokoitai*, because it accurately reflects the Hebrew of Leviticus 18:22 and 20:13.

The Hebrew Bible prohibited all sexual relations between members of the same gender. The Septuagint translators rendered *zākār* (זָכָר, "male") with *arsenos* (ἄρσενος), while the periphrastic expression *miškĕbê ᵓiššâ* (אִשָּׁה מִשְׁכְּבֵי, "after the manner of lying with a woman") was translated by an equally periphrastic Greek expression: *meta arsenos ou koimēthēsē koitēn gynaikeian* (μετὰ ἄρσενος οὐ κοιμηθήσῃ κοίτην γυναικείαν) at Leviticus 18:22 and *koimēthē meta arsenos koitēn gynaikos* (κοιμηθῇ μετὰ ἄρσενος κοίτην γυναικός) at Leviticus 20:13. One does not have to be a Greek scholar to see the term *coitus* in this expression. The Greek accurately conveys the meaning of the Hebrew. When the compound *arsenokoitai* is formed from its two components used separately in Leviticus 18 and 20, a convenient and concise expression faithful to the original is created. Thus the term *arsenokoitai*, based on the reading of the Septuagint, means "a male who has sexual intercourse with another male."

There is no reason to restrict the meaning of *arsenokoitai* to "male prostitute." Boswell cites no authorities when he says (p. 107), "The best evidence, however, suggests very strongly that it did not connote homosexuality to Paul or his contemporaries but meant 'male prostitute' until well into the fourth century, after which it became confused with a variety of words for disapproved sexual activity and was often equated with homosexuality." Boswell fails to stand where Paul stood and look back to the Septuagint and the Hebrew text, the real sources of Paul's language, and he therefore misses the meaning of *arsenokoitai*. The term *arsenokoitai* is the counterpart of the Classical Greek term *erastēs*, the active member of the sexual act between males. So Paul explicitly addresses both the passive and active homosexual roles at 1 Corinthians 6:9. Both terms would have been well understood by his Corinthian audience, where homosexuality was common. We do not need to look to the fourth century for an explanation of the term.

A debate continues on the meaning of *arsenokoitēs* (ἀρσενοκοίτης). David F. Wright rejects the conclusions and methodology of Boswell in a thorough analysis of *arsenokoitēs* (1984, 1987), adding support to my view (on the opposite side, see Pedersen 1986: 187). Wright's work is especially valuable for his review of the patristic sources. He concludes (1984: 145):

> That Hellenistic Jewish writings unambiguously condemned the homosexuality encountered among the Greek world is not in doubt. At the same time the moral philosophers of the Hellenistic era were increasingly coming to question homosexual indulgence. The presumption is thus created that *arsenokoitai* came into use, under the influence of the LXX of Leviticus, to denote that homoerotic vice which Jewish writers like Philo, Josephus, Paul and Ps-Phocylides regarded as a signal token of pagan Greek depravity.

To accurately reflect the Hebrew underlying the Septuagint of Leviticus 18:22, *arsenokoitai* cannot refer to male prostitution as Boswell claims. It appears to be a term that signifies to the male aggressor in homosexual relationships.

One of the greatest problems in the debate on homosexuality in the Bible is the assumption that the New Testament writers no longer cared for the Old Testament. This becomes true for the aging church, and by the twentieth century, it is true in practice, if not in principle. The New Testament writers, however, depended heavily on the Old Testament for their understanding of God's revelation in history, law, theology, and prophecy. It is only in the context of the Old Testament that the New Testament can be understood. This is particularly true of the passages that deal with homosexuality.

Neither Jesus nor Paul abrogate the Old Testament law in Marcionite fashion. To the contrary both hold that "the Law is good" and that "law is not made for a righteous man, but for those who are lawless and rebellious, for the ungodly (*asebesi*, ἀσεβέσι) and sinners, for the unholy and profane, for those who kill their fathers or mothers, for murderers and immoral men (*pornois*, πόρνοις) and homosexuals (*arsenokoitais*, ἀρσενοκοίταις) and kidnappers and liars and perjurers, and whatever else is contrary to sound teaching" (1 Tim. 1:8–10). Notice the association of homosexuality with terms from the semantic field of purity and impurity, terms like "ungodly," "unholy," and "profane." What source would inform the meaning of these terms if not the levitical writings and the Old Testament view of order?

John Yates addresses the theological aspect of this emphasis by pointing to the male-female complementarity of Genesis 1 as a reflection of the internal diversity of the trinity. The analogy to the unity of God constitutes ontological differences between male and female that do not exist in homosexual relations. According to Yates, homosexual practice is disordered and dehumanizing. He concludes (1995: 85):

> It necessarily follows that to seek sexual fulfilment outside of the heterosexual arrangement is to violate the order of creation. Homosexuality, as a displacement within the ontological order, must have the status of a dysteleology. It fails on each of the counts represented as the purpose of sex in the first two chapters of Genesis. The homosexual act does not contain within it even the possibility of a willingness to procreate. As such it is an implicit denial of one of the good ends to which God has ordered sexuality, it is on this basis vocationless, unable to generate a new centre outside of itself around which a family grows, develops and serves society. In the case of homosexuality, sex adds nothing essential to the love of a couple.

A final note. To understand Paul's view of reconciliation of the homosexual, one must fully appreciate the unity of 1 Corinthians 5–6 (Deming 1996: 289) and his view of sexual sin as body defilement. The unity question is important because the discussion about homosexuality in 1 Corinthians 6:9–11 is framed by two analogies: incest (5:1–13) and prostitution (6:12–20). These issues should not be judged by a human court (6:1–9); they belong to the realm of divine jurisprudence, as we might expect from our study of Leviticus 18. These chapters present a sexual treatise, culminating in the conclusion that sexual sins are uniquely defiling. Bruce Fisk concludes his study of this issue as follows (1996: 558): "Paul can declare sexual sin to be fundamentally different. Other sins may be physically destructive (e.g. suicide, gluttony), corporately destructive (e.g. gossip, divisiveness), or spiritually defiling (e.g. idolatry), but for Paul, because sexual sin is uniquely body-joining, it is uniquely body-defiling." The term for body-defiling sexual acts is *porneia*.

A distinction should be made between *porneia* (πορνεία) and the other terms we have been discussing. By the time Paul wrote to Timothy, *porneia* had come to be a general term for sexual immorality (translated "immoral men" in the New American Standard Bible). In Classical Greek literature, it meant "male prostitute," the same meaning it has in the Septuagint as a rendering of *qādēš* (קָדֵשׁ, "male temple prostitute"; Deut. 23:18; 1 Kings 14:24; 22:46). Even though Demosthenes (*Orations* 19.200) used *porneia* of homosexuality in the fourth century B.C., Paul could not use it to refer to homosexuality because *porneia* had by then assumed the more general meaning of "sexual immorality," and it may even have carried the older meaning of "temple prostitute." Perhaps for this reason, he chooses to invent the compound *arsenokoitai* and use the term *malakos*. He did not want to allow room for ambiguity. On this basis, both active and passive homosexuality are forbidden in Paul's correspondence to the Corinthians and Timothy.

Paul's Language of Reconciliation

No discussion of homosexuality in the Bible can be complete without a careful analysis of 1 Corinthians 6:11, for it is the source of certainty in an otherwise tumultuous sea of confusion. In the following paragraphs, each term is examined in detail. It is essential to understand the meaning of four Greek verbs in order to appreciate the New Testament perspective on reconciling the homosexual. The first provides a point of transition, contrasting the status of the homosexual before the action presented by the remaining three verbs.

The expression *and such were some of you* at 1 Corinthians 6:11 introduces three verbs that clarify the means by which the categories of sinners in the previous verses have access to the kingdom of God. The imperfect-tense verb *ēte* (ἦτε, "were") depicts a change that has occurred. Greek tenses describe "kinds of action," defined by grammarians as continuous, complete, or occurring (Dana and Mantey 1927: 178). The imperfect tense may be interpreted in one of several ways. The "descriptive imperfect" describes what was actually happening at some time in the past. The "durative imperfect" represents prolonged action in the past: "An act which began in the past is depicted as having continued over a period of time up to some undefined point. Presumably the action has been completed, else the present tense would have been used" (Brooks and Winbery 1979: 83). The "iterative imperfect" emphasizes the repetition of the action: "Sometimes the repetition takes the form of a practice or custom. Such expressions as 'kept on' and 'used to' may be used in the translation" (p. 84). Instead of a mere snapshot, the imperfect tense gives a kind of video or movie of consecutive frames as it describes action in the past. It portrays the conduct of whoever is described. Hence, the sinful actions of the Corinthians were progressive, customary, or repeated in the past; they kept on doing them. But what they were in the past is not what they are in the present, because they have been changed.

In describing this change in the Corinthians, Paul uses verbs that recall the language of impurity and cleansing seen earlier in the levitical purifying of the sanctuary with the blood of the slain goat (Lev. 16). The agent for this cleansing is the blood of Christ: "For it was the Father's good pleasure for all the fulness to dwell in him, and through him to reconcile all things to himself, having made peace through the blood of his cross" (Col. 1:19–20a). Entrance into the kingdom's favored status is based on an act of God according to Paul: "For he delivered us from the domain of darkness, and transferred us to the kingdom of his beloved Son, in whom we have redemption, the forgiveness of sins. And he is the image of the invisible God, the firstborn of all creation" (Col. 1:13–15; see also 2 Cor. 4:4).

Two metaphors are merged by Paul: the image of God and the temple. He transfers the imagery of the temple/sanctuary in the levitical system to the temple of the body, aware that Jesus had compared his own body to the temple: "Jesus answered and said to them, 'Destroy this temple, and in three days I will raise it up.' The Jews therefore said, 'It took forty-six years to build this temple, and will you raise it up in three days?' But he was speaking of the temple of his body" (John 2:19–21). Earlier in his letter to the Corinthians, Paul made the explicit comparison of the body to the temple: "Do you not know that you are a temple of God, and that the Spirit of God dwells in you? If any man destroys the temple of God, God will destroy him, for the temple of God is holy, and that is what you are" (1 Cor. 3:16–17). It is possible to see the whole picture that Paul is painting with respect to homosexuality and other sins that exclude people from the kingdom of God. From his understanding of the creation of humans in God's image and the sanctuary/temple as the focal point for God's presence; from the legal restrictions about the danger of impurity generated by deliberate sins and his knowledge of the penalties imposed for homosexual acts; and from his knowledge that Christ is the image of God in human form, the temple or body par excellence to which all believers must conform because their "bodies are members of Christ" (1 Cor. 6:15)—it is not surprising that Paul concludes with a categorical imperative regarding sexual purity: "Flee immorality (*porneian*, πορνείαν). Every other sin that a man commits is outside the body, but the immoral man sins against his own body. Or do you not know that your body is a temple of the Holy Spirit who is in you, whom you have from God, and that you are not your own? For you have been bought with a price: therefore glorify God in your body" (1 Cor. 6:18–20).

It remains for us to consider what Paul means when he writes, "But you were washed, but you were sanctified, but you were justified in the name of the Lord Jesus Christ, and in the Spirit of our God" (1 Cor. 6:11). These three verbs summarize aspects of the change that transfers a person from the bondage of sin to the kingdom of God. In order, they describe the transformation of the individual with respect to self, to society, and to God.

Each verb is introduced by the strong adversative conjunction *alla* (ἀλλά). Normally translated "but," expressing sharp contrast to what has come before, this conjunction also has a confirming or emphatic nuance (Dana and Mantey 1927: 240). The repeated use of *alla* by Paul suggests that he meant to put some distance between what the Corinthians were before and what they are after the change. Paul could have used either the imperfect tense or the aorist tense to express action in past time. The aorist or "indefinite" tense is used when a writer wishes to show that action has been completed. (One Greek scholar compares the aorist to a sort of flashlight picture and the imperfect to a time exposure; Robertson 1914: 1380.) In choosing the aorist for these three verbs, Paul emphasizes that the actions of cleansing, sanctifying, and justifying have been accomplished. They have completed a change in the condition and orientation of those who were practicing homosexuality and the other vices listed in 1 Corinthians 6:9–10.

Apelousasthe

The first term, *apelousasthe* (ἀπελούσασθε, "you were washed"), is the aorist middle form of *apolouō* (ἀπολούω, "to cleanse, wash oneself"). *Apolouō* is used elsewhere in the New Testament only at Acts 22:16: "And now why do you delay? Arise, and be baptized, and wash away your sins, calling on his name." The middle voice in Greek has several meanings, none of which is exactly paralleled in English. Syntactic or contextual evidence is therefore essential in translating the middle voice. Eugene Goetchius (1965: 104) isolates three main features:

1. The middle voice may express a direct reflexive meaning; i.e., the subject of a verb in the middle voice may indicate both the performer *and* the receiver of the action indicated by the verb. This is probably the least common meaning of the middle voice.
2. The middle voice may express an indirect reflexive meaning; i.e., the subject of a verb in the middle voice may indicate both the performer of the action and "that to or for which the action is performed." When so used, a verb in the middle voice may govern a noun or pronoun in the accusative case, which functions in the same way as the direct object of a verb in the active voice.
3. The middle voice may express a causative meaning; i.e., the subject of the verb in the middle voice may indicate the person who causes or allows an action to be performed.

The second feature does not apply since there is no noun or pronoun governed by the verb in our case. But the direct reflexive and causative meanings may be implicit in 1 Corinthians 6:11.

The reflexive meaning would suggest that believers appropriate the cleansing for themselves, as though they were applying soap and water to themselves in a literal washing procedure, but perhaps also figuratively as they become personally involved in the process of applying the blood of Christ to cleanse from sin. According to this meaning of the middle voice, believers show their participation in the cleansing process by performing an act of faith in the effectiveness of Christ's blood to cleanse, the outward symbol of which is the act of baptism according to Acts 22:16. In this view, baptism itself may be reflected literally in the term *apelousasthe*.

The causative meaning of the middle voice shows the subject of the verb as the person who allows the cleansing to take place. This meaning of the verb is closer to the aorist passive. In fact, there may not have been much difference between the middle and passive voices, for in speaking of the aorist passive, Archibald Robertson (1914: 816), whose work has become the standard New Testament Greek grammar, comments that "in Homer the aorist middle form, like the other middle forms, was sometimes used as passive." Thus we should be careful not to make too much of the possible theological nuances of the reflexive middle voice, especially because we want to avoid the suggestion that sinners can cleanse themselves from sin apart from the blood of Christ. Nevertheless, in Paul's use of the middle voice we can see that the intent of the individual is necessary before the act of cleansing from sin can be accomplished by God. There is no synergism in salvation. It is the work of God through Christ. The sinner, however, by an act of the will through faith, must appropriate the cleansing blood of Christ, which purges from sin. In this view, the verb *apelousasthe* suggests that the sinner is involved in the cleansing event by placing himself or herself in the proper frame of mind to permit God to do the work of cleansing.

The background for Paul's thought on cleansing may be found in the metaphorical use of the term *ṭāmēʾ* (טָמֵא) by Ezekiel. The prophet associated purification with deliverance from sin in the areas of unclean conduct as well as idolatry. The cleansing has import not only for the sinner but also for the name of God: "By cleansing Israel, Yahweh vindicates the holiness of his profaned name. In similar fashion, Ps. 106:34–39 states that Israel has become unclean through its idolatry, which has polluted (*ḥānēp* [חָנֵף]) the land and made the people of Yahweh abhorred (*tʿb* [תעב] piel, v. 40)" (G. André, *TDOT* 5:338). Given his rabbinic training, it is likely that Paul would have thought of the profanation of God's name in the context of his reference to homosexual conduct and the requirement for cleansing.

Hēgiasthēte

The verb *hēgiasthēte* (ἡγιάσθητε, "you have been sanctified") at 1 Corinthians 6:11 is cast in the aorist passive of the verb *hagiazō* (ἁγιάζω, "to be holy, sanctified, set apart, consecrated"). The background of this term for Paul was most certainly his knowledge of the Hebrew *qādôš* (קָדוֹשׁ, "holy, sacred"), calling to mind the entire complex of purity-impurity rules that informed the levitical system. According to BAGD (p. 8), *hagiazō*, when used of persons, means to "include in the inner circle of what is holy, in both relig[ious] and moral uses of the word. . . . So of the Christians, who are consecrated by baptism." Thus the act of setting apart or sanctifying is focused on the body of believers, the kingdom of God. Baptism is a sign of entrance into the kingdom of God. Surely this must have occurred to the apostle in writing this verb. However, holiness in ancient Israel carried an additional emphasis of the relationship of those who were set apart to the surrounding nations. Israel as a holy people was to stand in sharp contrast to the impure nations in the matter of their faith in Yahweh and moral conduct. In this verb, we see the relationship of the cleansed sinner to society. Implied in this verb is the idea that any act of sin has an effect on society and therefore cannot be perpetrated without impunity.

Edikaiōthēte

The term *edikaiōthēte* (ἐδικαιώθητε, "you were justified"), from the verb *dikaioō* (δικαιόω), is also aorist passive—the subject is the recipient of the action. The aorist tense may be described as "punctiliar," represented as a point (.), as opposed to "linear," represented as a continuous line (___); the kind of action in the aorist is therefore completed action or finished work (Robertson 1914: 823). If we understand the term *edikaiōthēte* in this sense, Paul states that based on the completed works of cleansing and sanctifying, the sinner is justified by God. God declares the sinner righteous or just. The declaration of righteousness is a forensic act of God on behalf of the sinner, cleansed and sanctified. God's wrath toward sin is appeased through the blood of Christ. Whatever the sinner may have done before this declaration has been forgiven, and a positive relationship to God has been restored. Thus in this verse, the cleansed and sanctified homosexual is no longer liable to divine punishment, and entrance into the kingdom of God is assured. Paul's attitude toward the homosexual may be inferred by his stance regarding someone who had committed incest.

The Incest Analogy

Paul certainly would have been familiar with the list of sexual violations in Leviticus 18, for there homosexuality is juxtaposed to incest (vv. 6–18). The apostle left no references to cases of homosexuality, but he does record an incident of incest in his correspondence to the Corinthians. From his management of the incest case, it is not difficult to predict how Paul might have handled homosexual conduct in the churches of his affiliation. Since the analogy of incest to homosexuality has not been broached before, this case must be discussed in some detail, first as to the nature of the case, next as to the specific rule by which the severe penalty is imposed by Paul, and finally as to the implication for homosexual conduct.

The case is stated at 1 Corinthians 5:1–13. Someone in the church at Corinth is guilty of having sex with his father's wife. Aware of the universal law against incest, Paul states that this custom is not even practiced among the Gentiles who are spiritually unenlightened, implying that someone who has experienced God's favor through Christ should avoid such heinous conduct. Incest falls under the general term of *porneia* ("immorality"). Boswell (1980: 115 n. 74) suggests that "the exact meaning of πορνεία [*porneia*] in NT writings is unclear," but it is plain in this case that the term encompasses the crime of incest. This is exactly opposite to what Boswell says in another place (p. 104) that "the word πορνεία occurs in discussions of sexual immorality as a specific type of behavior, not as the general designation for such activity." He deduces this view from two verses, both of which are from Paul:

> I may mourn over many of those who have sinned in the past and not repented of the impurity (*akatharsia*, ἀκαθαρσία), immorality (*porneia*, πορνεία) and sensuality (*aselgeia*, ἀσελγεία) which they have practiced. (2 Cor. 12:21)

> Now the deeds of the flesh are evident, which are: immorality (*porneia*, πορνεία), impurity (*akatharsia*, ἀκαθαρσία), sensuality (*aselgeia*, ἀσελγεία), idolatry, sorcery, enmities, strife, jealousy, outbursts of anger, disputes, dissensions, factions, envyings, drunkenness, carousings, and things like these, of which I forewarn you just as I have forewarned you that those who practice such things shall not inherit the kingdom of God. (Gal. 5:19–21)

Over several pages, Boswell wrings out of the New Testament text any reference to condemnation of homosexuality and concludes (p. 115) that

> for Paul, Christian sexuality had little to do with "purity" of seed ("All things are lawful unto me," 1 Cor. 6:12) or of procreative justification for sexual pleasure . . . but was, rather, a question of good stewardship—of using sexuality in a way that was not obsessive ("All things are lawful for me, but I will not be brought under the power of any," 6:12), did not cause scandal, and did not distract Christians from the service of the Lord ("that ye may attend upon the Lord without distraction," 7:35 . . .). There is no inherent reason why unions between persons of the same sex could not have met these moral criteria.

Boswell's libertarian view of the apostle Paul's words does not agree with the incest story. It is precisely on the ground of impurity in the levitical law that incest and homosexuality were categorically forbidden, and it is precisely on this ground that Rabbi Paul forbade them also. The penalty for the sexual violations recorded in Leviticus 18 was *kareth*, the divine penalty of extinction of the individual and offspring. Paul complains that the Corinthians "have become arrogant, and have not mourned instead, in order that the one who had done this deed might be removed from your midst" (1 Cor. 5:2). One can see in this an amelioration of the death penalty that was to be carried out by the community according to our understanding of the law in Leviticus 20. Excommunication is expected by Paul, but the church has not carried it out. Therefore, as with the *kareth* penalty, which befell the sinner and the community in the Old Testament economy in the event that responsibility was not assumed for execution, Paul appeals to divine intervention via a curse on the individual in order to bring about true repentance. His advice is "to deliver such a one to Satan for the destruction of his flesh, that his spirit may be saved in the day of the Lord Jesus" (1 Cor. 5:5). It is precisely on an analogy to the levitical writer's concept of impurity that Paul chooses this severe penalty: "Do you not know that a little leaven leavens the whole lump of dough? Clean out the old leaven, that you may be a new lump, just as you are in fact unleavened. For Christ our Passover also has been sacrificed" (vv. 6–7). When immorality is permitted in the church, the contagion of impurity may infect everyone. Thus with respect to believers, Paul's exhortation is "not to associate with immoral people" (v. 9). "Remove the wicked man from among yourselves" (v. 13).

By what rule does Paul impose this penalty? The eighth hermeneutical rule of Rabbi Ishmael is summarized as follows:

> If a particular instance of a general rule is singled out for special treatment, whatever is postulated of this instance is to be applied to all the instances embraced by the general rule. For example, "A man, also, or a woman that divineth that by a ghost or a familiar spirit, shall surely be put to death; they shall stone them with stones" (Lev. 20:27). Divination by a ghost or familiar spirit is included in the general rule against witchcraft (Deut. 18:10f.). Since the penalty of stoning is applied to these instances, it may be inferred that the same penalty applies to all the other instances embraced by the general rule. (Louis Jacobs, *EJ* 8:369–70, citing the Babylonian Talmud, *Sanhedrin* 67b)

As we saw in the chapter on biblical sanctions and homosexuality, the death penalty and *kareth* are imposed for all of the sex crimes of Leviticus 18 because of the impurity generated by them. That is the general rule. In 1 Corinthians 5, Paul singles out the case of incest for severe penalty, at the very least separation from the body of believers, at worst perhaps the full import of the *kareth* penalty with respect to eternal life. According to the strict guidelines of rabbinic exegesis, the penalty advocated by Paul for incest would also apply to homosexual practice, since it too is embraced by the general rule. Perhaps Paul meant that by deliverance to Satan a premature death might ensue for the offender, while the *kareth* penalty would remain intact unless repentance intervened.

If so, he would be well within the bounds of rabbinic interpretation on the sanctions for incest and by inference for homosexuality.

The clear implication from this analysis of the incest analogy is that any homosexual conduct would have been viewed by Paul as a source of impurity that must be removed at once lest the entire church be destroyed. It is a postulate of biblical religion that individual conduct has a profound effect on society. That "all things are lawful for me" should not be taken literally as modern writers sometimes do to justify certain behaviors. Paul's view of homosexuality, like his view of incest, is firmly centered in the Old Testament law. As early as a century after Saint Paul, some expositors argued that the sin of incest placed the sinner beyond forgiveness. For example, in the second century Tertullian maintained that the

> sin of incest is *irremissible*, involving the "loss of baptism" and the impossibility of the restoration of the sinner to a state of grace and salvation. Accordingly, he insists that "it was not with a view to emendation but with a view to perdition that Paul delivered the incestuous fornicator to Satan, to whom he had already, by sinning above a heathen, gone over"; the condemned offender "had already perished *from the church* at the moment when he had committed such a deed." (Hughes 1962: 61)

As Philip Hughes ably shows, Tertullian's exegesis is unacceptable. Forgiveness awaits even the most egregious sinner according to 2 Corinthians 2:1–11, as long as true repentance and confession has occurred: "For the sorrow that is according to the will of God produces a repentance without regret, leading to salvation; but the sorrow of the world produces death" (7:10). This statement is made by Paul with reference to the sorrow created by his first letter, which had its intended effect. The church at Corinth had repented of its laxity in overlooking the sin of incest in its midst, had expelled the offender, and had then reconciled him on the basis of this repentance. The case of incest is an excellent model for the offense of homosexual conduct from the apostle Paul's perspective. Discipline is required, but it must be discipline with mercy. Hughes (1962: 66–67) contends:

> Discipline which is so inflexible as to leave no place for repentance and reconciliation has ceased to be truly Christian; for it is no less a scandal to cut off the penitent sinner from all hope of re-entry into the comfort and security of the fellowship of the redeemed community than it is to permit flagrant wickedness to continue unpunished in the Body of Christ. The Christian who falls into sin, however deplorable his sin may be, may still look to Jesus Christ the Righteous as his Advocate with the Father (1 Jn. 2:1).

"Christian homosexuality" is an oxymoron. Christianity and the modern gay movement cannot share the same biblical underpinnings. From a biblical perspective, the homosexual, like the incestuous person, falls under the law of condemnation, excluding him or her from the kingdom of God and alienation from the church. At the same time, the homosexual comes under the canopy of God's grace, which permits repatriation to the body of Christ after appropriate repentance, confession, and forgiveness. There is total consistency between the symbolic cleansing process in the levitical system and the cleansing through Christ.

Conclusion

In this chapter, I have argued that the terms *malakoi* and *arsenokoitai*, despite attempts by modern scholars to the contrary, were used by the apostle Paul to designate the passive and active roles in homosexual intercourse. While no background is available for *malakoi* in the Septuagint, it is likely that Paul formed the compound *arsenokoitai* from his knowledge of the terms *arseno* and *koitai* as they appear in the sexual legislation of Leviticus 18 and 20. Classical Greek sources reflect the passive and active roles for homosexuals. It is impossible to restrict the terms *malakoi* and *arsenokoitai* to masturbation, moral laxity, or prostitution. Attempts to do so seem to derive from an interest to remove the sin of homosexuality from the Bible. In the language of Paul, the terms for homosexuality are combined with others in a list of sins, any of which precludes entry into the kingdom of God. Their seriousness cannot be mitigated.

On the other hand, Scripture does not simply condemn the homosexual. A merciful provision is made through the person and work of Christ so that a change in the homosexual's condition may take place. This change is represented by three verbs in 1 Corinthians 6:11 that reflect the transformed homosexual's new relationship to self, society, and God. These verbs are all placed in a completed tense, their results have been accomplished, so that the apostle to the Gentiles could say to the former homosexual believers at Corinth: "And such were some of you; but you were washed, but you were sanctified, but you were justified in the name of the Lord Jesus Christ, and in the Spirit of our God" (1 Cor. 6:11).

14

Conclusion: The Road Ahead

In each individual choice of what the Enemy would call the "wrong" turning, such creatures are at first hardly, if at all, in a state of full spiritual responsibility. They do not understand either the source or the real character of the prohibitions they are breaking. Their consciousness hardly exists apart from the social atmosphere that surrounds them. And of course we have contrived that their very language should be all smudge and blur; what would be a bribe in someone else's profession is a tip or a present in theirs. The job of their Tempters was first, of course, to harden these choices of the Hellward roads into a habit by steady repetition. But then (and this was all-important) to turn the habit into a principle—a principle the creature is prepared to defend. After that, all will go well. Conformity to the social environment, at first merely instinctive or even mechanical—how should a jelly not conform?—now becomes an unacknowledged creed or ideal of Togetherness or Being Like Folks. Mere ignorance of the law they break now turns into a vague theory about it—remember, they know no history— a theory expressed by calling it conventional or Puritan or bourgeois "morality." Thus gradually there comes to exist at the centre of the creature a hard, tight, settled core of resolution to go on being what it is, and even to resist moods that might tend to alter it. It is a very small core; not at all reflective (they are too ignorant) nor defiant (their emotional and imaginative poverty excludes that); almost, in its own way, prim and demure; like a pebble, or a very young cancer. But it will serve our turn. Here at last is a real and deliberate, though not fully articulate, rejection of what the Enemy calls Grace.

—C. S. Lewis, *The Screwtape Letters*

T he commencement address by Screwtape to the denizens of hell summarizes my viewpoint regarding the treatment of the biblical text. C. S. Lewis might have been describing the manner in which revisionists treat the subject of homosexuality in the Bible. In so many ways, they try to strip the plain meaning from the text when it does not conform to their agenda. But the language of Scripture cannot be twisted to one's own advantage. When language becomes "smudge and blur," when "conformity to the social environment" becomes an "unacknowledged creed," and when "ignorance of the law turns into a vague theory about it," it is time to reevaluate the language, creed, ideal, or ignorance of the law. To reject the grace of God after having heard the message of reconciliation in plain, unadulterated language is one thing; to reject it on the basis of "smudge and blur" is quite another.

My purpose throughout this book has been to lead the reader through the unfamiliar territory of the language of homosexuality in the ancient Near East, the Hebrew Bible, and the New Testament, interpreting the Hebrew and Greek expressions for same-gender sexual relations in the context of the different cultures in the ancient world. In the process of pursuing this goal, of necessity we have encountered a wide range of subject matter from both primary and secondary sources. I have attempted to handle all of these sources carefully.

The methods of Humpty Dumpty and Screwtape cannot be applied to the biblical text. We cannot give to the biblical expressions concerning homosexuality whatever meanings we choose. Rejecting textual and literary criticism and other hermeneutical methods that might be described as "deconstructive," let us stay on the high road of a "rehabilitative" approach, a term applied to the work of C. S. Lewis by Bruce Edwards. The Bible must be read as a real, objective text. Let the work of Lewis serve as a model:

> Lewis, in his rehabilitative way, maintained a balance among the components of the reading process that has been lost in the cacophony of competing contemporary critical theories. While believing in the integrity of

the text he avoided the excesses of New Criticism by taking authorial intention seriously and approached the text from within its historical context.
Against the nihilistic and solipsistic extremes of deconstructive critics,
one may extrapolate from Lewis' work a sane model for confronting literary texts. (Edwards 1986: 213)

This method runs in the opposite direction of the modern traffic in literature on the topic of homosexuality. Lewis's approach suggests that
there is a particular meaning to language and a particular direction and
destination toward which language leads. For evangelicals, Scripture is
the guide to this journey. Its author is none other than the Creator himself. But the number of writers who take "authorial intention seriously"
is remarkably few when the issue is socially or politically unpopular,
as in the case of homosexuality. Only a handful of authors write in
defense of the biblical text (Taylor 1995: 4). On the other hand, the traffic is heavy if one goes in the direction of the revisionists, but to do so
is to move without a moral map, influenced by every billboard of tolerance, situation ethics, and relativism.

Since I have provided summaries at the end of each chapter, only a
few points must be underlined here with regard to homosexuality in the
ancient Near East, the Old Testament, and the New Testament. I conclude this chapter with a personal appeal.

The limited resources currently available for the study of homosexuality in the ancient Near East impose certain limitations on any conclusions. There is still much information about the ancient Orient and
homosexuality that must come to light. Some of it no doubt lies hidden in dusty bins of cuneiform tablets in the basements of some of the
world's great museums. More lies beneath the sands of Near Eastern
tells yet untouched by the archeologist's spade. Further research is
required before the biblical picture of homosexuality will be complete
against its ancient cultural background.

A synthesis of sexual practices in the ancient Near East has not been
written, nor has much attention been paid by scholars to the subject of
homosexuality. Examination of homosexuality in the ancient Near East
reveals that the data is sparse, presenting at best a puzzle of which we
have but a few pieces. Consequently, it is possible only to guess at the
larger picture that might lend support to our conclusions. The pieces
we do have suggest that same-gender sexual relations throughout the
ancient Near East were practiced on a limited scale as part of religious
rituals within the strict confines of the cultus or possibly as an expression of sociopolitical dominance. At present, we cannot determine the
precise nature or extent of such practices. To date, no categorical pro-

hibition against homosexual practices has been found for Mesopotamia, Anatolia, or Egypt.

In Mesopotamia, for example, sexual aberrations have been noticed, but the extant legal sources do not provide a concise catalog of sexual crimes like that found in Leviticus 18. The observation by Robert Biggs (1969: 103) is apropos the Mesopotamian data: "There was apparently no taboo against anal intercourse of either a homosexual or a heterosexual nature, so such activity cannot be considered a perversion." Anal intercourse was practiced by temple prostitutes, probably of both genders, perhaps as a means of population control in addition to generating income for the temple.

Egyptian sources depict a possible homosexual relationship between Seth and Horus, and it is possible that certain pharaohs engaged in same-gender sexual contact. No extant legal sources provide a judicial view of homosexuality in Egypt. The Egyptian evidence is very scant.

Homosexuality is mentioned in the Hittite law code, but only with respect to a man who has sexual relations with his son. While the Hittite sources prohibit other aberrant sexual relations (e.g., between man and some beasts) and adulterous unions, documentation for homosexuality from Anatolian sources is lacking. The Hittite sources are most valuable for their detailed presentation of impurity, providing a background against which the biblical purity-impurity concepts can be evaluated. They are also of interest when they omit aspects of the discussion covered in the biblical sources. Thus while the Bible sanctions incest, homosexuality, and bestiality, the Hittite code bans only incest and bestiality (except with a horse).

Same-gender sexual relations are categorically forbidden in the Bible. This is not a new conclusion but is the dominant historical position of the church and the synagogue. In the Old Testament, the Israelites are presented in sharp contrast with their Canaanite and Egyptian neighbors who are said to have practiced homosexuality. A similar contrast is made in the New Testament between the righteous, who have access to the kingdom of God, and the unrighteous, among them homosexuals, who do not. Both the Old and New Testaments make provisions for the transformation of individuals who offend the law so that they may be repatriated to society or the kingdom of God.

In the Old Testament, homosexual acts are portrayed in three narratives: the postdeluvian Noah story, in which the drunken father seems to have been raped by his son Ham, whereupon a curse befalls the Canaanite peoples (Gen. 9:20–27); the Sodom story (Gen. 19); and the account of the men of Gibeah (Judg. 19). The story of Noah provides an etiology for the customs of the Canaanites whose homosexual conduct is condemned in the law (Lev. 18 and 20). Some modern scholars attempt to show that the Sodom story reflects primarily or only inhospitality rather than homosexuality. Our analysis of the linguistic data, however, counteracts this view. Hebrew *yādaᶜ* (יָדַע) and Greek *synginomai* (συγγίνομαι) suggest a homosexual motif in the Sodom story.

We have thoroughly investigated the language of biblical law on the question of same-gender sexual intercourse. The Bible makes a categorical statement against homosexuality: "You shall not lie with a male as one lies with a female; it is an abomination" (Lev. 18:22). A careful study of this law establishes beyond doubt that all same-gender sexual relations are prohibited. The law sanctioned homosexuality and other sexual sins on the premise that they generated an impurity inconsistent with the holiness of Yahweh, Israel's God. This impurity jeopardized both the individual and society, exposing them to the wrath of God. Homosexuality in the Bible cannot be understood apart from appreciation of the biblical writer's concept of impurity. Impurity as the rationale for homosexuality in the law has been virtually ignored in modern discussions of this subject, short of caricatures of cultic practices in ancient Israel.

Two penalties for homosexuality are imposed in biblical law: death at the hand of humans and the *kareth* penalty. Not synonymous, these penalties presume that human conduct as well as its consequences are the product of choice. The transcendent God of Israel demands an absolute holiness consistent with his own attributes; the law, therefore, stipulates the boundaries of sexual behavior. For the violations of Leviticus 18 and 20, death was probably carried out by stoning, not merely as punishment for the individual sinner but as protection for society against the wrath of God. The *kareth* penalty, in its original form a divine curse of extinction of the individual and progeny (with possible implications for the afterlife), is imposed only for deliberate sins and is strictly the prerogative of the deity. It follows in the absence of the death penalty, which the ancient Israelite community was responsible to carry out. The imposition of *kareth* for same-gender sexual relations, heretofore not discussed in the light of the homosexual question, establishes that such acts follow from choices for which the individual bears moral and social responsibility.

Deliberate sins are not covered by the sacrificial system (Num. 15:30–31), but the merciful God of Israel provides a means through which deliberate sins may be commuted to unintentional sins and thereby receive atonement. Confession and repentance enable even the deliberate sinner to participate in the annual Day of Atonement rituals of cleansing the sanctuary, expiating the sin, and appeasing God's wrath. On these conditions, the *kareth* penalty could be avoided.

In my approach to the New Testament and homosexuality, I have addressed the work of certain modern scholars who suggest that Jesus himself may have had homosexual inclinations or even sexual relations—conjectures that are contrary to the biblical data and should be rejected out of hand. Jesus was not a homosexual nor did he in any way support homosexual conduct. At the same time, Jesus had compassion for homosexuals, since his person and work serve as "a ransom for many" (Mark 10:45). No person is excluded from the gospel message that Jesus died and rose again to free the world from bondage to sin.

This freedom is clearly expressed in the correspondence of the apostle Paul to the young churches at Rome and Corinth and to the young pastor Timothy. According to Paul in Romans 1, choice determines homosexual conduct. The sin condition (*yēṣer*, יֵצֶר) is the foundation for homosexual conduct (as it is for all sin). The individual is morally responsible for this inclination, which can be directed toward either good or evil, toward the Spirit or the flesh (Rom. 8). Only the power of God through the Holy Spirit can enable a person to live beyond the power of the sin condition. All sin is generic to the human species, including the sin of homosexuality, but no sin is genetic. Because it is a function of choice, God holds everyone accountable for it. To overcome the tendency to sin, the sinner must be transformed: "Therefore if any man is in Christ, he is a new creature; the old things passed away; behold, new things have come" (2 Cor. 5:17).

Thus, as in the Old Testament, the New Testament does not condemn the homosexual to a life without hope, despite being excluded from the kingdom of God by the practice of homosexuality. The language of 1 Corinthians 6:9–11 makes it abundantly clear that a change is both necessary and possible. By repentance, confession of sin, and faith in Christ Jesus, the homosexual is washed, sanctified, and justified before God. To assume the levitical metaphor, moral impurity is cleansed from the sanctuary, which is the body in the New Testament: "Flee immorality. Every other sin that a man commits is outside the body, but the immoral man sins against his own body. Or do you not know that your body is a temple of the Holy Spirit who is in you, whom you have from God, and that you are not your own? For you have been bought with a price: therefore glorify God in your body" (1 Cor. 6:18–20). Sanctification is the ongoing work of the Holy Spirit in a person's life after regeneration. Justification implies that the requirements of God have been met and his wrath is appeased. The homosexual changed in this way has an open door to the kingdom of God. This change is neither a temporary readjustment of behavior or lifestyle nor the product of a person's own effort. The Holy Spirit effects this change when the repentant sinner turns to Christ.

Because of the mercy extended to homosexuals by God, it is incumbent upon all who accept the Bible as God's authoritative revelation to faithfully represent the biblical model of holiness in their lives. How can an unholy church expect holiness from homosexuals? Too often we Christians condemn conduct in others that we accept in ourselves. It must be remembered that the practice of homosexuality is only one of many deeds of the flesh (Gal. 5:19–21). The fruit of the Spirit must be evident toward those who carry the burden of homosexuality. Homosexuals should not be hated or abused or presented with any other hazard to inhibit their entrance into the kingdom of God. On the other hand, neither should the biblical requirements for sexual conduct nor the measures established for reconciliation be compromised.

This caveat may be emphasized by a case in point. In his recent autobiographical book entitled *Stranger at the Gate: To Be Gay and Christian in America*, Mel White (1994) rejects the interpretation I have given to the biblical texts, largely on the authority of John Boswell's *Christianity, Social Tolerance, and Homosexuality*—very shaky ground indeed. A former evangelical, he is now openly homosexual and currently dean of Dallas's Cathedral of Hope, an affiliate of the gay Universal Fellowship of Metropolitan Community Churches. The position he takes with respect to the Bible and homosexuality deserves mention here, both because he claims to be an authority of Biblical Hebrew and Greek and because his rhetoric is inflammatory against traditional interpretations of the biblical text. White holds (1994: 238) that even though the sixty-six books of the Bible are ancient, written in languages and cultures different from our own, it "is inspired by God and a trustworthy guide for matters of Christian faith and practice." This is no statement of sincere elevation, however, for White continues by denying the Bible's relevance for today (p. 239):

> If you know anything about those six biblical passages used to attack and condemn us [homosexuals], you will admit that the authors never once speak of "sexual orientation." The fact that some people are shaped at conception, at birth, or conditioned in earliest childhood to a lifetime of same-sex intimacy is a scientific discovery less than a century old. And yet Moses lived approximately thirteen hundred years before Christ, and the Apostle Paul wrote his letters to the churches in Rome and Galatia [*sic*] almost two thousand years ago. The ancient prophet and the fiery missionary-preacher were fighting pagan idolatry, temple prostitution, child molestation, and irresponsible sexuality, heterosexual and homosexual alike. They didn't know about today's gay and lesbian people living in committed relationships who lead normal, productive lives, who love God and cherish and honor their families.

This from a man who abandoned his wife and family to pursue his homosexual lifestyle. It is evident that White's view of the Bible as a "guide for matters of Christian faith and practice" is far removed from the one advocated in this book.

It is presumptuous for White to suggest that anyone who takes the Bible seriously will support his view of homosexuality. Thus he comments (p. 239): "My old friends from the religious right say they take the Bible seriously, and I believe them. But I must ask, why do they go on denying the historic, cultural, and linguistic evidence (and modern scientific discoveries) that would help them understand the meanings of those passages for our times?" Even Pope John Paul II comes under attack from White. In a 1993 letter, White disclaims (p. 317): "Because you are unwilling to deal forthrightly with the new biblical, pastoral, psychological and scientific data about homosexuality, you are advocating an anti-gay policy that leads to the suffering and death of God's children in your care." It does not occur to White that his view cannot be supported from the linguistic data. My investigation of the evidence demonstrates that no new biblical data supports homosexuality, nor do current psychological, sociological, or scientific data provide proof for homosexual orientation at birth or through conditioning. One simply cannot ignore the biblical statements about homosexuality and treat Christianity willy-nilly as a kind of no-fault insurance policy against any and all types of behavior, including same-gender sexual intercourse. To own such a policy is far from gaining assurance of eternal life according to the biblical rules of the kingdom.

In a spirit of vindictiveness against the so-called religious right, White presents an agenda to "keep the religious right from doing more wrong." He encourages (p. 320): "Start your own version of a local 'to prevent a gay/lesbian' holocaust museum. Demonstrate the similarity between Hitler's Third Reich and the current tactics of the religious right." He advocates censorship (p. 321): "Organize your new coalitions to call radio and television stations quoting the offenders, suggesting they be taken off the air. Follow up with public or even legal pressure when the inflammatory rhetoric continues. Write letters to the editors against the columnists of the religious right." Above all, White counsels that homosexuals not "give in to the barrage of misinformation, hyperbole, half-truths, and lies. Believe in our cause. It is just. Truth will win the war even though some of us will be wounded and even killed in the battle. Love your enemies. It is still the best weapon we have against the religious right and those who believe their lies" (p. 322).

These references will serve to give the flavor of White's view of the Bible and homosexuality. I agree with him that the Bible requires the believer to love one's enemies. I agree that truth will win in the end. I do not believe in the cause of homosexuals who take White's position on the Bible, for careful study of the biblical text demonstrates the fallacy of it. According to biblical religion, homosexuality is not, as White suggests, a natural and God-given orientation. The Christian response to White's view of homosexuality is plain: the Bible places Mel White and every other homosexual under obligation to be changed through faith in the blood of Christ to be made worthy of the kingdom of God.

Finally, as the debate on homosexuality and the Bible continues, I ask once again that we dedicate ourselves to the method of linguistic analysis, asking that the text become to us what it is, rather than making its words what we wish them to be in the manner of Humpty Dumpty. The biblical writers did not work in a cultural or linguistic vacuum; they were part of a larger sphere of influences that streamed across their paths in a more or less steady flow from Mesopotamia, the Levant, and Egypt. It is hoped that much will come to light in the future from these cultures to enlighten our understanding of homosexuality in the biblical world, since much of what the Bible teaches about homosexuality and many other subjects was part of a concentrated effort to define and maintain the identity of the people of Israel against the background of a cosmopolitan milieu. Listen to the sage advice of Arno Karlen, whose article "Homosexuality in History" offers important balance to subjectivist and revisionist interpretations of homosexuality (1980: 97):

> It is not only inevitable but useful to keep reexamining the past and seeking more from it. But such efforts must always stay rooted in fact and probability. This is difficult if one feels that the integrity of society is threatened. It is equally difficult when concern for public opinion and civil rights tempt one to smudge the line between the world as it is and the world as one would like to see it.

It would be of great benefit to the future of exegesis and interpretation on the subject of homosexuality in the Bible if this advice were heeded.

To bring all thoughts and actions into agreement with the will of God is the goal of biblical religion. To this end the Bible directs all humanity. To this end the blood of Christ was shed on the cross. I cannot close this book without repeating the personal appeal of the apostle Paul with respect to those who are struggling with homosexual desires. It should be the appeal of every Christian: "Therefore, we are ambassadors for Christ, as though God were entreating through us; we beg you on behalf of Christ, be reconciled to God. He made him who knew no sin to be sin on our behalf, that we might become the righteousness of God in him" (2 Cor. 5:20–21). The appeal is made because the stakes are exceedingly high. In the final judgment, all will be measured by whether they have committed abominations (Rev. 21:1–9).

How then does one avoid eternal punishment? From first to last, on this subject Scripture is very clear. From the law that has engaged our attention throughout much of this book, the frequently reiterated solution is found: "You are to perform my judgments and keep my statutes, to live in accord with them; I am the LORD your God" (Lev. 18:4). From the pen of the same apostle who condemned the practice of homosexuality comes the merciful solution: "There is therefore now no condemnation for those who are in Christ Jesus. For the law of the Spirit of life in Christ Jesus has set you free from the law of sin and death. For what the Law could not do, weak as it was through the flesh, God did: sending his own Son in the likeness of sinful flesh and as an offering for sin, he condemned sin in the flesh, in order that the requirement of the Law might be fulfilled in us, who do not walk according to the flesh, but according to the Spirit" (Rom. 8:1–4).

Obedience to the will of God keeps a person in the state of purity required to please the Creator. As the writer of the Apocalypse anticipates the return of the Messiah and the establishment of his kingdom, one last time he reminds his readers of the need for moral purity (Rev. 22:12–17):

> "Behold, I am coming quickly, and my reward is with me, to render to every man according to what he has done. I am the Alpha and the Omega, the first and the last, the beginning and the end." Blessed are those who wash their robes, that they may have the right to the tree of life, and may enter by the gates into the city. Outside are the dogs and the sorcerers and the immoral persons (*pornoi*, πόρνοι) and the murderers and the idolaters, and everyone who loves and practices lying.
>
> "I, Jesus, have sent my angel to testify to you these things for the churches. I am the root and the offspring of David, and the bright morning star."
>
> And the Spirit and the bride say, "Come." And let the one who hears say, "Come." And let the one who is thirsty come; let the one who wishes take the water of life without cost.

In light of our findings about homosexuality in the Bible, what can be said about the road ahead? It is clearly not broad and straight and free of hazards. Modern society is inclined toward tolerance and acceptance of homosexual conduct. The religious factor is diminished in many quarters. On the other hand, a growing number of people are returning to biblical principles for the conduct of their lives. The biblical directives on sex and marriage drive these people to reject homosexuality as a viable alternative to the creative order. Whatever course is taken, the stakes are eternally high according to the biblical view.

In this book I have attempted to set the record straight on what the Bible teaches about same-gender sexual relations. The biblical directive is clear. Two roads lie before us: one way leads to destruction, the other to eternal life. Whatever pleasures may be enjoyed along the way are not worth the pain of choosing the wrong direction. If we are persuaded that the biblical revelation is a guide to eternal life, we can no longer simply wave at those who are traveling in the opposite direction. We must stop, care, and communicate the biblical message to our generation. It is a message of love and hope for everyone, homosexual and heterosexual alike.

The message can be summarized in two words: Choose life! From beginning to end, this is the theme of Scripture. To choose life is to align oneself with the order and design of creation. The tree of life was freely accessible to Adam and Eve until they chose to obey the tempter rather than God (Gen. 3:22–24). Their alienation from God symbolizes the broken relationship that all people experience when sin enters the picture. The prototypes of humanity were made in the divine image, which, I have maintained, is the pattern provided by the incarnate Christ (Col. 1; Phil. 2). Sin, then, is ultimately whatever is out of order with respect to the divine pattern.

In the law, life and death are apposed in the order of Israel's sanctuary. Impurity is associated with death; holiness is linked to life. In the very passage where homosexuality is legislated, the choice of life is proffered: "Observe my statutes and requirements; whoever among men shall do them shall live as a result. I am the LORD" (Lev. 18:5, my translation). The blessing of obedience to God's covenant is life; the curse is death (Deut. 30:19).

I have emphasized throughout this work the importance of blood as the vehicle prescribed for the removal of impurity from God's dwelling place, whether Israel's sanctuary or the individual who is described as the temple of the Lord (1 Cor. 6:19–20). Based on the principle that life is inviolate and the seat of life is in the blood (Lev. 17:11), when a life is forfeit, only another life will compensate (Exod. 21:23). Because the soul that sins deserves to die (Rom. 6:23), by God's grace a ransom is provided through the person of Christ. He is qualified as the "high priest," who presented to God in the heavenly sanctuary not the blood of goats and bulls, as did Israel's high priest in the tabernacle on the Day of Atonement, but the redemption price of humanity paid with his own blood on the cross. "How much more will the blood of Christ, who through the eternal Spirit offered himself without blemish to God, cleanse your conscience from dead works to serve the living God?" (Heb. 9:14).

The biblical hope for homosexuals is in the new covenant of Christ's blood that cleanses from sin and empowers one to live a transformed life, pure in body and mind. Recall that the apostle Paul speaks of homosexuals as those who have "a depraved mind" (Rom. 1:28) and are alienated from God, but near the end of his letter to the Romans he offers the solution to reconciliation:

> I urge you therefore, brethren, by the mercies of God, to present your bodies a living and holy sacrifice, acceptable to God, which is your spiritual service of worship. And do not be conformed to this world, but be transformed by the renewing of your mind, that you may prove what the will of God is, that which is good and acceptable and perfect. (Rom. 12:1–2)

The transformed mind is in order with the divine plan. Choose life!

Works Cited

Adams, Jeremy duQ.
   1981   Review of *Christianity, Social Tolerance, and Homosexuality* by John
           Boswell. *Speculum* 56:850–55.
Albright, William F.
   1965   "The Role of the Canaanites in the History of Civilization." Pp.
           438–87 in *The Bible and the Ancient Near East*. Edited by G. Ernest
           Wright. New York: Doubleday.
Aldred, Cyril
   1980   *Egyptian Art*. London: Thames & Hudson.
   1988   *Akhenaten: King of Egypt*. New York: Thames & Hudson.
Alt, Albrecht
   1968   *Essays on Old Testament History and Religion*. Translated by R. A.
           Wilson. Garden City, N.Y.: Doubleday.
Anderson, Bernhard W.
   1993   "The Biblical Circle of Homosexual Prohibition." *Bible Review* 10
           (June): 52.
Assmann, Jan
   1990   *Maʾat: Gerechtigkeit und Unsterblichkeit im Alten Ägypten*. Munich:
           Beck.
Bailey, Derrick Sherwin
   1975   *Homosexuality and the Western Christian Tradition*. Reprinted Ham-
           den, Conn.: Archon. (Originally London: Longmans, Green, 1955.)
Baines, John, Leonard Lesko, and David P. Silverman
   1991   *Religion in Ancient Egypt*. Edited by Byron E. Shafer. Ithaca: Cor-
           nell University Press.
Baltzer, Klaus
   1971   *The Covenant Formulary in Old Testament, Jewish, and Early Chris-
           tian Writings*. Translated by David Green. Philadelphia: Fortress.
Barton, John
   1978   "Understanding Old Testament Ethics." *Journal for the Study of the
           Old Testament* 9:44–64.

Bechtler, Steven R.
1994   "Christ, the Telos of the Law: The Goal of Romans 10:4." *Catholic Biblical Quarterly* 56:288–308.

Bigger, Stephen F.
1979   "The Family Laws of Leviticus 18 in Their Setting." *Journal of Biblical Literature* 98:187–203.

Biggs, Robert
1969   "Medicine in Ancient Mesopotamia." *History of Science* 8:94–105.

Boswell, John
1980   *Christianity, Social Tolerance, and Homosexuality*. Chicago: University of Chicago Press.

Bottéro, Jean
1992   *Mesopotamia: Writing, Reasoning and the Gods*. Translated by Zainab Bahrani and Marc Van De Mieroop. Chicago: University of Chicago Press.

Bowman, Alan K.
1989   *Egypt after the Pharaohs*. Berkeley: University of California Press.

Brichto, Herbert C.
1973   "Kin, Cult, Land, Afterlife—A Biblical Complex." *Hebrew Union College Annual* 44:1–54.

Brooks, James A., and Carlton L. Winbery
1979   *Syntax of New Testament Greek*. Washington, D.C.: University Press of America.

Burkert, Walter
1995   *The Orientalizing Revolution: Near Eastern Influence on Greek Culture in the Early Archaic Age*. Cambridge: Harvard University Press.

Burton, J. W.
1974   "Some Nuer Notions of Purity and Danger." *Anthropos* 69:517–36.

Buss, Martin J.
1989   "Logic and Israelite Law." *Semeia* 45:49–65.

Byne, William
1994   "The Biological Evidence Challenged." *Scientific American* 270/5:50–55.

Campbell, Edward F., Jr.
1960   "The Amarna Letters and the Amarna Period." *Biblical Archaeologist* 23:2–22. Reprinted in *The Biblical Archaeologist Reader*, vol. 3, pp. 54–75. Edited by Edward F. Campbell Jr. and David Noel Freedman. Garden City, N.Y.: Doubleday, 1970.

Carter, Howard, and A. C. Mace
1977   *The Discovery of the Tomb of Tutankhamen*. New York: Dover.

Cassuto, Umberto
1983   *From Noah to Abraham*. Translated by Israel Abrahams. Jerusalem: Magnes.

Chiera, Edward
1966   *They Wrote on Clay*. Chicago: University of Chicago Press.

Dana, H. E., and Julius R. Mantey
1927   *A Manual Grammar of the Greek New Testament*. New York: Macmillan.

Davies, Douglas
1977   "An Interpretation of Sacrifice in Leviticus." *Zeitschrift für die Alttestamentliche Wissenschaft* 89:387–99.

Deming, William
1996   "The Unity of 1 Corinthians 5–6." *Journal of Biblical Literature* 115:289–312.

De Young, James B.
1988   "The Meaning of 'Nature' in Romans 1 and Its Implications for Biblical Proscriptions of Homosexual Behavior." *Journal of the Evangelical Theological Society* 31:429–41.
1990   "A Critique of Prohomosexual Interpretations of the Old Testament Apocrypha and Pseudepigrapha." *Bibliotheca Sacra* 147:437–54.
1991   "The Contributions of the Septuagint to Biblical Sanctions against Homosexuality." *Journal of the Evangelical Theological Society* 34:157–77.

Douglas, Mary
1966   *Purity and Danger*. London: Routledge & Kegan Paul.
1973   *Natural Symbols*. New York: Vintage.

Dover, Kenneth J.
1989   *Greek Homosexuality*. Cambridge: Harvard University Press.

Dresner, Samuel H.
1991   "Homosexuality and the Order of Creation." *Judaism* 40:309–21.

Driver, Godfrey R., and John C. Miles
1952–55   *The Babylonian Laws*. 2 vols. Oxford: Clarendon.

Durkheim, Émile
1915   *The Elementary Forms of the Religious Life*. Reprinted Glencoe, Ill.: Free Press, 1965.

Edwards, Bruce L.
1986   "Destruction and Rehabilitation: C. S. Lewis' Defense of Western Textuality." *Journal of the Evangelical Theological Society* 29:205–14.

Eichrodt, Walther
1961–67   *Theology of the Old Testament*. 2 vols. Translated by J. A. Baker. Philadelphia: Westminster.

Eissfeldt, Otto
1965   *The Old Testament: An Introduction*. Translated by Peter R. Ackroyd. New York: Harper & Row.

Eliade, Mircea
1959   *The Sacred and the Profane*. New York: Harvest.

Emery, W. B.
1987   *Archaic Egypt*. New York: Penguin.

Fagan, Brian M.
1992   *Rape of the Nile*. Wakefield, R.I.: Moyer Bell.

Ferro-Luzzi, G. Eichinger
  1974   "Women's Pollution Periods in Tamiland (India)." *Anthropos*
          69:113–61.
Fisk, Bruce N.
  1996   "*Porneyein* as Body Violation: The Unique Nature of Sexual Sin in
          1 Corinthians 6:18." *New Testament Studies* 42:540–58.
Fitzmyer, Joseph A.
  1967   *The Aramaic Inscriptions of Sefire.* Analecta Orientalia 49–51.
          Rome: Pontifical Biblical Institute Press.
Flannery, Kent V.
  1983   "Early Pig Domestication in the Fertile Crescent: A Retrospective
          Look." Pp. 163–88 in *The Hilly Flanks and Beyond: Essays on the
          Prehistory of Southwestern Asia, Presented to Robert J. Braidwood.*
          Edited by T. Cuyler Young Jr., Philip E. L. Smith, and Peder
          Mortensen. Studies in Ancient Oriental Civilization 36. Chicago:
          Oriental Institute.
Fohrer, Georg
  1968   *Introduction to the Old Testament.* Translated by David E. Green.
          Nashville: Abingdon.
Frankfort, Henri
  1974   *Before Philosophy: The Intellectual Adventure of Ancient Man.* New
          York: Penguin.
  1978   *Kingship and the Gods.* Chicago: University of Chicago Press.
Frymer-Kensky, Tikva
  1989   "Law and Philosophy: The Case of Sex in the Bible." *Semeia*
          45:89–102.
Gardiner, Alan
  1964   *Egypt of the Pharaohs.* London: Oxford University Press.
Geisler, Norman L.
  1989   *Christian Ethics: Options and Issues.* Grand Rapids: Baker.
Gelb, Ignace J.
  1963   *A Study of Writing.* Chicago: University of Chicago Press.
Geller, M. J.
  1990   "Taboo in Mesopotamia." *Journal of Cuneiform Studies* 42:105–17.
Gesenius, Wilhelm
  1910   *Gesenius' Hebrew Grammar.* Edited by Emil Kautzsch. Translated
          by A. E. Cowley. Oxford: Clarendon.
Gillett, Grant
  1987   "AIDS and Confidentiality." *Journal of Applied Philosophy* 4:15–20.
Goedicke, Hans
  1967   "Unrecognized Sportings." *Journal of the American Research Cen-
          ter in Egypt* 6:97–102.
Goetchius, Eugene Van Ness
  1965   *The Language of the New Testament.* New York: Scribner.
Gordon, Cyrus H.
  1965   *The Ancient Near East.* New York: Norton.

1987   *Forgotten Scripts*. New York: Dorset.
Greenberg, David F.
1988   *The Construction of Homosexuality*. Chicago: University of Chicago Press.
Greenberg, Moshe
1991   "Some Postulates of Biblical Criminal Law." Pp. 333–51 in *Essential Papers on Israel and the Ancient Near East*. Edited by Frederick E. Greenspahn. New York: New York University Press.
Grenz, Stanley
1990   *Sexual Ethics: A Biblical Perspective*. Dallas: Word.
Grosheide, F. W.
1976   *Commentary on the First Epistle to the Corinthians*. New International Commentary on the New Testament. Grand Rapids: Eerdmans.
Gurney, Oliver R.
1961   *The Hittites*. Baltimore: Penguin.
Habel, Norman C.
1972   " 'Yahweh, Maker of Heaven and Earth': A Study in Tradition Criticism." *Journal of Biblical Literature* 91:321–37.
Hamer, Dean H., et al.
1993   "A Linkage between DNA Markers on the X Chromosome and Male Sexual Orientation." *Science* 261 (July 16): 321–27.
Harland, J. Penrose
1942–43 "Sodom and Gomorrah." *Biblical Archaeologist* 5:17–32 and 6:41–54. Reprinted in *The Biblical Archaeologist* Reader, vol. 1, pp. 41–75. Edited by G. Ernest Wright and David Noel Freedman. Garden City, N.Y.: Doubleday, 1961.
Hays, Richard B.
1986   "Relations Natural and Unnatural: A Response to John Boswell's Exegesis of Romans 1." *Journal of Religious Ethics* 14:184–215.
Heidel, Alexander
1951   *The Babylonian Genesis: The Story of Creation*. Second edition. Chicago: University of Chicago Press.
Helyer, Larry L.
1994   "Cosmic Christology and Col 1:15–20." *Journal of the Evangelical Theological Society* 37:235–46.
Henley, Tracy B.
1993   "The History and Current Status of the Concept 'Behavior': An Introduction." *Journal of Mind and Behavior* 14:341–44.
Hiltner, Seward
1980   "Homosexuality and the Churches." Pp. 219–31 in *Homosexual Behavior: A Modern Reappraisal*. Edited by J. Marmor. New York: Basic.
Hoekema, Anthony A.
1986   *Created in God's Image*. Grand Rapids: Eerdmans.

Hoffner, Harry A., Jr.
  1973   "Incest, Sodomy and Bestiality in the Ancient Near East." Pp. 81–90 in *Orient and Occident*. Edited by Harry A. Hoffner Jr. Neukirchen-Vluyn: Butzon & Bercker.

Horner, Tom
  1978   *Jonathan Loved David*. Philadelphia: Westminster.

Hughes, Philip E.
  1962   *Paul's Second Epistle to the Corinthians*. New International Commentary on the New Testament. Grand Rapids: Eerdmans.

Jackson, Bernard S.
  1971   "Liability for Mere Intention in Early Jewish Law." *Hebrew Union College Annual* 42:197–225.

Jacobsen, Thorkild
  1976   *The Treasures of Darkness*. New Haven: Yale University Press.

Jenkins, James J.
  1993   "What Counts as 'Behavior'?" *Journal of Mind and Behavior* 14:355–64.

Jones, Tom B. (ed.)
  1969   *The Sumerian Problem*. New York: Wiley.

Karlen, Arno
  1980   "Homosexuality in History." Pp. 75–99 in *Homosexual Behavior: A Modern Reappraisal*. Edited by J. Marmor. New York: Basic.

Kaufmann, Yehezkel
  1972   *The Religion of Israel*. Translated by Moshe Greenberg. New York: Schocken.

Kilmer, Anne D.
  1972   "The Mesopotamian Concept of Overpopulation and Its Solution as Reflected in the Mythology." *Orientalia* 41:160–77.

Knapp, A. Bernard
  1988   *History and Culture of Ancient Western Asia and Egypt*. Chicago: Dorsey.

Kramer, Samuel Noah
  1963   *The Sumerians: Their History, Culture, and Character*. Chicago: University of Chicago Press.
  1981   *History Begins at Sumer*. Philadelphia: University of Pennsylvania Press.

Lambert, Wilfred G.
  1960   *Babylonian Wisdom Literature*. Oxford: Clarendon.

Lambert, Wilfred G., and Alan R. Millard
  1969   *Atra-ḫasīs: The Babylonian Story of the Flood*. Oxford: Clarendon.

Lance, H. Darrell
  1989   "The Bible and Homosexuality." *American Baptist Quarterly* 8:140–51.

Leahey, Thomas H.
  1993   "A History of Behavior." *Journal of Mind and Behavior* 14:345–53.

LeVay, Simon
    1991   "A Difference in Hypothalamic Structure between Heterosexual and Homosexual Men." *Science* 253 (Aug. 30): 1034–37.
LeVay, Simon, and Dean H. Hamer
    1994   "Evidence for a Biological Influence in Male Homosexuality." *Scientific American* 270/5:44–49.
Levine, Baruch A.
    1974   *In the Presence of the Lord*. Leiden: Brill.
    1989   *Leviticus*. Jewish Publication Society Torah Commentary 3. Philadelphia: Jewish Publication Society.
Levi-Strauss, Claude
    1963   *Structural Anthropology*. New York: Basic.
Lewis, C. S.
    1952   *Mere Christianity*. New York: Collier.
Lloyd, Seton
    1978   *The Archaeology of Mesopotamia*. London: Thames & Hudson.
    1980   *Foundations in the Dust*. London: Thames & Hudson.
Mallowan, Max E. L.
    1965   *Early Mesopotamia and Iran*. New York: McGraw-Hill.
Matthiae, Paolo
    1981   *Ebla: An Empire Rediscovered*. Translated by Christopher Holme. New York: Doubleday.
McCarthy, Dennis J.
    1978   *Treaty and Covenant: A Study in Form in the Ancient Oriental Documents and in the Old Testament*. Revised edition. Analecta Biblica 21. Rome: Pontifical Biblical Institute Press.
Mendenhall, George E.
    1954   "Covenant Forms in Israelite Tradition." *Biblical Archaeologist* 17:50–76. Reprinted in *The Biblical Archaeologist Reader*, vol. 3, pp. 25–53. Edited by Edward F. Campbell Jr. and David Noel Freedman. Garden City, N.Y.: Doubleday, 1970.
Meyers, Eric M.
    1971   *Jewish Ossuaries: Reburial and Rebirth*. Rome: Biblical Institute.
Milgrom, Jacob
    1970   *Studies in Levitical Terminology*, vol. 1. Berkeley: University of California Press.
    1983   *Studies in Cultic Theology and Terminology*. Studies in Judaism in Late Antiquity 36. Leiden: Brill.
    1990   *Numbers*. Jewish Publication Society Torah Commentary 4. Philadelphia: Jewish Publication Society.
    1991   *Leviticus 1–16*. Anchor Bible 3. New York: Doubleday.
    1993   "Does the Bible Prohibit Homosexuality?" *Bible Review* 9:11.
Morgenstern, Julian
    1931–32 "The Book of the Covenant, part III: The Ḥuqqim." *Hebrew Union College Annual* 8–9:1–150.

Moscati, Sabatino
    1962   *The Face of the Ancient Orient*. Garden City, N.Y.: Doubleday.
Moyer, J. C.
    1969   *The Concept of Ritual Purity among the Hittites*. Ph.D. dissertation,
            Brandeis University.
Nahmanides (Ramban)
    1974   *Commentary on the Torah: Leviticus*. Translated and annotated by
            Charles B. Chavel. New York: Shilo.
Neuhaus, Richard J.
    1995   "In the Case of John Boswell." *Evangelical Review of Theology*
            19:64–70.
Oates, Joan
    1986   *Babylon*. London: Thames & Hudson.
O'Flaherty, Wendy Doniger
    1976   *The Origins of Evil in Hindu Mythology*. Berkeley: University of Cal-
            ifornia Press.
Olsen, Glenn W.
    1981   "The Gay Middle Ages: A Response to Professor Boswell." *Com-
            munio* 8:119–38.
Oppenheim, A. Leo
    1977   *Ancient Mesopotamia: Portrait of a Dead Civilization*. Revised edi-
            tion, completed by Erica Reiner. Chicago: University of Chicago
            Press.
Otto, Rudolf
    1923   *The Idea of the Holy*. Oxford: Oxford University Press.
Parker, Simon B.
    1991   "The Hebrew Bible and Homosexuality." *Quarterly Review* 11:4–19.
Pedersen, William L.
    1986   "Can Ἀρσενοκοῖται Be Translated by 'Homosexuals' (1 Cor. 6:9;
            1 Tim. 1:10)?" *Vigiliae Christianae* 40:187–91.
Phillips, Anthony
    1980   "Uncovering the Father's Skirt." *Vetus Testamentum* 30:38–43.
Pope, Marvin H.
    1976   "Homosexuality." Pp. 415–17 in *The Interpreter's Dictionary of the
            Bible: Supplement Volume*. Edited by Keith Crim. Nashville: Abing-
            don.
Pope, Stephen J.
    1997   "Scientific and Natural Law Analyses of Homosexuality." *Journal
            of Religious Ethics* 25:89–126.
Porter, J. R.
    1976   *Leviticus*. Cambridge: Cambridge University Press.
Posener, Georges
    1957   "Le Conte de Neferkare et du Général Sisene." *Revue d'Egyptolo-
            gie* 11:119–37.
Primoratz, Igor
    1997   "Sexual Perversion." *American Philosophical Quarterly* 34:245–58.

Pronk, Pim
 1993   *Against Nature?* Grand Rapids: Eerdmans.
Rad, Gerhard von
 1962   *Old Testament Theology*, vol. 1. Translated by D. M. G. Stalker. New
           York: Harper.
Ramsey Colloquium
 1994   "The Homosexual Movement: A Response by the Ramsey Collo-
           quium." *First Things* 41:15–20.
Redford, Donald B.
 1992   *Egypt, Canaan, and Israel in Ancient Times*. Princeton: Princeton
           University Press.
Robertson, Archibald T.
 1914   *A Grammar of the Greek New Testament in the Light of Historical
           Research*. Nashville: Broadman.
Robins, Gay
 1993   *Women in Ancient Egypt*. Cambridge: Harvard University Press.
St. Louis Statement
 1995   "The St. Louis Statement on Human Sexuality." *Evangelical Review
           of Theology* 19:9–42.
Saggs, H. W. F.
 1968   *The Greatness That Was Babylon*. New York: Mentor.
Sarna, Nahum M.
 1989   *Genesis*. Jewish Publication Society Torah Commentary 1. Philadel-
           phia: Jewish Publication Society.
Schechter, Solomon
 1961   *Aspects of Rabbinic Theology: Major Concepts of the Talmud*.
           Reprinted New York: Schocken. (Originally 1909.)
Schmidt, Thomas E.
 1995   *Straight and Narrow?* Downers Grove, Ill.: InterVarsity.
Seele, Keith C.
 1957   *When Egypt Ruled the East*. Chicago: University of Chicago Press.
Smith, Christopher R.
 1996   "The Literary Structure of Leviticus." *Journal for the Study of the
           Old Testament* 70:17–32.
Soden, W. von
 1994   *Introduction to the Ancient World: The Background of the Ancient
           Orient*. Translated by Donald G. Schley. Grand Rapids: Eerdmans.
Speiser, Ephraim A.
 1964   *Genesis*. Anchor Bible 1. New York: Doubleday.
 1967   *Oriental and Biblical Studies*. Edited by J. J. Finkelstein and Moshe
           Greenberg. Philadelphia: University of Pennsylvania Press.
Stafford, J. Martin
 1988   "Love and Lust Revisited: Intentionality, Homosexuality, and Moral
           Education." *Journal of Applied Philosophy* 5:87–100.
Taylor, J. Glen
 1995   "The Bible and Homosexuality." *Themelios* 21/1 (October): 4–9.

Thomsen, Marie-Louise
    1992   "The Evil Eye in Mesopotamia." *Journal of Near Eastern Studies* 51:19–32.

Tobin, V.
    1992   Review of *Ma'at: Gerechtigkeit und Unsterblichkeit im Alten Ägypten* by Jan Assmann. *Biblica* 73:293–97.

Van Der Toorn, K.
    1985   *Sin and Sanction in Israel and Mesopotamia*. Studia Semitica Neerlandica. Assen/Maastricht: Van Gorcum.

Van Gennep, Arnold
    1960   *The Rites of Passage*. Chicago: University of Chicago Press.

Wehr, Hans
    1976   *A Dictionary of Modern Written Arabic*. Third edition. Edited by J. Milton Cowan. Ithaca, N.Y.: Spoken Language Services.

Wenham, Gordon J.
    1983   "Why Does Sexual Intercourse Defile (Lev. 15:18)?" *Zeitschrift für die Alttestamentliche Wissenschaft* 95:432–37.
    1991   "The Old Testament Attitude to Homosexuality." *Expository Times* 102:359–63.

White, Mel
    1994   *Stranger at the Gate: To Be Gay and Christian in America*. New York: Simon & Schuster.

Wold, Donald J.
    1978   *The Meaning of the Biblical Penalty Kareth*. Ph.D. dissertation, University of California, Berkeley.

Woolley, C. Leonard
    1965   *The Sumerians*. New York: Norton.

Wright, David F.
    1984   "Homosexuals or Prostitutes? The Meaning of *Arsenokoitai* (1 Cor. 6:9; 1 Tim. 1:10)." *Vigiliae Christianae* 38:125–53.
    1985   Review of *The New Testament and Homosexuality* by Robin Scroggs. *Scottish Journal of Theology* 38:118–20.
    1987   "Translating Ἀρσενοκοῖται (1 Cor. 6:9; 1 Tim. 1:10)." *Vigiliae Christianae* 41:396–98.

Wright, J. Robert
    1984   "Boswell on Homosexuality: A Case Undemonstrated." *Anglican Theological Review* 16:79–94.

Yates, John C.
    1995   "Towards a Theology of Homosexuality." *Evangelical Quarterly* 67:71–87.

Zohar, Noam
    1988   "Repentance and Purification: The Significance and Semantics of חטאת in the Pentateuch." *Journal of Biblical Literature* 107:609–18.

Scripture Index

General Index